Adoring *Outlander*

Adoring *Outlander*

*Essays on Fandom, Genre
and the Female Audience*

Edited by VALERIE ESTELLE FRANKEL

McFarland & Company, Inc., Publishers
Jefferson, North Carolina

ISBN (print) 978-1-4766-6423-1
ISBN (ebook) 978-1-4766-2487-7

LIBRARY OF CONGRESS CATALOGUING DATA ARE AVAILABLE

BRITISH LIBRARY CATALOGUING DATA ARE AVAILABLE

Front cover image © 2016 Yuri Arcurs

Printed in the United States of America

*McFarland & Company, Inc., Publishers
Box 611, Jefferson, North Carolina 28640
www.mcfarlandpub.com*

Contents

Introduction

On Modern Multi-Genre and a New Age for Fandom

With about 25 million books sold, *Outlander* has had a lively presence among its readers for decades before it hit the big time as a Starz show. Certainly, being on that network, with the implied nudity and big budget costumes along with an epic, character-based storyline, created its own image. To producers, it appeared to be *"Game of Thrones* meets *Downton Abbey"* in a dizzying blend of drawing room courtship and brutal violence (Hale).

Yet, before the show, genre fluidity had long been a sticking point for readers, and especially for author Diana Gabaldon. Doing her early signings, she shifted her recommendation to match her audience. As Gabaldon explained at Comic-Con 2014:

> Depending on who I was talking to, if it was a young woman I'd say, "Oh, historical romance, men in kilts"... If it was a slightly older lady, I'd say, "Oh, it's historical fiction—if you liked *Shogun*, you'll love this." Which is totally true! If it was a young man, I'd say, "It's fantasy, time travel, things like that: swords." And if it was an older man, I'd say it was military history [Bates].

Certainly, these all apply in a blend of near-countless elements. Gabaldon adds, "As my first editor used to say, these have to be word-of-mouth books, because they're too weird to describe to anyone" (Bates). They may be weird, but at Gabaldon's insistence, they're filed under general fiction, not romance. Gabaldon has regaled her fans with tales of her first book being handed out at the annual Romance Writers of America conference, only to have some members ecstatic but others appalled by a first-person weighty hardcover in which the hero spanks the heroine. Her scores for RWA's RITA Award were split—mostly the voters were ambivalent about whether it was a romance at all. Still, they awarded it Best Book of the Year. One reviewer writes:

> The surest way to irk Diana Gabaldon, whose latest novel, *A Breath of Snow and Ashes*, debuted atop the *New York Times* best-seller list last week, is to call her a romance writer. If so accused, she'll counter that her books are historical mysteries tinged with science-fiction, and that the love scenes are secondary [Koerner].

Certainly, the books' historical nature is plain, though Gabaldon had never visited Scotland before book one arrived, and several aspects of the history are specifically fictional.

Voyager is nautical fiction with pirates, press gangs, sea battles, and tropical islands. As Anthony Guy Patricia shows in this collection, there's also quite a lot of Romance, in its original meaning—adventure story. By the later books, there is more than a trace of generational saga as well. In book eight, Brianna discovers a modern conspiracy that's been tracking her lineage. Frank writes to her of government spooks tracking her to discover the secrets of time travel, as she and her line may be heirs to a great destiny. This takes on a touch of the thriller based in ancient legend popularized by *The Da Vinci Code* as Brianna goes on the run. (Describing this twist, Gabaldon simply says, "When you start thinking about time travel and so forth, you get all kinds of interesting possibilities"). Fascinated fans will be happy to hear this subplot will return in book nine ("An Interview with Diana Gabaldon").

Beyond all these, the romance (with a modern meaning) is central to the books, especially book one—by the later books, Jamie and Claire are an established couple, and burgeoning love affairs are left to the next generation. But book one offers all the elements expected in romance, so much so that Gabaldon's publishers preferred this category, forcing her to bargain her way onto the general fiction shelf. In this collection, critics Jodi McAlister and Eleanor Ty both systematically explore to what extent the series fits the definition of romance, with the former focusing on its melodramatic appeal and the latter setting it against traditional romances with their many rules. Celebrating Gabaldon's genre inversion, Michelle L. Jones examines Claire as the gender-flipped romantic hero with Black Jack threatening her and Jamie in ways wholly unconventional. In a groundbreaking study of subjects rarely tackled in academia or fan writing, Anthony Guy Patricia examines the series' homosexual appeal and fandom, and its effect on male readership. Meanwhile, Sandi Solis contrasts dreaded Black Jack and delightful Lord John as opposing emotional forces in Jamie's life pulling him toward darkness and light.

The range of genres continues as *Outlander* certainly offers classic fantasy elements—most of all the standing stones that incite the plot. Beyond this, however, Claire meets the Loch Ness monster, Jamie and his sister have second sight, and Mandy and Jem share a telepathic bond that blends their connection with the stones and their mystical Scottish heritage ("An Interview with Diana Gabaldon"). In a chilling fairy encounter, Jamie meets the Wild

Hunt in *The Scottish Prisoner*. Perhaps most compellingly, Master Raymond tutors Claire in manipulating auras and in ancient wisdom from the dawn of time.

Uncanny ghost stories form significant subplots, as Claire begins by learning of the phantoms of Inverness, then encountering a very particular Highland ghost—Jamie's. Otter-Tooth saves her in book four, and Frank's spirit comes to her, as Jamie's loved ones visit him before battle. Even Adso the cat is more than he seems. Roger, too, is guarded by his parents' spirits, and has a life-transformation and new purpose after his "half-death." Stella Murillo cleverly investigates this genre as the dead interact with those already touched by the grave in "Half-Ghosts and Their Legacy for Claire, Jamie and Roger."

Gabaldon's plot, too, mimics the heroine's journey structure perfectly, a pattern almost required in fantasy series. It's one more example of what makes the story a celebrated classic particularly for female readers, speaking to their depth psychologically. In a beautifully lyrical exploration of symbol and metaphor through the show, Patti McCarthy explores Claire's growth in terms of this story pattern through this specifically women's epic.

For the show's producer Ron Moore, already creator of science fictions *Battlestar Galactica* and *Star Trek: Deep Space Nine*, the comparison to speculative fiction, especially *Outlander*'s rival *Game of Thrones*, predominates. He says:

> It's about love and loyalty and trust and obligation. It's more eternal themes than it is really about time travel. It's not about different timelines, or if you change the past, how will it affect the future. Even though those questions do come up, periodically, it's not the central focus of the story. It becomes a more overt science fiction piece, once you really get into intense discussions of timelines and how one event can be like dominoes through history [Radish].

Jennifer Phillips analyzes this connection, working out how nudity, gaze, rape, and other gender issues are presented on the two popular television series, albeit with inverted audiences.

Similarly, the Lord John short stories (as well as *Outlander* short stories "Virgins" "The Space Between" and "A Leaf on the Wind of All Hallows") are shelved with sci fi–fantasy and appear in anthologies for Tor, a sci fi–fantasy publisher. "The Space Between" is a magical tale of Master Raymond, St. Germain, auras, and standing stones, while most of the Lord John short stories have him solving supernatural mysteries featuring succubae, zombies, ghosts, and devil-worshippers … or so it appears at first glance. With no paranormal-gothic section, these books are invariably mixed into the fantasy shelf (a topic I take on myself through analysis of the many, many mixed genres in the Lord John novels and stories). Gabaldon is also planning to write two independent mysteries and a Master Raymond novel, which will expand the types of stories she offers even further ("An Interview with Diana Gabaldon").

As an examination of the series by fans, for fans, this book also explores Gabaldon's fandom itself. Stephenie McGucken starts off this collection by lovingly exploring *Outlander* tourism in the Highlands, and the many locations adapted for use on the show. She reveals the increase in visitors and "the *Outlander* effect" while incorporating scholarly studies of fan tourism and the history of Fraser castles and coats of arms—this was the first essay I knew *had* to be included here. Jennifer Phillips and Katharina Freund team up to explore Gabaldon's treasured interactions with her fans, especially on Tumblr, and their teasing effect on the eager readers. In this new digital age, Gabaldon is seizing the technology and using it to greet her fans and welcome them into her world. One of Gabaldon's most intriguing releases is her stack of teasers—tiny excerpts of her books long before publication, as social media allows her to delight her fans with pre-publication snippets. Jessica R. Matthews explores how this changes the process of reading to find such spoilers out of order. Finally, Eleanor Ty analyzes what about the story is so terribly appealing and breaks down the qualities from heroism to drama that have brought millions of fans clamoring for each book. And yes, she also examines the careful crafting of the sex scenes and the appeals of sweet Jamie Fraser versus muscled Sam Heughan.

An obligatory spoiler warning might add that this collection spoils *everything*, from season one to the novels to the short stories. There is also graphic sexual language, quoted, of course, from the series. Within, episodes are cited as E101, etc., while books are cited by title and chapter.

As the show's second season approaches, with more books on the horizon as well, fans can come together as never before to celebrate the joys of all things *Outlander*. And perhaps explore, through genres and beyond, why this saga has such an overwhelming fascination.

WORKS CITED

Bates, Karen Grigsby. "Aye, Sassenach—Gabaldon's Appeal Is Timeless." *NPR*. 8 Aug 2014. http://www.npr.org/2014/08/08/338363871/aye-sassenach-gabaldons-appeal-is-timeless.

Gabaldon, Diana. *Written in My Own Heart's Blood*. New York: Delacorte Press, 2014.

Hale, Mike. "A Highland Fling Would Not Be Unexpected Here." *New York Times*. 1 Aug 2014. http://www.nytimes.com/2014/08/02/arts/television/outlander-a-starz-series-adapted-from-the-novels.html?_r=0.

"An Interview with Diana Gabaldon." *Outlander Podcast*. Episode 49. http://outlanderpod.wordpress.com/2014/08/03/episode-49-an-interview-with-diana-gabaldon.

Koerner, Brendan. "*A Breath of Snow and Ashes*: The Romance Novel at the Top of the *New York Times* Best-Seller List." *Slate*. 21 October 2005. http://www.slate.com/articles/arts/number_1/2005/10/a_breath_of_snow_and_ashes.html.

Radish, Christina. "Creator Ronald D. Moore Talks *Outlander*, Bringing This Story to TV, Deciding on 16 Episodes, Season 1 Ending, and More." *Collider*. 8 Sept 2014. http://collider.com/ronald-d-moore-outlander-interview.

PART I

Gabaldon's Fans, Forming Communities

"A love letter to Scotland"

The Creation and Conception of Heritage

STEPHENIE MCGUCKEN

Outlander showrunner Ronald D. Moore's oft-quoted description of the show as "a love letter to Scotland," provides a key to understanding the production's utilization of historic places as backdrops for filming (quoted in Canton). The Romantic view promoted in the show intentionally foregrounds Scottish heritage sites in such a way that the locations become key to the story's arc. From the first moments of the show's credits, Scotland is presented as an untamed, picturesque, and magical place steeped in unique history. Each historic site utilized in the course of filming comes with its own history, which is adopted, enveloped, and rejected by the production in favor of their constructed view of place and time. The impact is subtle, for both viewer of the show and visitor-viewer to the sites used in filming.[1]

Before going further, a few terms must be clarified, and certain limitations outlined. The *Oxford English Dictionary* defines heritage as "that which has been or may be inherited; any property, and esp[ecially] land, which devolves by right of inheritance." The entry goes further to define heritage tourism as "tourism to places of historical or cultural influence." Richard Zumkhwala-Cook broadens the definition to include "commonly inherited ideals, practices, and property transmitted from a readily accessible past and of an essential and timeless cultural identity" (111). Heritage is not necessarily history when history is presented as a set of "textbook facts." Heritage in this essay refers to extant historic sites that are re-packaged to tell a story (*Outlander*) crafted for a specific reason and for a specific audience. The employment of a historic site as a backdrop for a fictionalized story creates a desire to visit the site in order to relive the show, as well as experience the history to which such sites testify. This brings us to the limitations of a study such as the one before you. All of the sites considered here are from the first season of the show, in part, because of the information (interviews, podcasts, reviews, etc.) available now that the show has been screened. Ongoing production of season two makes specific comments on its use of heritage impossible at this moment. The selection of sites is varied, and it includes the screen time each received, the differences in approach to set dressing, and the differences in the buildings' established reputation as a heritage, and film, site. Furthermore, the term visitor-viewer is used here to mean the *Outlander* viewer who is inspired to visit the locations, distinguishing them from the site visitor who is not related to the *Outlander* fandom. This distinction is important as the strategies adopted to appeal to the visitor-viewer should not alienate the visitor, who may share similar interests in heritage and history, an idea to which we will return.

This essay explores the constructed view of three heritage sites featured in the first season: Doune (Leoch), Blackness (Fort William), and Midhope (Lallybroch). It begins with a brief history of each castle, and how it was adapted for filming. The essay then discusses the implications of the show on the heritage sites used over the course of production, and how such sites could capitalize on the "*Outlander* effect."

Castles as Castles, Forts and Houses

Doune Castle: Castle Leoch

Construction of Doune Castle began under Robert Stewart, Duke of Albany and Regent of Scotland, in the 1380s and 1390s; it remained in Albany's family until his son and grandson were executed in 1425. From them, it passed into the hands of the royal governors before coming into the jurisdiction of the Earls of Moray in the sixteenth century. The family carried out restoration works in the 1880s, which included the erection of the Great Hall's roof as it is seen today (Gifford and Walker, 378–79). During the 1745–6 Jacobite Uprising, it was used as a prison for government troops captured by Jacobites at the Battles of Stirling and Falkirk (Salter, 94; Mackay 5, 21).

Claire describes Leoch in the book as she rides up to it after being captured by the Highlanders: "The castle itself was blunt and solid. No fanciful turrets or toothed battlements. This was more like an enormous fortified house, with thick stone walls and high, slotted windows."[2] This could be any number of castles in Scotland, much less the Highlands. She goes on to compare it to what she knew of it in the 1940s: "When I had known it, Castle Leoch was a picturesque ruin" (*Outlander*, Ch. 4). This idea of the picturesque ruin is echoed in the Revised Network Draft (RND) from April 2013: "The picturesque ruins of a medieval SCOTTISH CASTLE… The structure is abandoned, with weeds and grasses encroaching on what were once neatly kept grounds."

When the viewer first sees Doune/Leoch, it is a picturesque ruin. The castle has been digitally altered to make it appear as such. The tower's first floor was removed, while the north range was also reduced by about a floor level, with some parts lowered even further. The entire front façade of the castle is covered in vines, while the grass surrounding it is overgrown. An abandoned mower is strategically placed alongside the path towards the castle to reinforce that the castle has been turned over to the wild, abandoned by its caretakers. As Moore notes in his podcast, this first impression is not actually of the castle as it stands today: "instead of taking a ruined castle and building it up into a good looking castle, we took a good-looking castle and digitally made it into a ruin" (Moore 101). This first impression of the castle that the viewer is left with is not, however, the one that forms the bulk of the castle's screen time, and ultimately the viewer's relationship with the castle. Rather, it is in the views at the end of episode 101, "Sassenach," and over subsequent episodes that Leoch is shown as a whole, warm, and an active part of history.

Apart from the courtyard, Doune's interior was not used for production. The interiors of Leoch were instead filmed on the soundstages at the production's studio in Cumbernauld, outside of Glasgow. In order to maintain a certain air of authenticity, moulds of Doune's stonework were taken, which were then used in the construction of the sets. "All the stonework and the colours and textures are replicating what's really on [Doune's] interior" (Moore 101). The kitchen set was modeled on the actual kitchen of Doune, with the enormous hearth reproduced. "It's all predicated on the actual place" (Moore 101). The "actual place" is the historic Doune, which gives birth to the fictional Leoch. It is easy to forget where Doune ends and Leoch begins.

Leoch becomes integral to the story and *Outlander*'s presentation of history and historic sites. In her discussion of costume drama, Amy Sargent notes "historical films grant sight of places we go to imaginatively" (181). Stables and small structures erected in the courtyard provide a long-lost view into daily life at a castle and, with the aid of the Cumbernauld sets, present Doune/Leoch as a living, thriving building. History, normally only seen in the imagination, has been brought to life in vivid color. This contrived presentation of Doune/Leoch in the past creates a layer of fictionalized time, where history, heritage, and cultural production collide. *Outlander*'s audience becomes Doune's audience. Rather than walking the walls of the castle or exploring its multiple rooms with an audio guide, the audience is walked through the castle by the show's characters, most often by Claire (Caitriona Balfe).

Blackness Castle: Fort William

Approximately sixteen miles outside of Edinburgh, and situated on the banks of the Firth of Forth, Blackness Castle dates from the fifteenth century, when the Crichton family began construction. Its distinctive ship plan dates from the sixteenth century, with additions and alterations reflecting its varied use. In the late seventeenth century it was used as a prison for Covenanters who were arrested after the restoration of Charles Stewart. It was maintained as a defensive structure under the 1707 Act of Union, with a small garrison stationed there. Over the course of the eighteenth century, it served once again as a prison for prisoners of war captured in France, Spain, and the United States. It eventually became an ordnance depot in the 1870s, before falling under state guardianship in 1912 (McWilliams 105–106; Tabraham 2, 6, 31).

Blackness Castle's history as prison and fortress is re-created in *Outlander* over a series of scenes that span the central episodes of the first season. Standing in for Fort William, Blackness becomes the formidable prison where the show's hero Jamie Fraser (Sam Heughan) is taken after his arrest by Captain Black Jack Randall (Tobias Menzies). In a series of gut-wrenching flashbacks over episode 106 ("The Garrison Commander"), the audience learns that Jamie was brutally whipped there. While the castle features again in episodes 108 and 109 ("Both Sides Now" and "The Reckoning"), Blackness's appearance in 106 is largely what concerns us here, as the castle became the stage for events that are referenced throughout the season.

Blackness, in comparison to Doune/Leoch and Midhope/Lallybroch, was minimally dressed, with the whipping post and platform constructed in its courtyard. The castle's existing atmosphere was left largely alone to convey the scenes' darker tones. In his podcast for the episode, Moore speaks at length on the castle's feel. As he recalls in his earliest impressions of Blackness:

> I immediately said "This is a potential Fort William," because it is such a forbidding, barren, just heavy, fortress … as soon as you walked into that courtyard … you feel the oppression, you feel the heavy nature of it and those giant walls and all that rock and stone and you just feel the brutality of it.

Rather than the warm Romantic view of the laird's castle, Blackness/Fort William is the dark, dangerous castle in which the hero and heroine confront their enemy in order to survive. Fans and reviewers have noted poignant, physical reactions to 106's whipping scene, with one reviewer describing it as "powerful, disturbing, [and] stomach-turning" (Conrad). Heughan has commented that filming the scene was "hard work," saying that "it had to be visceral" in order to demonstrate the impact it would have on his character. Blackness/Fort William forces the viewer to witness Randall's brutality in direct comparison to the nostalgic warmth largely created at the other locations. The castle's history as prison is reshaped and highlighted. By not dressing the set extensively and by embracing the castle's history and menacing atmosphere, the show highlights its historical function as defensive post, garrison, and prison without saying explicitly that this is the location's history. Fiction meets history in graphic detail.

Midhope Castle: Lallybroch

Midhope Castle is situated on the Hopetoun Estate in West Lothian, approximately thirteen miles outside of Edinburgh's city center. The first record of Midhope is in the fifteenth century during a land dispute between Henry Luigstone (Laird of Manerston) and John Martyne (Laird of Medhope). As a result of the dispute's resolution, it fell into the Livingston family, who maintained it until Alexander Drummond took over the property about 1582. The majority of the extant building dates to Drummond's time, with the arched basement floor dating to the early fifteenth century (Cadell 31–32). The doorway, which features in the show, dates to the seventeenth century, as does the gateway. Drummond's initials and the date of 1582 survive in an inscription (possibly part of a lintel) to the left of the gateway (McWilliam 327). A series of repairs was undertaken in the late 1980s–early 1990s with the intention that the building would be left a shell upon the completion of the works (Cadell 40).

In the book, Lallybroch is described by Claire, who comments that the broch, or tower, "that gave the small estate its name was no more than another mound of rocks." She continues, Lallybroch "was larger than I had expected; a handsome three-story manor of harled white stone, windows outlined in the natural grey stone, a high slate roof with multiple chimneys, and several smaller whitewashed buildings clustered about it, like chicks about a hen" (Ch. 26). Rather than the harled stone with natural gray stone accents, Midhope is made of ashlar stone of slightly varying colors. Its stone façade stands out against its surroundings, giving the impression of historic isolation, despite the proximity of a number of modern buildings. There is not a crumbling tower on the site, as described in the book.

The crumbling tower as seen in the show is part of a CGI composition of Claire's first view of the homestead (from above, as in the book's description) as she and Jamie approach it. This is the viewer's only glimpse of the tower. To bring Lallybroch itself to life, small structures were erected around the exterior of Midhope, including stables in the back (conveniently covering a ruined building), and animal pens and beehives in the front. Plants were added to further fill in the space around the house. A false wall extended the reach of the boundary wall (today a ruin). The wall's extension also served to block the drive to the wood mill a few hundred feet beyond the house. The Fraser coat-of-arms covered the empty space on the gate's archway, which likely held the Crichton family coat-of-arms, lost prior to 1885, and based on photographic evidence (Fleming 1885).

The Fraser coat-of-arms as seen in the show are not the historical arms, nor are they the arms Diana Gabaldon establishes in *The Outlandish Companion* (215). As with many historic families, the arms of the different branches of the family vary slightly. The historical Clan Fraser arms feature three argent (silver) symbols of the strawberry (*fraise*) on an azure (blue) field. The arms of the Lovat branch of Clan Fraser feature the strawberry symbol (argent on an azure field) quartered with three crowns (gules on white field) (Paul 70, 113). Gabaldon adds a bordure of gules (red) and or (gold) to the arms to signify Broch Turach (215). The arms used in the show draw on the strawberry motif, but are quartered and halved differently. The left half (normally quadrants one and three) features three crescents stacked. The right half is quartered with a single strawberry emblem in quadrant two (top) and a spear in quadrant four (bottom). Apart from the incorrect quartering, the selection of the heraldic emblems is interesting.[3] Three crescents are found on the Seton family arms, but not alone on any Fraser arms. Of the recorded arms prior to 1800, only one has crescents: Fraser of Eskdell (bordure with eight crescents).[4] Nowhere is a spear found on Fraser arms. However, the spear is a symbol of readiness for battle, and could therefore refer to the clan's motto, *Je suis prest* (I am ready). The strawberry, as to be expected, is found throughout the Fraser variants. While this might seem like historical nitpicking in a show that goes to great lengths to present history and heritage authentically, it is precisely this moment of constructed authenticity that reminds of the show's fiction. Constructed authenticity in set design helps bring history to life elsewhere, but here it does the opposite by reminding that this is a fictional Fraser. As elsewhere, history is drawn on and manipulated to tell a story. Nowhere else is that manipulation as blatant or character-driven.[5]

The manipulation seen in the coat of arms is evidenced elsewhere at Midhope. Its interiors are largely ruinous, which made filming inside the castle impossible (Moore 112). Rather than attempting to base the interior sets on the interior of Midhope itself, similar to what had been done for Doune Castle, Jon Gary Steele created the sets largely from scratch. Interestingly, while the interior sets recreate the feel of a grand eighteenth-century house, they appear as if they would not fit into Midhope. Midhope/Lallybroch becomes a TARDIS-like space where TV set (the inside) is bigger than the historic home (the outside). Rather than detracting from or undermining the show's attempts at historic authenticity, the subtle Midhope/Lallybroch size differences remind us, like the Fraser arms, that the show is fiction, albeit a fiction that seeks to create an artistic impression of history.

Outlander: *Heritage on the Small Screen*

Johan Huizinga has argued that "to the world when it was half a thousand years younger, all experience had yet to the minds of men the directness and absoluteness of the pleasure and pain of child-life.... We, at the present day can hardly understand the keenness with which a fur coat, a good fire on the hearth, a soft bed, a glass of wine, were formally enjoyed" (qtd. in Woods 38). Fictionalized accounts of history, such as *Outlander*, seek to show a familiarity with the past through universal themes (love, hate, triumph, tragedy). The re-enactment of daily life makes the viewer wonder if, in Claire's words, "life on this alien world was not so different after all" (E102). Yet, for all of the truth it presents, there is inevitably a difference between textbook veracity and created fiction just as there is between living and recreating history. These differences collide in the use of historic sites.

Compared to other productions filmed in Scotland, *Outlander* is unique in its use of the country's surviving heritage as a backdrop. Chairman of VisitScotland Mike Cantaly has said that "Scotland really is the star of *Outlander*, and its focus on stunning scenery, romance, adventure, and ancestry make it a fantastic advert for Scotland" (qtd. in Ruggia). Scotland's heritage is certainly no stranger to film and television productions, with the likes of *Braveheart*, *The DaVinci Code*, and *Brave* all drawing upon Scotland's heritage to tell their stories and testifying to a relationship between film and tourism in Scotland.

Specific parallels can be drawn between *Braveheart* and *Outlander*: most noticeably, the use of Scotland's history to tell character-driven stories, and the impact of the movie/television show on historic sites referenced in the story or used for filming. The newly-coined *"Outlander* effect" has its origins in the established *"Braveheart* effect." *Braveheart* was undeniably responsible for an increase in visitor numbers to several historic sites in and around Stirling related to William Wallace (Karpovich 14). Sue Beeton pointed out that no filming occurred around Stirling itself, despite it being the "real" location of events portrayed in the movie (Beeton, *Film-Induced Tourism* 58). The historic locations used in *Braveheart* are overwhelmingly Irish. *Outlander*, by contrast, utilizes *Scottish* locations to ground its fictionalized story. Both participate in Zumkhawala-Cook's history-turned-heritage "spectacle of reenactments [and] performances ... [that include] life-like icons that illustrate the way it [history] really was" (Zumkhawala-Cook 112). However, *Braveheart* demonstrates a different type of film-induced tourism to that inspired by *Outlander*.

Braveheart is about retracing the often-fictionalized steps of a historic person, William Wallace. *Outlander*-inspired tourism is about retracing the steps of a fictional character, James Fraser, throughout history and at specific historic locations. Still, the way these locations are used by production, as we have seen, do not always explicitly state the history of the location on screen, but do imply it visually in certain cases such as at Blackness/Fort William and Doune/Leoch. Visits to these places, then, become two-fold: a pilgrimage both to historic site and filming location, with these two related narratives competing for attention. At Doune, this multiplicity of narratives is split again.

Doune Castle, unlike the other castles under consideration, is unique for its notoriety as a film location prior to *Outlander*.[6] Featured in *Monty Python and the Holy Grail*, and briefly in *Game of Thrones*, Doune Castle is no stranger to film-induced tourism. In recounting her own experiences at Doune, Beeton described how "those in the know" asked for coconuts at the front desk, and were rewarded with a pair that they were then allowed to use around the castle to recreate iconic moments from *Holy Grail* (2005 36). Doune had already "taken on mythical, spiritual connotations" prior to *Outlander*'s use of the castle (Beeton, *Film-Induced Tourism* 36). *Outlander*, rather than making Doune's name for it (as it has arguably done for places such as Midhope), is enhancing this mythical connotation as Castle Leoch. Reports have suggested that the castle's visitor numbers were up 30.2 percent for 2014–15 ("Outlander Visitors to Doune Castle"). Rather than supplanting *Holy Grail* as an incentive to visit Doune, *Outlander* is providing a second set of incentives, increasing the pool of possible visitors. The two fictional narratives compete for the attention of visitors. The gift shop is stocked with Historic Scotland exclusive *Outlander*-inspired merchandise, including tote bags, mugs, and t-shirts. The audio guide available, by contrast, is narrated by Monty Python's Terry Jones, who takes the listener through the castle pointing out various features of the castle, while providing insight into the filming of *Holy Grail*. As of yet, there is not an *Outlander* trail that takes a visitor-viewer through the castle from the perspective of the show. The only opportunity that visitor-viewers had to experience Doune as Leoch at the site itself was in the period between October 2013 and February 2014 when, as noted, part of the courtyards were left up while production shot elsewhere. A small sign explained what the sets were for, as well as why one could not wander through them.

Not only do visitors at Doune have to negotiate the *Holy Grail–Outlander* divides, they also have to negotiate the history of the castle. Their visit to the castle becomes a triangulation of history and fictionalized history. In the case of *Outlander*, it also provides an opportunity to visualize possible uses of the castle in the past. The kitchen, because of the awareness to detail in the set design, can be mentally re-imagined by the visitor-viewer with historic costumes and implements rather than solely experienced as a context stripped of vitality. While the audio guide can recreate some parts of life in the kitchen, visual literature, such as *Outlander*, goes one step further to help the visitor imagine the past in the present. If Berger is correct in his assertion that "we never look just at one thing; we are always looking at the relation between things and ourselves," the experience of the visitor-viewer to Doune, and other locations, is enhanced by their ability to locate themselves in the castle's history through its use as a film location of a favored television show (qtd. in Urry and Larsen 32). This connection could be furthered by the employment of specific references to the show and its implied use of heritage and history to help inspire visitor-viewers to further their own conception of their relationship to story, history, and place.

Furthermore, certain framing of visits to film-heritage sites, as Beeton notes, "can create a situation where people are basing their knowledge on false information as well as developing false expectations of sites they choose to visit" (Beeton, *Film-Induced Tourism* 31). This false information and expectation can, as Beeton goes on to argue, lead to disappointing experiences. More than these unsatisfactory experiences, this false basis can further jeopardize perceived history, and ultimately, heritage. Without the careful employment of references to constructed heritage, in this case *Outlander*, a location visit might be deemed unsatisfactory because the familiar is made unfamiliar. Some encouragement for the visitor-viewer to recreate their visual knowledge of the site through the mental recall of the scenes filmed there is beneficial. It could help increase the chance of a pleasant experience "on location," which in turn helps maintain visitor numbers through word-of-mouth recommendations. As Urry and Larsen note, "gazing is not merely seeing, but involves cognitive work of interpreting, evaluating, drawing comparisons, and making mental connections between signs and their referents" (17). Sites that encourage an active gaze (one that looks, interprets, evaluates, and connects) open up a dialogue between heritage and visitor-viewer that shows such as *Outlander* encourage as accidental by-products of their employment of heritage and history.

The active gaze can be seen in the deployment of imaginative recreation/recollection and subsequent reactions over the course of a visit. Scholars such as Broomhall and Spinks have noted that tourist literature about historic sites makes a greater demand on the traveler's imagination rather than on the tourist's bodily sensations (277). *Outlander* becomes a visual tourist literature when fans embrace the location, visiting it to retrace the steps of the characters. While Broomhall and Spinks's observations are certainly the case for the locations considered, sometimes the location also evokes bodily sensations as visitors remember the scenes filmed there, such as the whipping at Blackness/Fort William in episode 106. When some visitor-viewers recall the whipping of 106, it is not about heritage or remembering the scene, but recalling the impact of it. As they recreate it in their mind on location, their own response is recalled and intensified. While a visit to Blackness/Fort

William might encourage bodily and emotional sensations in a unique way, it goes one step further in the case of Blackness. Fiction is not real, but the fiction at this location is truth in part: it was, after all, a prison at a bloody moment in Scottish history. Imagination leads to bodily, and emotional, responses. Fiction helps demonstrate history by encouraging the viewer to confront its darker sides.

What does this mean for heritage sites and institutions in Scotland? Further work is needed as the show unfolds, and the number of locations increases, to trace the individual impact of the show on specific sites. It is clear that visitor increases at various locations are substantial. While some comments can be made now on the heritage tourism impact, some distance will be necessary to further measure it. At the same time, investment must be made (sooner rather than later) to maintain at least some percentage of the gains in visitor numbers and revenue. Historic Scotland, the National Trust for Scotland (NTS), and VisitScotland have all adopted different approaches to increasing and maintaining visitor numbers. Historic Scotland and NTS have a variety of exclusive merchandise, and arrange *Outlander*-specific workshops at their properties.[7] VisitScotland has produced digital maps of locations as part of its hodgepodged campaign "Scotland: The Land That Inspired *Outlander*." The campaign's website features various links on planning a visit, researching one's Scottish heritage, and other already-established tourist information on the VisitScotland website rather than new dynamic materials.[8] A coherent program that brings the three together intentionally to cross-advertise is needed. (Why does VisitScotland's campaign website, for example, not link to the heritage institutions?)

In general terms, there are programs and strategies that can be adopted by several of the locations (including those not under consideration here). For example, a heritage trail that provides insight to each site's history would be beneficial for educational purposes, as well as could be used to provide insight into how the sites were transformed. From that, temporary or semi-permanent exhibitions of costumes, set pieces, and/or photographs of each could be used to further tie location to show and help increase interest in visiting the site (and in the case of local fans turned visitor-viewers, encourage repeat visits). A strategic employment of such programs in phases would help sustain the "*Outlander* effect" past the immediate present. Doune Castle, as the most prominent site in terms of film-induced heritage tourism, seems the most likely candidate for piloting such programs.

Specific programming at different sites also needs to be introduced. For example, Doune hosts annual *Monty Python* events that include movie nights, re-enactments, and costume contests. An *Outlander* equivalent would create an event for visitor-viewers that could generate repeat visits. At the time of writing, an event planned around the castle's history in the Jacobite Rebellion is being advertised, but not in conjunction with the castle's use in *Outlander*. Such programming has the potential to appeal to local fans, and some level of targeted advertising would be appropriate.[9] Furthermore, incorporating an *Outlander* strand into the existing audio guide would further capitalize on the increase in visitor-viewer and visitor numbers in general.

While Blackness and Doune Castles both have an existing infrastructure to engage visitors, Midhope does not. It is on private land, which creates an obstacle for possible visitors. However, the estate does offer passes (available at the Hopetoun Farm Shop), allowing people to visit the site. Midhope/Lallybroch, of all the locations, is possibly the one that would benefit most from a concentrated attempt to bring the show to the site.[10] Hopetoun House, the main attraction for many heritage tourists on the Hopetoun Estate, was also used as a location in the first season. A concerted effort to help connect the locations would help the estate control the visitor-viewer who wanders to Midhope, as well as provide a fuller experience for that visitor-viewer while in the area. Its proximity to Blackness Castle (just under five miles) further demonstrates an interconnectivity of the filming locations, which independent tour guides have begun tapping into.

While visitor-viewers would undeniably welcome specific *Outlander*-inspired programming, sensitivity must also be given to the visitor who is not a viewer or *Outlander* fan. Despite the fact that some may share similar interests in history and heritage with the visitor-viewer, the programming should not alienate them, nor should it turn heritage into an outright *Outlander* advertisement. An example of an appropriate display of television costumes at a historic site can be found at Christ Church Dublin. A location for the popular history-inspired television show *The Tudors*, Christ Church maintains a display of costumes in its crypt, just outside of the treasury. The display is easily disregarded by non-fan viewers and does not distract from the experience of the crypt and treasury. While the small exhibition has its flaws (for example, the lighting is too low to completely appreciate the richness of detail and fabric), its sensitive placement helps meet the differing needs in regards to visitor and visitor-viewer.

Of course, the issue of funding and responsibility for programming has not been considered, and that consideration is a necessary part of the process of implementing such programming. There is not an easy answer here, nor a guarantee that such programming would be successful across the board. What works at Doune or Blackness, for example, may not work at Midhope, Culross, or Linlithgow Palace. Is the monetary risk worth it? Based on increased numbers, the multiplication of tours billed as *Outlander* tours, and the current interest on various social media platforms, it seems that a risk would be worth it—especially as the "*Outlander* effect" continues to grow. In an ideal world, heritage institutions, such as NTS and Historic Scotland, as well as government organizations, including VisitScotland, would work together with independent tour groups, to help subsidize and implement such programs. Furthermore, they could work with Sony, Starz, and the on-going production in general to establish programming and events that can generate interest in both visiting locations and the show itself.

Conclusion

In an exchange between Claire and Roger MacKenzie in the second book in the *Outlander* series, *Dragonfly in Amber*, Roger questions Claire about her feelings towards historians. Claire responds, saying that she does not hold historians responsible for creating the popular Romantic view of Bonnie Prince Charlie. Rather, she lays the blame elsewhere: "'No, the fault lies with the artists,' Claire went on. 'The writers, the singers, the tellers of tales. It's them that take the past and re-create it to their liking. Them that could take a fool and give you back a hero, take a sot and make him a king'" (ch. 47). Similarly, in terms of *Outlander* as TV show, it is not the historians who attempt to recreate the past for the present, but rather the artists—producers, actors, designers—who re-enact and recreate it for the screen. Rather than faulting them, those in *Outlander* have sought to engage the audience through a constructed, yet authentic, heritage. In a Twitter Q&A, Co-Executive Producer Maril Davis commented that the production is "striving for authenticity in all areas" (Ksiazek 2014). Designer Jon Gary Steele in an interview with *Variety Magazine* commented that the producers did not want its audience picking out inaccuracies, so his team worked to create "an 18th century slice of life in Scotland. Architectural detail, drapery, props, all of it authentic" (Verini). Authenticity is clearly at the forefront of the production's concerns.

Constructed authenticity and fictionalized history are not to be dismissed. As we have seen, they bring history to life for an audience in ways that are otherwise impossible. They are not meant to be historical re-enactments, but a backdrop for a fictionalized story based on history. The properties are rejuvenated, encouraging visitors to relive the story that inspired them to visit. A by-product of this imaginative recreation is the mental recreation of history in its physical context. By using Scottish historic properties in the course of filming, *Outlander* opens a gateway to the past that places history firmly in the audience's mind. Furthermore, the financial gains that these locations report help to preserve the site for the future, thereby becoming entrenched in the history of the location itself. Capitalizing on the current trends through strategic programming is the next step in ensuring that the "*Outlander* effect" is not temporary, but a lasting impact on Scottish heritage as used in the show.

Urry and Larsen note that "modern tourism is tied into, and enabled by, various technologies" including film and television where "vision [is] constructed through mobile images and representational technologies" (2). In the case of *Outlander*, its imagery inspires and shapes tourism within Scotland in ways not yet fully understood. Doune/Leoch, Blackness/Fort William, and Midhope/Lallybroch, as well as other locations, tell a story of Romanticized history that frames the locations amidst an artistic framing of dressing, costumes, and story. How that constructed history will impact heritage (in the broadest sense) in the future largely depends on how heritage institutions, production, tour companies, and fans proceed from here.

NOTES

1. This essay would not have been possible without the assistance of a wide variety of people, including friends and family who obligingly not only discussed aspects of my argument with me, but also accompanied me to locations (before, during, and after filming). Specific thanks must be given to the members of the Late Antique & Medieval Postgraduate Society at the University of Edinburgh who heard this essay in its first iteration, and allowed me to shepherd them around locations while discussing heritage issues.

2. While Castle Leoch is often associated with Leod, the seat of Clan MacKenzie, the connection is not explored here, because author Diana Gabaldon has acknowledged that this association was not intentional, as she did not realize Leod was a real place at the time of writing. The later association between Leoch and Leod, and eventually Doune, is best saved for another discussion. It is sufficient to acknowledge the association, and the fact it was briefly considered by the producers as a location at Gabaldon's insistence. For more information, see *The Outlandish Companion*.

3. My thanks to Callum Watson of the University of Edinburgh for the observation that the quartering and halving was unusual and unknown on historic arms, as well as the Seton Arms' utilization of the three crescents.

4. Fraser Heics (centered on the joining of the four quadrants), Fraser RN (centered on the joining of the four quadrants), and Fraser-Tytler of Balnain (three in the upper right quadrant surrounding a lion's head) all utilize crescents in the 19th century. See Paul, "Crescents."

5. It is worth noting that while Doune/Leoch sets were left up between filming blocks so that visitors could have an impression of what the castle was closed for, and only dismantled completely after filming ended, the coat of arms remained at Midhope/Lallybroch for a time after the other set dressing was removed.

6. It is worth noting that Blackness Castle has also been used in film productions, most noticeably in 1989 when Mel Gibson shot scenes of Franco Zeffirelli's film version of *Hamlet* there (Tabraham 31). While Tabraham in the *Official Souvenir Guidebook* remarks that Blackness has "served as a location for several films" only *Hamlet* is mentioned. Nor have such film connections been used in the promotion of and programming at the castle to the same extent as at Doune.

7. One such workshop was held in Culross, the NTS-owned Crainesmuir location, in August 2015 led by the show's herbalist, Claire Mackay.

8. For VisitScotland's campaign, visit: http://www.visitscotland.com/about/arts-culture/outlander.

The first iteration of the map (still available on the website) has few filming locations preferring locations related to the book. The second lists filming locations, and what they were used for, but does not give the viewer any information on access, opening times, physical location, or who manages the property. For a campaign that seeks to encourage visiting, it lacks key information that the prospective visitor would likely find useful.

9. For example, event organizers could appeal to local fan groups, such as Outlandish UK, to help promote the event on the groups' Facebook pages and Twitter accounts.

10. At the time of writing, no *Outlander* merchandise was yet available at the Hopetoun shop, but plans to introduce it were underway.

WORKS CITED

Beeton, Sue. *Film-Induced Tourism*. Clevedon: Channel View Publications, 2005. Aspects of Tourism 25.

_____. "Location, Location, Location: Film Corporations' Social Responsibilities." *Journal of Travel & Tourism Marketing* 24.2–3 (2010): 107–114.

BOP Consulting. *Review of the Film Sector in Scotland*. Creative Scotland, 2014. http://www.creativescotland.com/__data/assets/pdf_file/0018/25245/Review_of_the_Film_Sector_in_Scotland_-_Jan_2014.pdf.

Broomhall, Susan, and Jennifer Spinks. "Interpreting Place and Past in Narrative of Dutch Heritage Tourism." *Rethinking History* 14.2 (2010): 267–285.

Cadell, William. "Midhope Castle." *Restoring Scotland's Castles*. Ed. Robert Clow. Glasgow: John Smith & Son Ltd., 2000. 30–42.

Canton, Maj. "Interview with Outlander EP Ron Moore, Creator Diana Gabaldon, Stars Sam Heughan & Caitriona Balfe." *TV Tango* (2014). http://www.tvtango.com/news/detail/id/553/qa-with-outlander-ep-ronald-p-moore-creator-diana-gabaldon-stars-sam-heughan-and-caitriona-balfe.

Connell, Joanne. "Film Tourism: Evolution, Progress, and Prospects." *Tourism Management* 33 (2012): 1007–1029.

Conrad, Erin. "Outlander: The Garrison Commander, Episode 106." *ThreeIfBySpace*. Sept. 2014. http://www.threeifbyspace.net/2014/09/outlander-the-garrison-commander-episode–106–review/#.Vb96X3j_RUQ.

Faircloth, Kelly. "Outlander's Ron Moore & Terry Dresbach on Tartans, Redcoats and KNITS." *Jezebel*. 23 Apr. 2015. http://themuse.jezebel.com/outlanders-ron-moore-terry-dresbach-on-tartans-redco–1698084923.

Ferguson, Brian. "Doune Castle Film Set 'Besieged' by Outlander Fans." 12 Mar. 2014. http://www.scotsman.com/what-s-on/tv-radio/doune-castle-film-set-besieged-by-outlander-fans-1-3336639.

Fleming, John. "View from the Southeast," 1885. CANMORE.

Frost, Warick. "Braveheart-ed Ned Kelly: Historic Films, Heritage Tourism, and Destination Image." *Tourism Management* 27 (2006): 247–254.

Gabaldon, Diana. *Dragonfly in Amber*. New York: Random House, 1992.

_____. *Outlander*. New York: Random House, 1991.

_____. *The Outlandish Companion*. New York: Delacorte Press, 2015.

Gifford, John, and Frank Arneil Walker. "Doune Castle." *Stirling and Central Scotland*. London: Yale University Press, 2002. 378–382. The Buildings of Scotland.

Hennig, Christopher. "Tourism: Enacting Modern Myths." *The Tourist as a Metaphor of the Social World*. Ed. Graham Dann. New York: CABI Publishing, 2002. 169–188.

"Heritage, N." *Oxford English Dictionary Online* June 2015.

Jamal, Tazim, and Steve Hill. "The Home and the World: (Post)touristic Spaces of (In)authenticity?" *The Tourist as a Metaphor of the Social World.* Ed. Graham Dann. New York: CABI Publishing, 2002. 77–108.

Karpovich, Angelina. "Tourism and Hospitality Planning and Development." *Theoretical Approaches to Film-Motivated Tourism* 7.1 (2010): 7–20.

Ksiazek, Sarah. "Twitter Q & A with Maril Davis/Tall Ship Productions and Ron Moore." 17 Jan. 2014. Web.

Lengkeek, Jaap. "A Love Affair with Elsewhere: Love as a Metaphor and Paradigm for Tourist Longing." *The Tourist as a Metaphor of the Social World.* Ed. Graham Dann. New York: CABI Publishing, 2002. 189–209.

Mackay, Elspeth. *Investigating The Jacobite Risings.* Edinburgh: Historic Scotland, 2010. Investigating Historic Sites: Events.

Martin-Jones, David. "Film Tourism as Heritage Tourism: Scotland, Diaspora, and *The Da Vinci Code.*" *New Review of Film and Television Studies* 12.2 (2006): 156–177.

McGee, Patrick. "Appearance, Apparition, and History." *Cinema, Theory, and Political Responsibility in Contemporary Culture.* Cambridge: Cambridge University Press, 1997. 66–70. Literature, Culture, Theory 24.

Moore, Ronald. *Outlander: Episode 101 Podcast "Sassenach."* Audio Recording. Ronald D. Moore's Outlander Podcast.

_____. *Outlander: Episode 106 Podcast "The Garrison Commander."* Audio Recording. Ronald D. Moore's Outlander Podcast.

Moore, Ronald, and Anne Kenney. *Outlander: Episode 112 Podcast "Lallybroch."* Audio Recording. Ronald D. Moore's Outlander Podcast.

Moore, Ronald, and Terry Dresbach. *Outlander: Episode 102 Podcast "Castle Leoch."* Audio Recording. Ronald D. Moore's Outlander Podcast.

_____. *Outlander: Episode 103 Podcast "The Way Out."* Audio Recording. Ronald D. Moore's Outlander Podcast.

Moore, Ronald, and Toni Graphia. *Outlander: Episode 111 Podcast "The Devil's Mark."* Audio Recording. Ronald D. Moore's Outlander Podcast.

Morkham, Bronwyn, and Richard Staiff. "The Cinematic Tourist: Perception and Subjectivity." *The Tourist as a Metaphor of the Social World.* Ed. Graham Dann. New York: CABI Publishing, 2002. 297–316.

Nicola. "7 Outlander Locations in 7 Hours." Apr. 2015.

"Outlander Visitors to Doune Castle Near Stirling Increase." *BBC: Tayside and Central Scotland* Apr. 2015. http://www.bbc.co.uk/news/uk-scotland-highlands-islands–32194927.

Palmer, Catherine. "Tourism and the Symbols of Identity." *Tourism Management* 20 (1998): 313–321.

Paul, James Balfour. *An Ordinary of Arms Contained in the Public Register of All Arms and Bearings in Scotland.* Edinburgh: William Green & Sons, 1895.

Prudom, Laura. "'Outlander' Postmortem: Stars Discuss Black Jack's Acts in 'The Garrison Commander.'" *Variety.* 13 Sept. 2014. http://variety.com/2014/tv/news/outlander–106-sam-heughan-tobias-menzies-jamie-flogging-garrison-command-er–1201305304/.

Ruggia, James. "Scotland Banking on Outlander's Tourism Bump." 28 Aug. 2014. http://www.travelpulse.com/news/destinations/scotland-banking-on-outlanders-tourism-bump.html.

Sargent, Amy. "The Darcy Effect: Regional Tourism and Costume Drama." *International Journal of Heritage Studies* 4.3–4 (1998): 177–186.

Sobchack, Vivian. "'Surge and Splendor': A Phenomenology of the Hollywood Historical Epic." *Film Genre Reader II*. Ed. Barry Keith Grant. Austin: University of Texas Press, 1995. 280–307.

Tabraham, Chris. *Blackness Castle: The Official Souvenir Guide*. Historic Scotland, 2009. Historic Scotland Official Souvenir Guides.

Tidwell, Mandy. "The Outlander Effect or (in Gàidhlig) 'Buaidh Outlander.'" *Great Scot*. 23 May 2014. http://greatscotblog.com/2014/05/23/the-outlander-effect-or-in-gaidhlig-buaidh-outlander.

"Tourism Chiefs Eye Outlander Effect." *HeraldScotland* 13 Mar. 2015. http://www.heraldscotland.com/news/13205554.Tourism_chiefs_eye_Outlander_effect.

Urry, John, and Jonas Larsen. *The Tourist Gaze 3.0*. London: SAGE Publications Ltd., 2011.

Verini, Bob. "'Outlander,' 'Mad Men' Art Directors Strive for Authenticity." *Variety* 2 June 2015. http://variety.com/2015/artisans/news/art-directors-for-emmy-contenders-strike-for-authenticity–1201509690.

Zumkhawala-Cook, Richard. "Heroes, Thugs, and Legends: Celluloid Scotland at Century's End." *Scotland as We Know It: Representations of National Identity in Literature, Film and Popular Culture*. London: McFarland, 2008. 145–174.

_____. "The Mark of Global Scottishness: Heritage Identity and the Tartan Monster." *Scotland as We Know It: Representations of National Identity in Literature, Film and Popular Culture*. London: McFarland, 2008. 108–144.

Engaging with "Herself"
Fandom and Authorship in the Age of Tumblr

JENNIFER PHILLIPS *and* KATHARINA FREUND

Introduction

The Internet has allowed unprecedented levels of interaction between culture creators and the fandoms surrounding the texts they create. And yet, somewhat paradoxically, it seems to have given greater power both to the consumers as well as the creators of texts. Whereas fans are free to respond to the text in almost any way they choose, liberating it from the "tyranny" of the author (as Barthes called it), there is an elevation (almost deification) of the text's creator. Fans feel as connected to Joss Whedon as they do to Buffy and Angel; Chris Carter is as synonymous with *The X Files* as the names Mulder and Scully are; and Diana Gabaldon is so revered by fans of the *Outlander* book series (and, more recently, television adaptation) that she is often given the honorary title "Herself"—a reference to the Scottish lairds depicted in her books.

Since Internet fandoms rose to prominence in the mid–1990s, creators have had varied responses to the online communities surrounding their texts. Not only did writers of *The X Files* lurk in online message boards to see how fans were reacting to the episodes, some admit to taking inspiration from these discussions in their writing of the show (Knibbs). The relationships between creators and their fans can change from reverence to revulsion: Joss Whedon was beloved by his online fans during the run of *Buffy* and *Angel*, but has recently faced such an online backlash for his depiction of Black Widow in *The Avengers: Age of Ultron* that he has quit Twitter altogether (Schenker, Van Camp).

Diana Gabaldon is no stranger to engaging with fans online. In fact, the first readers of early drafts of *Outlander* were fellow members of a Compuserve message board. It was the positive response of her first online "fans" which encouraged Gabaldon to seek publication for a novel she had originally set out to write only for herself and only for practice (*Companion* "Preface"). In the quarter of a century since *Outlander* was first published, Gabaldon has continued to engage with online fans, although the mode and means of that engagement has changed over time. Advents in technology (such as the birth of Web 2.0) and growth in Internet use and popularity were early catalysts for the shift in the fan/creator relationship. More recently, however, the *Outlander* fandom has been transformed by the adaption of the novels into a Starz television series.

In what follows, we trace the history of *Outlander* online fandom from its early days to the present, making note of Gabaldon's interactions and engagements with her online fans. In so doing, we show how the creator of the texts has sought to set limits and ethics for the "appropriate" engagement with her novels, and consider how effective and powerful such exertion of authorial authority has been. Following this, we discuss how this fan/creator conflict has become further complicated with the introduction of the network and marketing elements of the *Outlander* television series.

Engaging with the Text: Outlander Fandom and Fan Production (Pre-Adaptation, 1991–2013)

Tracking the early history of a fandom is not a straightforward task. As Coppa observes, "not only has a comprehensive history of media fandom not been written, but there also have been very few histories of individual fandoms and the works of art they have produced" (41). Early in the scholarship of fan studies, Henry Jenkins noted the difficulty in establishing a concrete history of fandom as fannish names change and people may leave fandom over time (225). Fandoms are globally dispersed, and in the pre–Internet era many existed in isolation, with only small groups of friends gathering from the same area.

Those fannish histories that have been written tend to focus on the so-called media fandom. Female-dominated and usually centered around science-fiction television shows, media fandom actively produces fan works such as fan fiction, art, and video mashups called vids (Coppa). These types of fannish communities are often separate from the literary science-fiction fandoms, comic book fandoms, and other groups, where fan works are not usually central to their engagement to the text. Romance fans, also, had their own book clubs and mailing lists in the early digital areas, and their own ways of engaging with their preferred texts (Radway).

Outlander, of course, does not sit comfortably in any of these categories. Gabaldon seems quite proud of this fact, as her website features a series of rolling quotes which all showcase the genre-bending nature of her work, including this line from her first editor, quoted prominently on her website: "These books have to be word-of-mouth books because they are too weird to describe to anybody." As mentioned above, Gabaldon began her authorial career in the message boards of the Compuserve Books and Writers Community and it was there she was encouraged to seek a publisher for the text that would become *Outlander*. She is still a contributor to this site, more than 27 years later. Gabaldon shared her experiences with the earliest public fan sites for the series in her 2007 podcast: "They inspire people to want to talk about them. Consequently people get very interested in them and go out looking for other people with enthusiasm for these books just so they'll have someone to talk to about them" (Gabaldon "Episode 16").

According to this podcast, the first fan website for the novels appeared in 1994, "which in computer terms is back in the stone age" when she was contacted by a fan who asked her blessing to make the site (Gabaldon "Episode 16"). This was followed in 1997 by another group of fans who met with Gabaldon in Vancouver and went on to create the largest and longest-running fansite, the *Ladies of Lallybroch* which has more than 10,000 members. The *Outlandish Voices* Yahoo group and mailing list is another long-running fan space for novel fans, which continues to be active to this day. Gabaldon has shared a list of endorsed fan sites on her official website.

It was in these spaces that *Outlander* fans congregated to discuss and share their thoughts and experiences of the novels. It is not possible, though, to fully grasp the scope of *Outlander* fandom as much of the interactions must happen in person, between friends, and in private communications and emails.

Outlander Fandom and Fan Production (Post-Adaptation, 2014–)

Since the announcement that Ronald D. Moore was seeking a network to pick up his adaptation of *Outlander* in 2012 (Anders), book fans have taken to social media and have since created extensive online communities and networks to discuss the series. Moving from the more book club/forum discussion spaces such as *Ladies of Lallybroch*, Yahoo Groups, and Gabaldon's preferred Compuserve forums, *Outlander* fans spread into spaces like Twitter, Facebook, Tumblr, Pinterest, Instagram, and YouTube, as well as blogs on various platforms. These sites all feature large fannish communities, mostly focused around television and film.

In these spaces, one can find influential fans such as Connie Verzak (and others, discussed below), as well as endless fan pages and individual fans, the cast and production staff of the series, Gabaldon, and the STARZ network's official social media accounts for the series. Any of these may have multiple social media presences; for example, Gabaldon regularly uses Facebook, Twitter, her blog, and the Compuserve forums.

Fandom exists dispersed across all of them, and how this fandom interacts is informed by the affordances and communities already existing in these spaces. If fans want to communicate with their existing networks of friends, for example, Facebook or Twitter might be used, whereas fans might happen to follow an *Outlander*-related Instagram or Pinterest account as part of their more general use of the platform. As Perez writes, "If there's one thing fans excel at, it is sharing what they love. Sharing as a fan practice has increased the need for a simple and easy way to spread fannish content to friends and followers" (151). In the following section, we review some of the online sites where *Outlander* fandom engages before discussing Tumblr in detail.

Micro-blogging site Twitter allows users to follow each other and share messages of a maximum of 140 characters, organized around a key term known as a hashtag. It is widely used by Diana Gabaldon, the producers of the television series, and many of the actors. As it is difficult to access older Tweets, Twitter is most useful as a live or a nearly live medium. Twitter allows fans of the series to communicate directly with the production staff and the author and to share their reactions to news and episodes as it happens. As episodes air, the #outlander hashtag will be used by the fans to share their reactions, with Tweets directed at Gabaldon, Moore, and the actors. Twitter is also commonly used for fan petitions, such as the #emmysforoutlander campaign.

Arguably the world's largest social network, Facebook is also a key site for *Outlander* fans to share, like, comment, and post material related to the show. The network Facebook page for the series (facebook.com/Outlander TVSeries.starz) has more than 890,000 people following it (as of August 2015), and it coordinates much of the online fanbase by organizing contests, quizzes, and games to engage the audience for the series (starz.com/originals/out-lander/more). Often connected to Twitter and Facebook is Instagram, a site solely used for sharing images and short videos. Actors such as Caitriona Balfe (Claire) commonly post behind-the-scenes shots from the set or fan events like San Diego Comic-Con, which are then discussed and commented on by the fans.

YouTube is another tangential site for *Outlander* fandom, with thousands of videos shared by fans and the network. Much of this is paratextual material: interviews, public appearances of the cast and crew, trailers, behind-the-scenes videos, video responses to episodes or fan theories, as well as fan-created remix videos set to music which usually highlight Claire and Jamie's relationship (known as fan-vids or vids).

Pinterest, a curation site, is commonly used to find ideas for decorating, fashion, and crafts. It allows fans to collect "boards" of images, quotes, and memes as well as items such as jewelery, crafts, and knitting patterns inspired by the series. Many of these sorts of items fall afoul of copyright lawyers of the network and are issued with "Cease and Desist" letters (see discussion below). Blogs are another common space for *Outlander* fandom, with groups such as *Outlandish Observations* and *My Outlander Purgatory* discuss and speculate on the novels, series, and how they relate to each other. Several key blogs are discussed further below, but each of these blogs might also utilize any of the other social media sites as part of their online presence.

Without a doubt, though, the majority of contemporary fan communities interact using Tumblr. With around 250 million blogs as of August 2015, Tumblr allows fans to post text, photos, quotes, music, links, and so on with an easy-to-use interface that promotes sharing among the community ("About Tumblr"). The fans on Tumblr mostly commonly share animated gif image sets, quotes, screenshots of favorite scenes, actor or behind the scenes photos, fan fiction, and discussions and responses to the episodes. These posts are organized using hashtags, such as #outlander, #outlander spoilers, #jamie and claire, #sassenach, and many more.

Unlike fandom's previous home in Livejournal, which has community and group pages, Tumblr, Twitter, and Pinterest are organized entirely folksonomically (Trant). All posts are dependent upon the user adding the appropriate hashtag or keywords for it to be found by others. These hashtags are entirely generated by the community and can be represented in different ways. For example, posts showcasing the "ship" of Jamie and Claire might be tagged #jamie and claire, #jamie x claire, #clairexjamie, or many others. This leads to a community that grows organically, but is decentralized. Fans need to participate in order to learn the best hashtags and blogs to follow. "As a result [of this fragmentation], it is harder to get a comprehensive sense of a fandom and harder still to build a truly inclusive sense of community" (Hellekson and Busse 15).

Endorsed by Herself: Diana Gabaldon's Online Fandom Interactions

When the *Outlander* television adaptation premiered on August 9, 2014, it found its biggest fan in none other than Diana Gabaldon. In the lead up to the series' run, Gabaldon was active on social media—via her blog, message boards as well as her Twitter and Facebook accounts—promoting the show and interacting publicly with the show's creators and actors. Increasingly, it seems, it is the role of the author to become a prominent online voice in promotion of their works. Certainly Gabaldon's numerous posts in favor of the adaptation lending it a sense of legitimacy tied to her authority as originator of the source text.

Over the course of the first season of *Outlander*, Gabaldon has not only continued to promote the show online, but began to interact with the fandom to a greater extent than she had previously. Specifically, Gabaldon used her Facebook feed to share numerous fan-creations that responded to the adaptation. Thus, Gabaldon has used her power as the text's original author to endorse not only the television adaptation, but fans' opinion pieces, fan vids and video manipulations, twitter hashtags, fan-captioned images, and fan music video mashups, among others.

These online endorsements are in addition to those which Gabaldon officially sanctioned in a section in *The Outlandish Companion* ("I Get Letters"). Here, Gabaldon refers to fan-response texts as "other manifestations," such as "documents, pictures, and objects they've made, showing [her] some personal vision of Jamie and Claire, or some special expression of attachment to the books." These include sketches of the characters, handmade jewelery, kilt-clad teddy bears named "Jamie," pictures of babies named after *Outlander* characters—even one picture of a racehorse named after the novel *A Dragonfly in Amber*. Gabaldon's promotion of fan content allows us to form a picture of her personal opinion of "appropriate" engagement with her text. What becomes clear is that while Gabaldon does promote fan-made texts, they are almost exclusively response texts, informed by and closely related to the source text.

A clear example of fan-made text that responds to *Outlander* while remaining connected to the source text are Connie Verzak's humorous episode recaps. Originally posted on her Tumblr blog (atom1cflea.tumblr.com), Verzak's recaps were picked up by the ScotlandNow website (Verzak "Lallybroch") after receiving promotion via Gabaldon's Facebook page. These recaps take the form of images captured from the episodes, superimposed with Verzak's often hilarious observations.

The recaps range in tone. Some are pop-culture mashups. In one image, Frank is captioned with the phrase "I liked it so I put a ring on it," in reference to Beyonce's well-known song. In another image, he is given a quote from an *Indiana Jones* film, calling himself a "Professor of Archaeology and … obtainer of rare antiquities." Others are humorous observations about the show itself, such as Frank claiming that "with a name like 'Black Jack' you know that's an ancestor I can be proud of!" or Verzak's observation that when Claire and Frank make love in episode one, there are two shots of their prominently-placed wrist-watches ("Recap 101").

Gabaldon's promotion of Verzak's recaps demonstrates a willingness to participate with an often-times irreverent, humorous and sometimes downright mocking take on both the adaptation and its source material. More than commenting on the episodes themselves, Verzak's captioned images also engage with larger discourses surrounding the series, such as a recent article Verzak wrote for the *Scottish Times* (and promoted by Gabaldon) entitled "10 Times Claire Fraser Sassasmacked the Patriarchy," in which Verzak highlighted ten ways *Outlander*'s central character refused to adhere to gendered expectations not only for women in the 1740s, but also in her original 1940s context.

This article by Verzak is similar in tone to another blog promoted by Gabaldon through her Facebook page: *Feminist Jamie Fraser*. An *Outlander* twist on the *Feminist Ryan Gosling* meme, the blog claims to provide "your daily dose of feminism, *Outlander* style." This blog is similar in form to Verzak's—screen captures from the series have been accompanied by additional text. Some of these text quotes are taken directly from the series— such as an image of Jamie and Claire sitting in the Laird's room in Lallybroch overlaid with the word "ours," an indication of Jamie's progressive opinion of property ownership—particularly in in his eighteenth century context. Similarly, another image shows a screencap from the episode "The Reckoning" (E109), in which Jamie controversially administers corporal punishment to Clare for her disobedience of his order, which led to her being captured by Black Jack Randall. The image comes from later in the episode after Jamie realizes their relationship need not mirror those around him. Over an image of Jamie and Claire kissing are the words: "Wives obey their husbands. Husbands discipline them when they don't[…]. But, maybe for you and me it has to go a different way." This quote is a turning point not only for Claire and Jamie's relationship, but for the series itself, as it shows how their relationship manages to transcend two centuries of gendered expectations.

A completely different type of fan-response text promoted by Gabaldon is the *Outlander Anatomy* blog. Run by a "professor of gross and microscopic human anatomy" who claims to have taught over a thousand medical students in the U.S., this blog attempts to teach lessons in human anatomy "through the lens" of *Outlander*. One such lesson about ears and cartilage is illustrated with images of the tanner's boy whose ear is nailed to a pillory ("Hear, here"). Other lessons range from a purely academic analysis of Jamie's gluteus maximus ("Tush"), in-depth analysis of the anatomical elements of kissing ("Kiss"), or an article utilizing the numerous shots of Claire and Jamie's naked bodies in the wedding episode to test readers about the anatomical knowledge they have obtained ("Hallelujah").

While the blog uses the *Outlander* adaptation as a starting point, its goal is educational, rather than satirical like Verzak's is or theoretically engaged as *Feminist Jamie Fraser*. Much like *Feminist Jamie Fraser*, *Outlander Anatomy* is another fan-made text endorsed by Gabaldon which uses the *Outlander* novels and television adaptation as a springboard for a tangentially-related discussion. Both of these blogs are using the popularity of the series and Gabaldon's novels to reach a new audience and educate them with something external to the series itself.

On top of the blogs she has promoted, Gabaldon also participates in slightly tangential fandom activities, such as promoting a #50shadesofplaid hashtag that satirized the release of the *50 Shades of Grey* movie. Gabaldon's Facebook feed isn't beyond her own representation of fandom, specifically that surrounding Sam Heughan, the actor who plays Jamie Fraser. Gabaldon shared a Twitter image from a fan who was encouraging followers to rate Sam Heughan's different facial hair looks, or reposting "nice" pictures of Sam from magazine photo shoots. On a political note, she also reposted an image Heughan posed for in favor of the failed Scottish independence vote.

What all of these promoted fanworks have in common is that they are closely tied to the source materials themselves. Verzak's reviews, *Feminist Jamie Fraser* and the *Outlander Anatomy* guides are essentially annotated screencaps from the television series. While each shows the creator's extensive creativity with the source material, each of these fan creations endorsed by Gabaldon is inextricably linked to its original source materials. Moreover, these blogs are essentially tributes to the novels and the television series. Any criticisms are mild and wryly mocking at worst—such as when Verzak used an image of Mrs. Graham talking to Frank in "Both Sides Now" (E108), which was captioned with the phrase "let me patiently & carefully give you a summary of episode 101" ("Recap 108"), as a slight to the writers of the scene.

One interesting departure from Gabaldon's promotion of fan-related texts is her advertisement for KC Dyer's novel *Finding Fraser*. Dyer's novel is a chick-lit tale about one woman's trip to Scotland to find a man like Gabaldon's fictional hero. Not only is the central character obsessed with Jamie, she also spends her time in Scotland on an *Outlander* fan pilgrimage, visiting sites mentioned in the novels. Not only did Gabaldon encourage her followers to read Dyer's novel, her endorsement is emblazoned on the front cover. This departure is particularly interesting when read in light of the one area of fan-created works with which Gabaldon expressly takes issue—fanfiction.

Herself and Her Text: Gabaldon's Opinion of Fanfiction

While it seems that Gabaldon has placed her authorial seal of approval on quite a few examples of fannish engagement, there is one area of fandom which she has been vocal about in her disapproval: fanfiction. In a blog post in 2008 (subsequently removed, but reposted in various places including Kate Nepveu's blog), Gabaldon called fanfiction "immoral," "illegal," "simple-minded sex-fantasies." While Gabaldon does admit that not all fanfiction is pornographic, "enough of it *is* that it constitutes an aesthetic argument against the whole notion" (emphasis in original). Furthermore, Gabaldon goes on to align fanfiction to breaking into someone's house (even if the goal isn't to steal anything) or trespassing in someone's backyard (even if there is no plan to plant illegal drugs on the property) and cites the difference between someone expressing their fondness for Jamie Fraser by dating a red-haired man rather than "seducing my husband" (qtd. in Nepveu). The latter issue would seem that Gabaldon is placing herself firmly within Claire Fraser's shoes. Perhaps even more controversially, Gabaldon considered fanfiction akin to selling children into "slavery" before adding "it makes me want to barf" (qtd. in Nepveu). In a more measured statement on her website (current at the time of writing), while she finds it "flattering" that people wish to "engage" with her novels by writing fanfiction, she says she's not comfortable with it and requests that people not write it, not send it to her, and not publish it (either in print or on the Internet).

Gabaldon's argument consistently returns to the theme of fanfiction's illegality, at one point claiming "I'm not making it up; this is International Copyright Law." Gabaldon justifies this by arguing that her tacit acceptance of fanfiction may lead to her losing all control of her characters. Although Gabaldon herself admits that this is a "specious legal argument," she claims she has seen it being made (although doesn't cite when or where). Despite the lack of legal precedent, Gabaldon admits that she (or her agent) have been known to contact fanfiction authors and ask them to remove their works from the Internet. Because of her opinion of its legal status Gabaldon implores fanfiction writers to use characters whose copyright has expired (such as Sherlock Holmes) (qtd. in Nevpeu).

However, Gabaldon is not entirely correct. Much has been written about the legal status of fan works (in particular, Tushnet, Denison, Jenkins). Copyright law is notably complex, and fan works constitute a murky area between adaptation and transformative work. But legal scholar Rebecca Tushnet frequently argues that fanfiction should be protected under the "fair use" exemption to copyright as it is non-commercial and it does not interfere with the market for the original work. There is, though, no case law or legal precedent that conclusively rules on fanfiction in relation to copyright of the original work.

More than just relying on a (potentially incorrect) argument about fanfiction's illegality, Gabaldon's opposition to fan-inspired written works is also in ironic contrast to the inspiration for the character of Jamie Fraser, as well as her own descriptions of her initial drafting process, both of which have elements akin to the process of writing fanfiction. Firstly, Gabaldon was inspired by a source text. In the *Outlandish Companion*, Gabaldon describes watching rerun of a *Doctor Who* episode in which the second Doctor is joined by a young Scotsman from 1745—Jamie MacCrimmon. Not only was Gabaldon attracted to how the young man looked in a kilt, she also appreciated his "pigheaded male gallantry," particularly shown in his attempts to look after the Doctor's female companion, Polly ("Prologue"). Of course, Gabaldon not only based Jamie Fraser on Jamie MacCrimmon, but the historical setting for *Outlander* was also taken from *Doctor Who*. MacCrimmon is picked up by the Doctor in the aftermath of the ill-fated Battle of Culloden—the specter of which haunts the *Outlander* novels. Just like Gabaldon, fanfiction authors are also inspired by the characters and settings of source texts and use them as starting points for their own writing.

Not only does Gabaldon share the process of inspiration with fanfiction authors, her first readers were online. Also in *The Outlandish Companion* (1999), Gabaldon describes how part of what helped her write the original novel was her participation in an online message board called the *Literary Forum* ("Prologue"). Here Gabaldon met a group of people from diverse backgrounds all united in their love of books—both reading them and writing them. One night, in order to win an argument with a male member of the forum about what it felt like to be pregnant, Gabaldon shared a passage online which would later go on to be a scene between Jenny Murray and her brother Jamie. Gabaldon instantly received feedback, encouragement and requests for more. It was this feedback that made Gabaldon see that the novel she had written for "practice" ("Prologue") might actually have a readership. This process of writing "practice" texts, posting them online, receiving feedback and having a captive audience of like-minded fans is very similar to communities of fanfiction writers.

This irony has not escaped the notice of *Outlander* fans. In a *reddit* thread about *Outlander* fanfiction, user MaryPopNLockins asks if there is any "decent" *Outlander* fanfiction. Subsequent posters on the thread explain Gabaldon's position in opposition to fanfiction. Many users are happy to accept the creator's "prerogative" in requesting fanfiction not be written based on their works. However, user electrobolt believes that because of its origin as a "transformative work" with "Jamie based on Jamie McCrimmon from Doctor Who," fanfiction based on *Outlander* is therefore "fair game." Later in the thread, that same user has a more emotive response to Gabaldon's request, citing it as hypocritical.

> […] if there's one thing I can't abide it's hypocrisy. "I stole Jamie from Doctor Who, and that's okay, but you can't use him, because I am a REAL WRITER and you are just a LAZY THIEF." (I'm paraphrasing, but this is basically the absurdity of what she said in her original crazy statements […])

In an open letter in response to Gabaldon's original posts about fanfiction, LiveJournal user kate_nepveu expresses a similar sentiment:

> I particularly urge you to not revile fanfic on the grounds that much of it contains sex, when your own works, first, are *full* of sex, some of it involving characters not of your own creation, and, second, were inspired in part by Dr. Who. Because not only have you insulted some vocal fans of your books, but you look a bit foolish to boot.

Another potential complication to Gabaldon's rejection of fanfiction is her extreme endorsement of the television adaptation, which, at its core, could be deemed a form of fanfiction itself. Ronald D. Moore has often been quoted as claiming that his wife, costume designer Terry Dresbach, is the number one fan of the *Outlander* books and that his chief job in adapting them for television is to "not screw it up" (qtd. in Tedder).

Considering television adaptations as forms of "fanfiction" is not without precedent. Steven Moffat and Mark Gatiss, showrunners of the BBC adaptation *Sherlock*, have referred to themselves as men who "write fanfiction for a living" (qtd. in "Sherlocked"). The inspiration for a key set piece of the episode "The Sign of Three," wherein Holmes gives the Best Man speech at Watson's wedding, was based on Moffat's long-held desire to see such a scene when he discovered that it was missing from the Conan-Doyle canon (Asher-Perrin). Writing missing scenes or filling in narrative gaps are frequent impetuous for fanfiction writers (Jenkins 1992). This type of public admission aligns the writers with the fans, creating commonality between them and emphasizing their similar goals.

While Moore isn't adapting *Outlander* with the same freedom that Gatiss and Moffat are—where they pick and choose scenes and stories from the originals, rearranging them for their own purposes in what they call a "magpie" approach to adaptation (qtd. in Jefferey)—he is, in essence, creating a fiction which is based on and inspired by Gabaldon's work, characters and story. One reviewer went so far as to posit that the additional storyline in the *Outlander* mid-season finale "Both Sides Now" (E108) would not be out of place on a fanfiction website (Beth).

This episode's break from strict adaptation is evident in its title. Whereas all of the other episodes are named after chapters from Gabaldon's novel, this episode is not. More than simply breaking with adaptation in naming the episode, the plot includes several scenes that are never shown in the novels in which Frank is never given his own point of view. Such is this episode's relationship to fanfiction that the reviewer goes so far as to re-write Moore's additional scenes in the format of a summary as it would appear on a popular fanfiction website:

> Rated: Fiction, M—English—Thriller/Romance—Char: Frank Randall, Claire Randall, Rev. Wakefield, Mrs. Graham, Wee Roger, Alley Sally—Chapters: 18—

Words: 29,810—Reviews: 345—Favs: 87—Follows: 102—Updated: 1h ago—Published: Apr 20 Summary: *After the disappearance of his wife, Frank turns to the local police to locate her and a suspicious highlander. But incompetence and ineffectual methods lead him to follow his own dark path to find his lost love* [Beth].

Despite the fact that there is a possibility to interpret the television show as "legitimate" fanfiction, Gabaldon doesn't see it that way. For Gabaldon, there is nothing inherently contradictory about her rejection of amateur, unpaid, fanfiction texts and the professional, commercial Starz adaptation. Of course, her public endorsement of the series would almost certainly be part of her official credited role as "series consultant."

Gabaldon is not alone in her dislike of fanfiction. In fact, her request that it not be written is quote similar to those which have been voiced by other authors (see Fathallah). Those who, like Gabaldon, are opposed to fanfiction include George R.R. Martin and Anne Rice—both of whom voice issues around fanfic authors' "laziness" and their rights as the original creators of their characters and worlds (Fathallah 4). J.K. Rowling, while permitting the existence of *Harry Potter* fanfiction, has voiced fears about a young reader stumbling onto Harry Potter in an X-rated situation in a fanfiction story (Fathallah 4). *Twilight* author Stephenie Meyer's criticisms of fanfiction are about how the fanfiction author's time and talents are best served writing something that can be published (Fathallah 4). These comments are ironic when considering that one fanfiction author has been quite successful in getting her *Twilight* fanfiction published (admittedly with changes in names, setting, situation, and so forth to make it legal), namely, E.L. James of *Fifty Shades of Grey* fame.

Not all authors are entirely opposed to fanfiction. Neil Gaiman has expressed a toleration and acceptance of it, whereas Orson Scott Card, who was initially opposed to fanfiction, has come to accept it. Other authors (such as *Princess Diaries* author Meg Cabot, young adult author R.J. Anderson and *Mortal Instruments* author Cassandra Clare) actually credit fanfiction writing as the place where they were able to hone their craft (see Fanlore).

Where some authors who have voiced their discomfort with fanfiction based on their works have softened in their positions over time (see Rice and Scott Card), Gabaldon has remained steadfast in her request that fans "do not write it, do not send it to [her], and do not publish it, whether in print or on the web" (Official Website). For the most part, *Outlander* fans have obeyed Gabadon's request (although it is hard to tell how much this has been impacted by Gabaldon's claims that both she and her agent have been known to request fanworks be taken down from the web).

Despite Gabaldon's prohibition against fanfiction, there are still some works of fanfiction based on *Outlander* which are available online. A quick search of the two most popular fanfiction publishing websites (*Fanfiction.net* and *Archive of Our Own* or AO3), shows that while some people still write

Outlander fanfiction, the number of published stories is dramatically lower than fandoms based on other adapted books. At the time of writing, there were thousands of the following: *Harry Potter* (721,000 ff.net; 78, 500 AO3), *Game of Thrones* (3,400 ff.net; 13,200 AO3) and BBC *Sherlock* (52,000 ff.net; 73,000 Ao3).

Of the fanfiction works which have been published, there are two distinct groups: stories based on the *Outlander* universe and characters and stories based on the actors who play Jamie and Claire (what is referred to among fandoms as Real Person Fiction or RPF). At the time of writing, on fanfiction.net, there were only sixteen stories listed as based on the *Outlander* book series. Of those, only three featured Gabaldon's characters, while others were either tagged with *Outlander* because they contained a time-traveling motif, or the author simply needed to assign her story to a pre-existing text (as per *fanfiction.net*'s publication rules). On *Archive of Our Own*, there were slightly more—56 works—based on the *Outlander* novels, with most featuring Claire and Jamie, but with a greater focus on other characters such as Brianna, Roger and Lord John Grey.

Fandom Identities

How is it, then, that in the online world of seemingly infinite modes of fan participation, where the creator truly has little or no control over interpretation and secondary works, Diana Gabaldon has been able, by polite request, all but stop one huge aspect of fandom response texts? Is the aura of her author-function (as Foucault calls it) that powerful? Do fanfiction authors respect her request at face value or is the lack of fanfiction a reflection of their fear of legal reprisals? And what is it about fanfiction which Gabaldon so opposes when (as we have seen) she seems to endorse almost all other aspects of fandom participation and response to her texts?

One possibility for the distinct lack of fanfiction texts based on *Outlander* could rest in the source text itself. The reasons for writing fanfiction are numerous and well-documented (for example, Jenkins; Bury; Hellekson and Busse). While often considered in how it deviates from "canon" (i.e., the "officially" published or screened output of a novel, film or television franchise), many fanfiction texts bear distinct relationships to the canon which spawns them. Jennifer McGee observes how some fanfiction stories seek to explain the canon, fill in gaps in the canon, expand the canon in time (either backwards or forwards) and of course, alter the canon completely (to the extent that the story is described as an AU or "Alternate Universe" story) (162). Another key reason that many people write fanfiction is to see a relationship taken in a different direction from the canon (known as "shipping").

The sheer size of Gabaldon's literary output may, in part, fulfill the needs that most fanfiction supplements. Over the course of eight novels of over 1,000 pages each, Gabaldon has been able to explain many of the questions raised by the earlier novels—with the promise of answering more. Another reason for the lack of fanfiction could be the nature of the relationship between Claire and Jamie, which doesn't follow the traditional "will-they/won't they" pattern of many central pairings in film and on television.

However, if, as Becca Schaffner (2009) asserts, fanfiction is "valuable and powerful" because it causes "a large community of readers unconstrained by time, distance, age, or talent" to gather online and share their passion for the source text, then we must ask, what impact has Gabaldon's banning had on the *Outlander* fandom? A central feature of much fanfiction writing is to express support for a non-canonical romantic pairing, or "shipping" two characters (Freund, "Veni, Vidi, Vids!"). This practice, while cementing fan identities, also tends to create sub-groups within fandoms. For example, fans of the original *The X-Files* series were split about the very idea of a romantic relationships in the series (Knibbs). Followers of MSR (or, "shippers," perhaps the original usage of the term) believed that Mulder and Scully should be more than merely friends and partners. By contrast, No-Romos believed, as their name suggests, that there should be no romance within the series, and instead the show should remain focused on chasing aliens and other paranormal monsters (Scodari and Felder 240). There were also groups supporting other pairings such as Scully/Skinner, Mulder/Krycek, even a polyamorous relationship between Mulder, Skinner and Krycek (Knibbs).

Later fandoms became more focused on relationship pairings: "Team Edward" and "Team Jacob" was a key split within the *Twilight* fandom. Similarly, often wars erupt between fans of BBC *Sherlock* based on which "ship" they follow. Johnlock fans believe Sherlock and John have always been in a homoromantic relationship, despite any evidence to the contrary on the show. Adlock fans cite the episode "A Scandal in Belgravia" as evidence of Sherlock Holmes' enduring love for "the Woman," Irene Adler. These fans not only produce fanfiction which supports their relationship preferences, but they also congregate on Tumblr blogs and support members of their own communities against anything deemed as an "attack" from another corner of the fandom.

The *Outlander* fandom has very little evidence of such groupings. This may be due to the fact that the adaptation is still relatively new. This may also be due to the fact that most popular relationship pairings are already represented within the source text. Claire/Jamie, Brianna/Roger, and Jenny/Ian are completely stable, without serious love triangle possibilities even presented. These and other later relationships are presented in the original series as near-perfect, with nothing for fans to change with their "what-ifs." Further, these were all cemented by 1996, in contrast with the mystery of how *Twilight* and *Harry Potter* would end just as social media and fanworks spiked in popularity. This could also be in part because there are very few fans creating their own takes on the characters through fanfiction and other fandom-specific outlets. On Tumblr, where many fandoms congregate through personal microblogging pages, a search of posts tagged "Outlander" returns mostly promotional images rather than pages with unique fan output. The fan-creations within the Tumblr community are mostly gif captures from the series, arranged with quotes either from the show or the original novels. There is very little departure in these texts from the source materials. This is unlike Tumblr communities surrounding shows *Sherlock*, *Supernatural* and *Arrow*, whose Tumblr tags are full of original drawings, mashups, and pages and pages of fanfiction.

If anything, the tension in *Outlander* fandom rests not on shipping fictional characters, but on the growing number of Tumblr blogs in which promotional clips featuring Sam Heughan and Caitriona Balfe are re-posted as gifs and dissected in minute detail. Hypothesizing about the real-life relationship of two actors, using clips of their interactions as "proof" is somewhat different to writing a story in which the two people interact. For one, writers of "real-person fiction" are quick to admit that their versions of the "real people" are as fictional as any other literary character. Moreover, they cite the role of publicists and publicity in "creating" a version of the actor for public consumption which is a "carefully crafted fairy-tale to meet with public standards" (Theoria). Thus, even the "real" Sam and Cait accessed through media interviews and news articles are fictional constructs. However, theorizing about any real-world relationship between the two is a source of friction within the *Outlander* fandom on Tumblr. Some fans believe their theorizing is totally harmless, while others believe that if the actors have decided to keep their private lives private, then the fans have no right to pry.

Despite the lack of fanfiction and "shipping wars" common to most online fandoms, the fan-made content promoted by Diana Gabaldon through her Facebook page does demonstrate that while *Outlander* fans are not engaging with the television series (as well as the books) in the same way as most other fandoms, there is no lack of fan participation with the series. Fan spaces are easier to find and engage with than ever before, with reblogging, sharing and searching built into systems like Tumblr, Twitter, and Pinterest.

Still, as network marketing departments engage in these same spaces, all the media from the show (official or fan-generated) becomes part of the overall paratextual and transmedia experience (Sarachan 138). The fannish media landscape has blurred with official network Facebook pages sharing gifs and memes and fan-generated sites sharing official merchandise. Sarachan asks, "With all of these options for creating and sharing, the question arises whether such contributions define a 'fan' or merely a 'viewer'" (142).

Corporate Ownership and Fandoms

Indeed, since the *Outlander* adaptation, setting the limits of acceptable fannish engagement is no longer solely in Gabaldon's hands (if it ever really was). As with many other adaptations, *Outlander* fans have found their beloved books now under the care of a television or film studio, in this case parent company Sony Pictures. The Starz network, which bought the TV rights to *Outlander,* maintains its own web presences on Facebook, Twitter, and other social networks. Like Gabaldon, Starz also has a list of endorsed fan sites on the Starz Facebook page, including regional Facebook pages such as "Outlander Denmark," blogs, wiki pages, and Tumblr blogs.

The network's marketing team did extensive promotion and fan engagement through these sites in the lead up to the series premiere. Many of their social media posts used the fannish vernacular common to Tumblr, such as the #Droughtlander campaign during the long mid-season break. Gifs, memes, quizzes, and other fannish engagements were commonly seen produced by the official network accounts for the series. In particular, they caught much attention around the web for the #PocketJamie campaign, where fans were given a small paper image of Jamie Fraser and encouraged to take photos of it in locations all around the world to win a prize. This campaign was so effective it was nominated in the advertising industry's Shorty Awards.

The contestation of ownership over a text is a complicated affair, with Starz, Moore, Gabaldon, and the fans all having vested interests in the text and how it is perceived. Early studies of fandom cast the fan engagement as resistant to mainstream corporate power, as they created subversive homoerotic "slash" fanfiction and shared VHS tapes of fan-made mashup videos through the mail (Jenkins). However, fans are now courted by marketing teams and their engagement is actively encouraged. Due to the plethora of options now available for audiences, television marketing has moved towards a model of *engaging* the audience to promote sustained and loyal viewership, rather than relying on Nielsen ratings or market share (Wood & Baughman).

Meanwhile, the legal team of the Starz network has issued notices of copyright infringement to Terry Matz, an avid knitter who shared patterns for *Outlander* knitwear on her website. In the new fannish spaces post-adaptation, the network and copyright owners have defined what types of uses of their material are considered acceptable. Sharing the network-distributed and endorsed Pocket Jamie was allowable as it was initiated by their marketing team. Distribution of fan-created works such as knitting patterns was considered a copyright violation by the network, despite the fact that Gabaldon has endorsed such works in *The Outlandish Companion*, as discussed above.

Many fans are familiar with this sort of contradictory online experience, where networks foster certain types of engagement and punish others. Despite author J. K. Rowling's signaling her approval of fanfiction (as long as it did not include adult content), *Harry Potter* fan sites and fanfiction writers were issued cease-and-desist letters and notices of copyright infringement after the rights to the series had been purchased by Warner Brothers (Jenkins). *Doctor Who* fans have also been issued similar orders for sharing knitting patterns inspired by characters from the long-running series (Bloxham).

Murray has characterised this as "an uneasy dance in which conglomerates' desire for maximum circulation of content chafes uncomfortably against fans' resourcefulness in eluding the prescribed legal and economic frameworks for the circulation of that content" (9). In this model, fan participation in a media franchise is encouraged, but only to the limits prescribed by the corporate legal team:

> Corporations have thus manoeuvred themselves into the paradoxical position of seeking to generate maximum emotional investment by consumers in a given content brand, but of needing to corral such emotional attachment into purely consumptive-as opposed to creative-channels. It is this irresolvable tension which gives rise to the multiple fronts of fan/producer antagonism [Murray 10].

While there is often significant negative publicity surrounding intellectual property and trademark suits against loyal fans, Gabaldon and Starz have both engaged in this to prevent unwanted fan incursions into "their" text.

Conclusion

Digital communication tools have enabled fans and creators to interact directly, and also enabled fans to easily adapt source material into new forms. Since the announcement of the *Outlander* television adaptation, the community has grown from discrete community spaces such *Ladies of Lallybroch* and *Outlandish Voices* into the social media sites commonly used by fans and television viewers. Fannish images, reactions, and fanfiction can be easily discussed and shared by reblogging. As discussed above, questions have been raised as to how much these fannish practices differ from more casual viewing practices. The lines between viewer and fan have become blurred. *Outlander* fandom now exists alongside personal social interactions on Facebook, Twitter, Instagram, and Pinterest.

As a participant in these social spaces, Diana Gabaldon promotes and endorses much of the fan content generated around the series. Gabaldon also uses her social media presence to answer fan questions and share new content from upcoming books. However, she remains steadfastly opposed to fanfiction as "morally" and "legally" inappropriate interactions with *her* text. Now, post-adaptation, the legal and marketing departments of the network also work to define the limitations of acceptable audience engagement. The network simultaneously courts fans using guerrilla marketing campaigns, memes, and quizzes while at the same time issuing takedown notices to things they feel violate "their" intellectual property.

Outlander fandom presents one of many examples of how audiences now inhabit a complex mediascape moderated by copyright law and discourses of authorial control. This uneasy relationship between audience, author, marketing, and copyright lawyers is not a new phenomenon; complex concepts of ownership, fair use, and authority are part of the reality in which all popular creative works, such as *Outlander*, now exist.

WORKS CITED

"About Tumblr." *Tumblr.* https://www.tumblr.com/about

Alter, Alexandra. "The Weird World of Fan Fiction." *Wall Street Journal.* 14 June 2012. http://www.wsj.com/articles/SB10001424052702303734204577464411825970488

Anders, Charlie Jane. "Ron Moore will turn Diana Gabaldon's *Outlander* Series into a TV Show!" *io9.* 17 July 2012. http://io9.com/5926841/ron-moore-will-turn-diana-gabaldons-outlander-series-into-a-tv-show.

"Archive of Our Own." *Organization for Transformative Works.* http://archiveofourown.org.

Asher-Perrin, Emily. "Sherlock's Best Man Speech is Basically Fanfic, Moffat Says He's Absolutely Not a Sociopath." Torwww. 28 Jan 2014. http://www.tor.com/2014/01/28/sherlocks-best-man-speech-is-basically-fanfic-moffat-says-hes-absolutely-not-a-sociopath.

Balfe, Caitriona. "Instagram Photo." *Instagram.* https://instagram.com/p/rFwqpxt-Eg.

Barthes, Roland. "The Death of the Author." *Image, Music, Text.* New York: Hill and Wang, 1977, 142–148.

Beth. "My Top Ten Moments from Outlander Midseason Finale: Both Sides Now." *That's Normal.* 27 Sep 2014. http://thats-normal.com/2014/09/top-ten-moments-outlander-midseason-finale.

Bloxham, Andy. "Doctor Who's New Enemy: The BBC Lawyers." *Daily Telegraph.* 14 May 2008. http://www.telegraph.co.uk/news/uknews/1953364/Doctor-Whos-new-enemy-the-BBC-lawyers.html.

Bury, Rhiannon. *Cyberspaces of Their Own: Female Fandoms Online.* New York: Peter Lang, 2005.

Calvert, Ben, Neil Casey, Bernadette Casey, Liam French and Justin Lewis,. *Television Studies: The Key Concepts.* London: Routledge, 2007.

Coppa, Francesca. "A Brief History of Media Fandom." *Fan Fiction and Fan Communities in the Age of the Internet.* Eds. Hellekson, Karen and Kristina Busse. Jefferson, NC: McFarland, 2006. 41–59.

Cover, Rob. "Audience Inter/Active Interactive Media, Narrative Control and Reconceiving Audience History." *New Media & Society* 8.1 (2006): 139–58.

"Dear Shippers." *Trust This Dialect.* 3 May 2015. http://trustthisdialect.tumblr.com/post/118007242362/dear-shippers

Denison, Rayna. "Anime Fandom and the Liminal Spaces between Fan Creativity and Piracy." *International Journal of Cultural Studies* 14.5 (2011): 449–66.

Dyer, K.C. *Finding Fraser.* Vancouver: Lions Mountain, 2015.

Fanfiction.Net. https://www.fanfiction.net.

Fathallah, Judith. "'Except That Joss Whedon Is God': Fannish Attitudes to Statements of Author/Ity." *International Journal of Cultural Studies* (2014): n.p.

Feminist Jamie Fraser. http://feministjamiefraser.tumblr.com.

Fiske, John. *Reading the Popular.* London: Routledge, 1989.

_____. *Television Culture.* London: Routledge, 1987.

Foucault, Michel. "What is an Author?" *Language, Counter-Memory, Practice: Selected Essays and Interviews.* Ithaca: Cornell University Press, 1970.

Freund, Katharina. "'Fair Use Is Legal Use': Copyright Negotiations and Strategies in the Fan-Vidding Community." *New Media & Society* (2014): 1461444814555952.

_____. "'Veni, Vidi, Vids!' Audiences, Gender and Community in Fan Vidding." University of Wollongong dissertation, 2011. http://ro.uow.edu.au/theses/3447.

Gabaldon, Diana. "Deal with Sony Pictures for Adaptation of *Outlander* for Cable TV Series." DianaGabaldonwww.2012.

_____. *Diana Gabladon's Official Webpage. DianaGabaldon.com.* 2015.

_____. "Episode 16: My History and Experience with the Web." 15 October 2007. DianaGabaldonwww.

——.*The Outlandish Companion.* New York: Delacorte Press, 1999. Kindle File.

Grassi, Laurie. "Meet Diana Gabaldon, Author of the Incredible Outlander Series." *Chatelaine.* 25 June 2014. http://www.chatelaine.com/living/chatelaine-book-club/interview-with-diana-gabaldon-author-of-outlander-series-soon-to-be-tv-show.

Hellekson, Karen, and Kristina Busse. *Fan Fiction and Fan Communities in the Age of the Internet: New Essays.* Jefferson, NC: McFarland, 2006.

_____. *The Fan Fiction Studies Reader.* Iowa City: University of Iowa Press, 2014.

Hills, Matt. "The Dispersible Television Text: Theorising Moments of the New *Doctor Who.*" *Science Fiction Film & Television* 1.1 (2008): 25–44.

_____. *Fan Cultures.* London: Routledge, 2002.

Jeffery, Morgan. "*Sherlock* Mark Gatiss Q&A: 'Horror is a big part of Sherlock Holmes.'" *Digital Spy.* 5 Jan 2012. http://www.digitalspy.com.au/british-tv/s129/sherlock/interviews/a358335/sherlock-mark-gatiss-qa-horror-is-a-big-part-of-sherlock-holmes.html.

Jenkins, Henry. *Convergence Culture: Where Old and New Media Collide.* New York: New York University Press, 2006.

_____. *Textual Poachers: Television Fans and Participatory Culture.* London: Routledge, 1992.

Knibbs, Kate. "How Horny *X-Files* Lovers Created a New Type of Online Fandom." *Gizmodo.* 5 May 2015. http://gizmodo.com/how-horny-x-files-lovers-created-a-new-type-of-online-f-1702083417.

Ladies of Lallybroch. http://www.lallybroch.com.

Lutes, Alicia. "Outlander Author Diana Gabaldon on the Finale, Its Controversy, and Season 2." *The Nerdist.* 2015. http://nerdist.com/outlander-author-diana-gabaldon-on-the-finale-its-controversy-and-season–2.

Matz, Terry. "Outlander Patterns No Longer Available." *In The Loop Knitting.* http://intheloopknitting.com/outlander-patterns-no-longer-available.

McGee, Jennifer. "'In the end, it's all made up': The Ethics of Fanfiction and Real Person Fiction." *Communication, Ethics, Media and Popular Culture.* Ed. Phyllis M. Japp, Mark Meister and Debra K. Japp. New York: Peter Lang: 2005.

Murray, Simone. "'Celebrating the Story the Way It Is': Cultural Studies, Corporate Media and the Contested Utility of Fandom." *Continuum Journal of Media and Cultural Studies* 18.1 (2004): 7–25.

Nepveu, Kate. "Diana Gabaldon & Fanfic Followup." *Dreamwidth.* 10 May 2010. http://kate-nepveu.dreamwidth.org/836748.html.

Nightingale, Virginia. *Studying Audiences: The Shock of the Real.* London: Routledge, 1996.

Outlander Anatomist. "Anatomy Lesson 1: Today's Anatomy Lesson: Jamie's Tush or Bottoms up!." *Outlander Anatomy.* 28 Sep 2014. http://www.outlanderanatomy.com/todays-anatomy-lesson-jamies-tush-or-bottoms.

_____. "Anatomy Lesson 14: 'Jamie and Claire' or 'Anatomy of a Kiss.'" *Outlander Anatomy.* 14 Feb 2015. http://www.outlanderanatomy.com/jamie-and-claire-or-anatomy-of-a-kiss.

_____. "Anatomy Lesson 18: 'Hallelujah Chorus Part Deux.'" *Outlander Anatomy.* 31 Mar 2015. http://www.outlanderanatomy.com/anatomy-lesson–18-hallelujah-chorus-part-deux.

_____. "Anatomy Lesson 24: The Ear—Part I." *Outlander Anatomy.* 23 Jun 2015. http://www.outlanderanatomy.com/hear-here-the-ear.

Outlander Anatomy. http://www.outlanderanatomy.com.

"Outlander Fanfiction?" *reddit.* Sep 2014. https://www.reddit.com/r/Outlander/comments/2ff5p6/outlander_fanfiction.

"Outlandish Voices." *Yahoo Groups.* https://groups.yahoo.com/neo/groups/DianaGabaldon/info

Perez, Nistasha. "Gif Fics and the Rebloggable Canon of Superwholock." *Doctor Who: Fan Phenomena.* Ed: Paul Booth. Bristol: Intellect, 2013.

"Professional Author Fanfic Policies." *Fanlore.net.* http://fanlore.org/wiki/Professional_Author_Fanfic_Policies

Radway, Janice A. *Reading the Romance: Women, Patriarchy, and Popular Literature.* Chapel Hill: University of North Carolina Press, 1991.

Sarachan, Jeremy. "Doctor Who, Slacktivism and Social Media Fandom." *Fan Phenomena: Doctor Who.* Ed. Paul Booth. Bristol: Intellect, 2013.

Schaffner, Becca. "In Defense of Fanfiction." *The Horn Book Magazine* 85 (2009): 613–18.

Schenker, Marc, and Jeffrey Van Camp. "Joss Whedon Quits Twitter: A Tale of Shame, Feminism and Angry Trolls." *Digital Trends.* 6 May 2015. Phttp://www.digitaltrends.com/social-media/joss-whedon-driven-off-twitter.

Scodari, Christine, and Jenna L. Felder. "Creating a Pocket Universe: 'Shippers,' Fan Fiction, and the *X-Files* Online." *Communication Studies* 51.3 (2000): 238–257.

Shefrin, Elana. "*Lord of the Rings, Star Wars,* and Participatory Fandom: Mapping New Congruencies Between the Internet and Media Entertainment Culture." *Critical Studies in Media Communication* 21.3 (2004): 261–81.

"Sherlocked: Steven Moffat Talks Fan Art and Fanfiction." *Sherlockology.* 3 June 2015. http://www.sherlockology.com/news/2015/6/3/steven-moffat-fan-fiction–030615.

Staiger, Janet. *Media Reception Studies.* New York: New York University Press, 2005.

Starz. "How #Pocketjamie Became a World Wide Sensation." *Industry Shorty Awards.* http://industry.shortyawards.com/nominee/6th_annual/Wu/how-pocketjamie-became-a-world-wide-sensation.

_____. "More Outlander." *Outlander on Starz.* http://www.starz.com/originals/outlander/more.

_____. "Outlander Facebook Page." *Facebook.* https://www.facebook.com/OutlanderTVSeries.starz.

Tedder, Michel. "Creator Ronald Moore Is 'very curious to see how people react to *Outlander* return.'" *Variety.* 2 April 2015. http://variety.com/2015/scene/vpage/creator-ronald-moore-is-very-curious-to-see-how-people-react-to-outlander-return–1201465369.

Theoria. "Dust of Every Writer." *The Fanfic Symposium.* 27 Aug 2001. http://www.trickster.org/symposium/symp80.html/

Tushnet, Rebecca. "I Put You There: User-Generated Content and Anticircumvention." *Vanderbilt Journal of Entertainment and Technology Law* 12 (2010): 889–946.

_____. "Judges as Bad Reviewers: Fair Use and Epistemological Humility." *Law & Literature* 25.1 (2013).

_____. "Legal Fictions: Copyright, Fan Fiction, and a New Common Law." *Loyola of Los Angeles Entertainment Law Review* 17 (1996): 651.

_____. "Payment in Credit: Copyright Law and Subcultural Creativity." *Law and Contemporary Problems* (2007): 135–74.

Trant, Jennifer. "Studying Social Tagging and Folksonomy: A Review and Framework." *Journal of Digital Information* 10.1 (2009).

Verzak, Connie. "All the *Outlander* Edits I Ever Edited." *Killing Time.* 24 Sep 2014. http://atom1cflea.tumblr.com/post/98346816211/all-the-outlander-photo-edits-i-ever-edited.

_____. "Ex-post facto, y'all. *Outlander* recap 101, Sassenach." *Killing Time.* 20 Mar 2015. http://atom1cflea.tumblr.com/post/114169679786/ex-post-facto-yall-outlander-recap.

_____. "Outlander recap: Episode 12, Lallybroch: Don't Make Jenny Have to Come over and Get You." *ScotlandNow.* 27 April 2015. http://www.scotlandnow.dailyrecord.co.uk/lifestyle/outlander-recap-episode–12-lallybroch–5590124.

_____. "*Outlander* recap 108, Both Sides Now, Part 2." *Killing Time.* 9 Oct 2014. http://atom1cflea.tumblr.com/post/99548532351/outlander-s1e08-photo-recap-both-sides-now.

_____. "*Outlander* recap 110, By the Pricking of My Thumbs." *Killing Time.* 16 Apr 2015. http://atom1cflea.tumblr.com/post/116582367351/outlander-recap–110-by-the-pricking-of-my.

_____. "10 Times Claire Fraser Sassasmacked the Patriarchy." *ScotlandNow* 3 August 2015. http://www.scotlandnow.dailyrecord.co.uk/lifestyle/10-times-claire-fraser-sassasmacked–6184482.

Williams, Rebecca. "Good Neighbours? Fan/Producer Relationships and the Broadcasting Field." *Continuum: Journal of Media & Cultural Studies* 24.2 (2010): 279–89.

Wood, Megan M., and Linda Baughman. "*Glee* Fandom and Twitter: Something New, or More of the Same Old Thing?" *Communication Studies* 63.3 (2012): 328–44.

Diana Gabaldon's Excerpts and Daily Lines

When the First Read Is a Re-Read

Jessica R. Matthews

Anticipation. It's what makes us turn the pages of a Diana Gabaldon book. The powerfully immersive nature of Gabaldon's storytelling heightens our expectations about "what happens next" in the saga of Highlander Jamie Fraser and his time-traveling wife, Claire. For some of us, the anticipation is so great that we read ahead to have our predictions confirmed or denied; for others, the anticipation flames out, and we may put the book aside for a while. But regardless of how we handle that anticipation, for most of us, it's based on a linear reading of a complete work. Few of us[1] begin reading a Gabaldon novel in the middle and then read one randomly chosen paragraph after another.

Yet for more than ten years, a cohort of Gabaldon's readers has been reading in just that way. These readers regularly consume excerpts of Gabaldon's work-in-progress by accessing the snippets she distributes to her various social media outlets. These excerpts vary in length from nearly complete scenes to a few lines of dialogue, and they appear unscheduled and in no particular order throughout the several years it takes Gabaldon to finish one of her lengthy novels. As of this writing, the aggregated excerpts from all of the social media outlets Gabaldon uses represent a substantial body of archived[2] work for readers to access, and the access is open to anyone. No passwords are required.

Though it's impossible to tell how many of Gabaldon's readers look through these excerpts,[3] those who enjoy them and post to the Diana Gabaldon folder of the Books and Writers Community forum on Compuserve, the focus of this paper, are grateful for these "nuggets" (Devane) and their easy access.[4] Many of these readers attribute their desire for excerpts to the addictive nature of the *Outlander* series, as the contributors to the "Symptoms of Outlander Addiction" thread on the Gabaldon Books and Writers forum attest.[5] Accustomed to starting *Outlander* and compulsively reading through the series, devoted fans of the story and its characters eventually run out of books but not an intense desire for them. Many of these fans resort to rereading the series[6] to satisfy that desire and describe themselves as in a near "perpetual" state of "re-reading" (Henry, "Symptoms"), while others turn to Davina Porter's audio versions of the books. But for those readers whose hunger for the story cannot be satiated in these ways, their need for a continuous emotional connection with the books drives them to Gabaldon's social media outlets where they quickly discover they can find *more* of the story, albeit in fragments only.

These readers are particularly susceptible to the allure of excerpts, as "Sally" noted in her post to the "Read or not read—that is the question" thread on the Gabaldon Books and Writers forum: "I do read every excerpt … because I have zero self-control and really enjoy having the excerpts to keep me thinking about the story between books" ("Sally").

Implied in "Sally's" comment is the need for instant gratification, a need cultivated and met by the very social media that makes the excerpt reading practice systematic and scalable, but which also raises questions about its impact on the reading process. In her 2014 blog post to *Romance Around the Corner*, Brie addresses these questions directly: "Is Anticipation is the New Gratification?" In her post, Brie bemoans the sharing of details about books that increase reader anticipation and often lead to disappointment when the book fails to live up to its hype, and wonders whether "the satisfaction we find in the public act of waiting, replacing the satisfaction found in the private act of reading?" If reading excerpts is just about getting a "fix" of the story while waiting for the complete novel, has the story itself been subsumed by the anticipation for it?

The emphasis on anticipation runs throughout many of the conversations about excerpt reading in the Books and Writers forum. After Gabaldon posted a comment stating she would "kill" one of her characters in *Echo in the Bone* (Gabaldon, "ECHO [spoiler!]"), "Riverlady" replied, "I just love it when you do that! It just ratchets up the anticipation. Drooolll, shiver…" Other excerpt readers convey that sense of anticipation in the language of addiction and note how excerpts provide a needed "fix" to make waiting for the complete novel easier to bear:

> I read the excerpts … all of them. In fact, sometimes, before Echo came out, I would re-read them. I enjoyed having them because A) I needed a "fix" and B) The element of surprise stresses me out!! Yes, I am one of those that likes to know what Christmas presents I have coming. I am also one of those that likes

to know the end of a movie so that I can prepare myself for the journey and enjoy it ["DanaB"].

Notable in "DanaB's" comment is her comfort with what many readers would consider a spoiler: knowing how things turn out ahead of time. Instead, she finds greater pleasure in knowing what will happen so that she can focus on "the journey and enjoy it." This focus on the journey rather than the destination is one of the most distinctive characteristics of the excerpt reader and explains why they are undisturbed by spoilers.

Gabaldon's novels have a seductive power that makes that journey so pleasurable that readers do not want it to end. Excerpt reading can extend that journey, which is part of their appeal. Excerpt readers argue that the pleasure to be had from a "virgin" read of the novel is far too fleeting than the amount of joy to be had reading excerpts over months and years, as "Sabine" explains:

> If the DL [daily line] would spoil the surprises in the book, it would still be worth it. Let me explain: The first, surprising, "everything is new" read of a new book can take about 3 hours to 2 days, depending on the reading speed. After that, you enjoy rereading 3 to a zillion times, until you get all the details....
> So on the one side, you have these hours, which might be more fun unspoilt. On the other side, however, you have the hours of fun reading and discussing the DL's. Waiting each day for a new excerpt. Putting it into place, trying to find out, what it could mean ["Sabine"].

As Sabine suggests, excerpt readers enjoy puzzling out the order and meaning of these textual fragments, but her comment about "waiting each day for a new excerpt" underscores how differently the reading process is for these readers: they crave the parts rather than the whole because the feeling of anticipation and suspense can be sustained over a longer period. Thus, consuming excerpts extends the reading experience—the recycling of the anticipation, suspense, and gratification—a useful strategy for fans of Gabaldon's work who have become addicted to her novels and have a more intense need for the story that rereading cannot fulfill.

But a steady diet of excerpt reading, as gratifying as it may feel at the time, has its consequences: excerpt readers can never have a pure "first read" of the complete novel. "I'll only get once chance to experience it brand new," explained Karen Henry, a veteran contributor and moderator of the Gabaldon Books and Writers forum, and she works hard to avoid excerpts in order to "preserve that pristine first-reading experience" (Henry, Message to the Author). Readers like Henry will always sense the ghost of the excerpts flitting in and out, as if the palimpsest of the novel rises to the surface and then submerges, producing a reading experience that is both a first read and a re-read at the same time.

> When I first came here (many years ago), I read excerpts. Then I discovered they kind of spoiled things for me once I began reading the published book. They didn't feel fresh; the sense of discovery that one gets from a first read would be missing in those parts ["BethS"].

Those who read excerpts are not bothered by the duality of first read/re-read experience; in fact, they enjoy it; others, like Karen Henry and "BethS" are. And yet these former excerpt readers still find themselves tempted to read excerpts over the years-long drought while they wait for the next novel, especially given how often Gabaldon releases them and how easy they are to find. The many comments to the "Excerpt Withdrawal Support Group" thread, with their language of addiction and recovery, illustrate how difficult it is for fans to resist the temptation to read excerpts.

Love them or evade them, Gabaldon's excerpts, a stellar example of social media marketing, have added a new dimension to the reading experience, one that emphasizes the interpretive experience of an *incomplete* text. More importantly, excerpt reading foregrounds anticipation through the steady feed of fragments readers come to expect, placing greater emphasis on immediate gratification for even a morsel of text rather than an appreciation of the text as a unified work. This explains why the language of addiction runs through so many of the posts about the excerpt-reading experience. But more interesting, perhaps, is that Gabaldon herself uses the excerpts for her own gratification: she not only enjoys watching how excerpt readers respond to her plot and characters, she also finds their activity encourages her to keep writing.

It is, perhaps, the gratification that Gabaldon seeks that is the most disruptive aspect of the excerpt reading process. Her interaction with excerpt readers overturns the presumption that the reading experience is a transaction solely between the reader and the text. She writes the excerpts, posts them to social media sites, and presides over the interpretive experience of excerpt readers with coy and sometimes subversive comments[7] intended to satisfy reader curiosity and heighten it at the same time. All of this, combined with the sheer volume of excerpts and the hive of conversation about them, have introduced a new type of meaning-making for excerpt readers that takes place before the novel's publication: For these readers, the interpretive desire is to make meaning from textual fragments, and to extend that meaning-making over the years rather than through a discrete reading of a complete text. Thus, their activity is on display for the consumption of the author, Diana Gabaldon, while she is writing her novel. She explains:

> No work of art is complete until someone else shares it. Communication requires two parties. Having written something, I feel that some small cosmic circle remains unclosed until that something is read. [Gabaldon, *Outlandish Companion* 389].

Several authors post excerpts from their work-in-progress to their social media outlets, some seeking feedback but most using it as a smart marketing tool that helps them remain engaged with their fan base. Diana Gabaldon, however, uses this strategy extensively, and she has for a long time. Her fondness for social media and excerpts goes back to her early days as a novelist. In 1988, she began writing her first novel, *Outlander*, and in 1990, she posted an excerpt from it to the early version of Compuserve in order to "win an argument with a gentleman about what it feels like to be pregnant" (qtd. in Pera). That excerpt, where Jenny Murray describes her pregnant state to her husband Ian, her brother, Jamie Fraser, and his wife, Claire (*Outlander*, ch. 30), is one of the most lyrical and moving in all of *Outlander*, and the other participants on Compuserve recognized Gabaldon's talent and encouraged her to keep posting excerpts. She did, and her excerpts eventually caught the attention of someone on the list who helped her find an agent to publish her manuscript. *Outlander* was published by Delacorte in 1991 and Gabaldon had a multi-book contract. There is nothing like success to reinforce a practice, so Gabaldon embraced the power of the excerpt to garner attention and elicit reactions from readers.

By 2003, Gabaldon was posting excerpts to her own Books and Writers Community forum on Compuserve, excerpts that were in turn picked up by some of the original *Outlander* fan forums, such as the *Ladies of Lallybroch* and *Outlandish Voices* on Yahoo. Other excerpts appeared on Gabaldon's blog and website. Still, her Books and Writers forum was the main vehicle for releasing excerpts until 2011 when she became a power user of Facebook and Twitter. At that point, she began referring to excerpts as "Daily Lines" (#DailyLines or DLs), and though not always released on a daily basis as the name implies, they appear regularly and sometimes with great frequency on these social media sites as well as the Books and Writers forum.

Gabaldon's excerpt practice differs in important ways from other social media promotional strategies. It is not a serial release of the book, chapter-by-chapter or episode-by-episode. HarperCollins tried this approach in 2012 with its Like to Read app for Elizabeth Haynes' *Into the Darkest Corner* (Habash). For each 500 likes that the book received on its Facebook page, readers got another chapter of this psychological thriller. While this was a new use of social media, the publisher did adhere to the linear narrative; chapters were not released out of order. The fragments of works-in-progress that Gabaldon releases, however, are mostly devoid of context and with no allegiance to plot sequence. While they are always polished—"I never show anybody anything that I don't think is fit for human consumption," she says (Gabaldon, "Pre-publishing and Audience," MSG. 795733.20)—they provide just enough information to kindle the interest of a knowledgeable reader who recognizes characters and locations, but not enough to see the themes and scope of the novel, nor get a sense of its aesthetic power. Major events in the plot are rarely provided, as one long-serving member of the forum, Marte Brengle, who has read Gabaldon's excerpts "right from the beginning," noted: "Diana *never* gives out the really juicy parts before publication" (Brengle).

Below is a typical example of a Gabaldon excerpt from Book Seven in the *Outlander* Series, *Echo in the Bone*, published in 2009. This brief exchange between Ian Murray, the nephew of the series hero, Jamie Fraser, and William Ransom, a young lieutenant in the British army and an emerging major character in the series, first appeared as an excerpt in 2008:

> Murray lifted the camp-kettle off the fire and set it on the ground. He laid the knife in the embers for a moment, then dipped the hot blade into the frying pan, now filled with water. The hot metal hissed and gave off clouds of steam.
> "Ready?" he said.
> "Yes."
> William knelt down by a big poplar log and laid his injured arm flat on the wood. It was visibly swollen, the bulge of a large remnant splinter dark under his skin, the skin around it stretched and transparent with pus, painfully inflamed.
> The Mohawk—he couldn't yet think of him as anything else, despite the name and accent—glanced at him across the log, eyebrows raised quizzically.
> "Was that you I heard? Screamin', earlier?" He took hold of William's wrist.
> "I shouted, yes," William said, stiffly. "A snake struck at me."
> "Oh." Murray's mouth twitched a little. "Ye scream like a lassie," he said, eyes returning to his work. The knife pressed down. William made a deeply visceral noise [Gabaldon, "Let's Laugh Snips!"]

This excerpt continues for a few more lines as Ian removes the splinter lodged in William's arm and then chides him for using foul language. Readers learn that Ian and William meet, and they get a taste of Ian's humor, but the excerpt itself withholds important information about what, exactly, Ian and William know about their familial relationship at this point. This is a classic Gabaldon excerpt: depict character through dialogue but show little else, including a chapter number or title (she often doesn't know them at this point because her writing process itself does not follow an outline).

While this excerpt did appear in the final version of *Echo in the Bone*, not all excerpts Gabaldon posted for that book did. Additionally, Gabaldon may resurrect excerpts posted long ago but never published and include them instead. For example, the highly controversial sexual encounter between Lord John and Claire in *Echo in the Bone*, published in 2009, first appeared as an excerpt many years before,[8] and Claire's sword-wielding rescue of Jamie, also published in *Echo in the Bone* ("One Just Man," ch. 62), appeared ten years prior in *The Outlandish Companion* in 1999 as the "King, Farewell" (435–439) excerpt planned for a novel then titled *Surgeon's Steel*. The "King, Farewell" excerpt appears virtually unchanged in *Echo in the Bone*, but readers can see how Gabaldon stitched it into the novel through prefacing paragraphs that situate it in the plot. Encountering this "stitching" is part of the surprise for excerpt readers when they finally read the complete novel. For example, the exchange between Ian and William above is fully contextualized in the final version so that readers grasp the importance of this encounter and recognize the dramatic irony operating in it. Gabaldon only hints at that irony in her excerpt and in her exchange with readers who commented on it in her Books and Writers forum.

For readers familiar with these excerpts, encountering them in a final version of the novel can also complicate their response to the text. Reader-response theorists like Stanley Fish,[9] Wolfgang Iser,[10] and Jonathan Culler[11] have written extensively about the reader's interpretive experience, and though they differ in the influence they attribute to the text and the author, all of them emphasized the reader's role in "creating" the text throughout the reading process. Yet they all assumed the reader's journey through the text would be primarily a *sequential* one that moved through a *completed* text in a mostly linear fashion, filling in gaps and resolving uncertainties along the way.

Gabaldon exploded the assumption of a linear reading of a complete text by dispensing her excerpts in out-of-order fragments. Not only must her dedicated excerpt readers process the textual gaps and uncertainties in the excerpts themselves, they must also fill in the literal gaps—missing sections and chapters—as they seek to shape a coherent sense of the *entire* novel before its publication. Readers derive great satisfaction from trying to decode the meanings in these fragments and piece them together, as if they were shards found in an archeological dig, a clear example, as suggested earlier, of how this reading practice places great emphasis on interpreting an *incomplete* text. They take these fragments, parse their meaning, and often work together to build the novel's plot from them. This means that in their shared meaning-making in the Gabaldon Books and Writers forum, they not only "create" the text by realizing a meaning for it, they are literally *creating a text* from these fragments. Thus, their reading practice has a dual interpretive burden: they seek to realize the meaning of the text without having complete access to it, and they try to create a sequential narrative that their very reading practice denies them.

As indicated before, this type of reading is not solely between the reader and the text. Gabaldon also disrupts the premise of reader-response theory by making herself a party to the reader's interpretive experience. The interactivity between Gabaldon and her readers made possible by social media is something reader-response theorists could not have anticipated when they were writing. Wolfgang Iser's "biactive" theory of reading depended upon a reciprocal participation of text and reader[12]; he did not consider a "triactive" theory that would have included the author as well. For someone like Stanley

Fish, who wrote extensively about authorial intention in reader response theory, this is a dramatic change. Fish could speculate about what Milton intended readers of *Paradise Lost* to experience, but Fish never had to worry that Milton would confirm or deny those intentions on Facebook and Twitter.

Gabaldon, however, is not a silent party. As she works through her own writing process, Gabaldon replies to excerpt readers as they seek to make meaning from the snippets she provides. Her comments never give away key plot points, but they do add contributions about the characters that only the author would know, and these can help readers fill in the gaps, a process they would typically do on their own. In the following example, Gabaldon responded to a question from a reader who posted to the Research and Craft folder of the Books and Writers Community forum who subtly fished for more information about Lieutenant William Ransom. In 2007, while in the midst of writing *Echo in the Bone*, Gabaldon (MSG. 56707.1) herself posed a question in the "Rank and Title" thread of Research and Craft about how a superior officer in the British army of 1777 would address a lieutenant by rank. This savvy reader, "mommio2000," replied by asking for more information before answering the question:

> Diana,
>
> It might be helpful to have more information about this lad. For example, his exact age, his length of service, the status of his knowledge of his true paternal descent, his feelings about said paternal descent, specific information (including transcribed conversations) from relationships he has with tall redheaded Scotsmen, etc.
>
> ;)
>
> I know, I know, in the fullness of time. I'm just very impatient. <g> And this is one of the areas of main interest for me.

Gabaldon quickly recognizes this response for what it is: a reader's attempt to get important information about characters that hasn't appeared yet in the excerpts: "Dear mommio—," Gabaldon replies, "Ha, you think I won't tell you, don't you? <g>" ("Rank and Title," MSG. 56707.6). This is Gabaldon in playful mode, calling the reader's bluff and yet already knowing she will not fully answer her question. Gabaldon proceeds to describe "the lad" in great detail to "mommio2000," to include his age, the context (the first battle of Saratoga), and his length of experience in the army. Still, none of this information tells "mommio2000" what she really wants to know about the lieutenant's relationship to Jamie Fraser.

Gabaldon then responds by appending an attachment with an excerpt from a scene involving Jamie, Claire, and the young Lieutenant Ransom. Readers familiar with the lengthy plot lines of the *Outlander* series could intuit additional information from that scene by having followed "mommio2000s" question and Gabaldon's excerpts, but it does not confirm what, exactly, Ransom knows about his parentage: it would require a reading of the entire section of the book to get that knowledge. Thus, the excerpt can only trigger speculation and spur debate among readers, all of which Gabaldon can observe, digest, and comment upon if she chooses.

In choosing to comment, however, Gabaldon's most common strategy is to covertly allude to plot elements and teasers without giving anything away. "Lori" praises the excerpt Gabaldon attached for how the scene "harken[s] back to or echo[es] some event in the earlier books. It has the effect of deepening the scenes 'set in stone' so to speak, years ago" (Benton). Gabaldon responds with another clue: "This particular bit actually has a *forward* echo, as well—i.e., something that won't resonate until you run into a future event—but of course I can't tell you about that yet..." ("Rank and Title," MSG: 56707.22). Both Lori and Gabaldon use the word "echo" intentionally; Gabaldon was working on *Echo in the Bone* at the time, and echoes in plot and character run throughout that novel, especially those involving familial relationships, the very information "mommio2000" sought. The thread continues with more excerpts from Gabaldon, none of which will provide a full answer to "mommio2000s" question, but taken together create a breadcrumb trail of clues upon which to build a preliminary prediction for what will happen in the novel. Master of the coy but incomplete response, Gabaldon confirms some inquiries without telling too much:

> Dear Diana,
>
> You know, on reading this excerpt from William's pov, I'm wondering anew if he'll ever remember the Scottish groom who he was so close to during the first years of his life. I know you probably won't tell me, but I do think about that from time to time.
>
> Elise [Skidmore].

> Dear Elise—
>
> Oh, he'll remember, all right. <g>
>
> —Diana ["Rank and Title," MSG: 56707.53].

Gabaldon does answer Elise's question in a literal sense, but she does not disclose what William will remember, which is the information that most piques readers' curiosity. Implied in Gabaldon's response is the pose of the imperial author who knows all, even though she has not yet finished the book. Still, this cat-and-mouse game that Gabaldon plays with readers, notable for its teasing wit, provides pleasure for both author and reader alike, and it is the pleasure that accounts for the extensive practice of posting excerpts that generate discussion in the forum.

Such an extensive practice is time consuming, and one might wonder what motivates Gabaldon to do it, given her track record of success. She has explained why many times, and her response is no different from the one she provided early on in her in her companion book to the *Outlander* series, *The Outlandish Companion* (1999):

> I never post more than a fraction of any book—only a few pieces are really appropriate for such independent reading—but being able to share my work periodically gives me great satisfaction, and encourages me to go *on* working. I'm not looking for critique or suggestion when I post something—the work is "finished," as I say—but I do enjoy hearing comments, either on posted excerpts, or on published books, both because that closes the circle for me, and because it's very interesting to see how readers respond to specific incidents and characters [389].

Gabaldon's explanation is worth noting for two reasons: her insistence that she is not seeking reader feedback for these excerpts because she has no intention of using it, and how she gains satisfaction and encouragement from watching how readers respond to the excerpts she provides. It is rare for a reader to criticize a Gabaldon excerpt in her own forum, so reader comments primarily fall into three categories: those who thank Gabaldon effusively, those who flatter her skills, and those who try to interpret the textual clues she provides. No doubt it is those meaning-making comments that most attract Gabaldon's attention.

There is something indulgent about Gabaldon's desire to bask in the adulation of fans and watch all that meaning-making, but her fascination with analyzing behavior should come as no surprise: she has a Ph.D. in quantitative behavioral ecology, or "animal behavior with statistics" as she characterizes it (Gabaldon, "About Diana"). The Diana Gabaldon Books and Writers forum, with its numbered posts, totaled and herded into threads, is a perfect habitat for observing the behavior of readers addicted to her novels, and her trained eye no doubt draws conclusions about what triggers an emotional response in them. The amount of time she devotes to posting excerpts and responding to readers suggests Gabaldon is as addicted as they are. Nevertheless, the fact remains that those who read and comment on excerpts in Gabaldon's forum can never trump her knowledge as the creator of the work; they can only play with what she gives them. That excerpt readers find that process gratifying means that there is a pleasure to be gained when trading narrative coherence for the gratification provided by regularly delivered fragments of a Diana Gabaldon book.

Notes

1. A handful of readers who contribute to the Books and Writers Community forum on Compuserve have admitted to an erratic reading process of Gabaldon's books. For example, "wynnleaf" states she reads in a "somewhat backward fashion—first quarter of the book, then the last few chapters, then start moving backward from

the end or forward from the start until I finally finish the book. Diana's writing style seems to lend itself to the way I read" ("wynnleaf").

2. Jari Backman maintains an extensive archive of the excerpts Gabaldon posts to several of the folders on the Books and Writers Community on Compuserve. His excerpt page for *Echo in the Bone* (2009) includes 119 entries ranging from 2006 to 2009, the novel's year of publication. In 2011, Gabaldon also began posting daily lines to Facebook and Twitter. Close to 400 entries from 2010 to 2014 appear on the excerpt page for *Written in My Own Heart's Blood* (2014), including excerpts and daily lines posted to the Diana Gabaldon folders of the Books and Writers forum and on Facebook and Twitter.

3. In June of 2013, Karen Henry polled readers of her *Outlandish Observations* blog to ask how many read "excerpts or #DailyLines from Diana Gabaldon's upcoming books." Of the 952 respondents, 56.30 percent said they "gladly devour any excerpt of #DailyLine I can find." Another 5 percent claim an addiction to #DailyLines and another 7 percent state they do more discretionary reading of excerpts and #Daily-Lines. (Henry, "June Poll Results").

4. Quotes cited in this article are excerpts from the Diana Gabaldon Books and Writers Community Forum on Compuserve. The author believes in good faith that inclusion of these quotes constitutes a Fair Use as per 17 U.S.C. Section 107.

5. See the "Symptoms of Outlander Addiction" (MSG: 67539) in the Gabaldon Books and Writers forum that appeared in 2010.

6. See the "How Many Times Have You Read the Books?" thread started by brandyannette621 on 4 Oct 2009 on Compuserve.

7. Gabaldon has admitted to such subversive strategies: "It's no secret that I enjoy messing with people's minds" (Gabaldon, "Pre-publishing Audience," MSG: 79573.25). Some of her readers agree: "Bedequus" accuses Gabaldon of using excerpts to encourage readers to reach incorrect conclusions about the story: "Naughty Diana. That's why we never guess anything right. She knows how to 'help' us get it wrong" ("Bedequus," "Read or Not Read—That Is the Question").

8. This excerpt has been taken down, but discussions of it took place in 2006 on the *Outlandish Voices* forum and in "Mattie" referenced it in a 2007 post to the Books and Writers forum in MSG: 55633.1. Gabaldon did not confirm that excerpt in her reply. Bedequus also alluded to this excerpt in 2010 in MSG: 69195.6. Gabaldon did not comment.

9. See the most recent edition of *Is There a Text in This Class: The Authority of Interpretive Communities* (1982) for Fish's explanation of how his reader-response theories evolved over time.

10. See Wolfgang Iser, *The Act of Reading: A Theory of Aesthetic Response* (Baltimore: Johns Hopkins University Press, 1978). Print; *The Implied Reader: Patterns of Communication in Prose Fiction from Bunyan to Beckett* (Baltimore: Johns Hopkins University Press, 1974). Print.

11. See Jonathan Culler, *On Deconstruction: Theory and Criticism after Structuralism* (Ithaca, NY: Cornell University Press, 1982). Print.

12. See Iser, *Prospecting: From Reader Response to Literary Anthropology* (Baltimore: Johns Hopkins University Press, 1989; 1993), 46. Print.

Works Cited

Backman, Jari, and Sini Backman. "An Echo in the Bone—Excerpts." *Welcome to Sini-jari.fi*. Web. 7 Oct. 2009. 27 Sept. 2015. http://www.sinijari.fi

_____ "Written in My Own Heart's Blood—Excerpts." *Welcome to Sinijari.fi.* Web. 4 Apr. 2014. 27 Sept. 2015. http://www.sinijari.fi/linkit/outlander/b8spoiler.htm

"Bedequus." "Read or Not Read—That Is the Question." MSG. 69195.6. Diana Gabaldon. *Books and Writers Community.* Compuserve. Online posting. 12 Nov. 2010. 27 Sept. 2015. http://forums.compuserve.com/discussions/Books_and_Writers_Community/_/_/ws-books/69195.6?nav=messages

Benton, Lori. "Rank and Title." MSG: 56707.20. Diana Gabaldon. *Books and Writers Community.* Compuserve. Online posting. 17 July 2007. 27 Sept. 2015. http://forums.compuserve.com/discussions/Books_and_Writers_Community/_/_/ws-books/56707.20?nav=messages

"BethS." "Read or Not Read—That Is the Question." MSG. 69195.11. Diana Gabaldon. *Books and Writers Community.* Compuserve. Online posting. 12 Nov. 2010. 27 Sept. 2015. 69195. http://forums.compuserve.com/discussions/Books_and_Writers_Community/_/_/ws-books/69195.11?nav=messages

Brengle, Marte. "Read or Not Read—That Is the Question." MSG. 69195.14. Diana Gabaldon. *Books and Writers Community.* Compuserve. Online posting. 12 Nov. 2010. 27 Sept. 2015. http://forums.compuserve.com/discussions/Books_and_Writers_Community/_/_/ws-books/69195.14?nav=messages

"DanaB." "Read or Not Read—That Is the Question." MSG. 69195.18. Diana Gabaldon. *Books and Writers Community.* Compuserve. Online posting. 13 Nov. 2009. 27 Sept. 2015. http://forums.compuserve.com/discussions/Books_and_Writers_Community/_/_/ws-books/69195.18?nav=messages

Devane, Diana. "Symptoms of Outlander Addiction." MSG. 67359.1. Diana Gabaldon. *Books and Writers Community.* Compuserve. Online posting. 11 May 2010. 27 Sept. 2015. http://forums.compuserve.com/discussions/Books_and_Writers_Community/_/Symptoms_of_Outlander_Addiction/ws-books/67359.1?nav=messages

"Excerpt Withdrawal Support Group" Thread. MSG. 73409.1-73409.941. Diana Gabaldon. *Books and Writers Community.* Compuserve. Online posting. 31 Dec. 2011–24 May 2015. 27 Sept. 2015. http://forums.compuserve.com/discussions/Books_and_Writers_Community/_/_/ws-books/73409.1?nav=messages

Gabaldon, Diana. "About Diana." *Diana Gabaldon.* Web. 17 Jan. 2014. 17 Sept. 2015. http://www.dianagabaldon.com/about-diana/

_____. *Echo in the Bone.* New York: Delacorte, 2009. Print.

_____ "Let's Laugh Snips!" MSG. 61651.44. Diana Gabaldon. *Books and Writers Community.* Compuserve. Online posting. 9 Nov. 2008. 27 Sept. 2015. http://forums.compuserve.com/discussions/Books_and_Writers_Community/_/_/ws-books/61651.44?nav=messages

_____. *Outlander.* New York: Dell, 1992. Print.

_____. *The Outlandish Companion.* Toronto, Ontario: Doubleday Canada, 1999. Print.

_____. "Pre-Publishing Audience." MSG. 79573.20. Research and Craft. *Books and Writers Community.* Compuserve. Online posting. 18 Jan. 2014. 27 Sept. 2015. http://forums.compuserve.com/discussions/Books_and_Writers_Community/_/_/ws-books/79573.20?nav=messages

_____. "Pre-Publishing Audience." MSG. 79573.25. Research and Craft. *Books and Writers Community.* Compuserve. Online posting. 19 Jan. 2014. 27 Sept. 2015. http://forums.compuserve.com/discussions/Books_and_Writers_Community/_/_/ws-books/79573.20?nav=messages

_____. "Rank and Title." MSG. 56707.1. Research and Craft. *Books and Writers Community.* Compuserve. Online posting. 16 July 2007. 27 Sept. 2015. http://forums.

compuserve.com/discussions/Books_and_Writers_Community/_/_/ws-books/56707.1?nav=messages

_____. "Rank and Title." MSG. 56707.6. Research and Craft. *Books and Writers Community*. Compuserve. Online posting. 16 July 2007. 27 Sept. 2015. http://forums.compuserve.com/discussions/Books_and_Writers_Community/_/_/ws-books/56707.1?nav=messages

_____. "Rank and Title." MSG. 56707.22. Research and Craft. *Books and Writers Community*. Compuserve. Online posting. 18 July 2007. 27 Sept. 2015. http://forums.compuserve.com/discussions/Books_and_Writers_Community/_/_/ws-books/56707.22?nav=messages

_____. "Rank and Title." MSG. 56707.53. Research and Craft. *Books and Writers Community*. Compuserve. Online posting. 22 July 2007. 27 Sept. 2015. http://forums.compuserve.com/discussions/Books_and_Writers_Community/_/_/ws-books/56707.53?nav=messages

Habash, Gabe. "HC Adapts App to Push Excerpts on Facebook." *Publishers Weekly*. Web. 22 June 2012. 27 Sept. 2015. http://www.publishersweekly.com/pw/by-topic/industry-news/publisher-news/article/52701-hc-adapts-app-to-push-excerpts-on-facebook.html

Henry, Karen. Message to the Author. 6 Apr. 2014. E-mail. 27 Sept. 2015.

_____. "Excerpt Withdrawal Support Group." MSG. 73409.7. Diana Gabaldon. *Books and Writers Community*. Compuserve. Online posting. 12 Nov. 2011. 27 Sept. 2015. http://forums.compuserve.com/discussions/Books_and_Writers_Community/_/_/ws-books/73409.2?nav=messages

_____. "June Poll Results." *Outlandish Observations*. Web. 1 July 2013. 27 Sept. 2015. http://outlandishobservations.blogspot.com/2013/07/june-poll-results.html

_____. "Read or Not Read—That Is the Question." MSG. 69195.7. Diana Gabaldon. *Books and Writers Community*. Compuserve. Online posting. 12 Nov. 2010. 27 Sept. 2015. http://forums.compuserve.com/discussions/Books_and_Writers_Community/_/_/ws-books/69195.7?nav=messages

_____. "Symptoms of Outlander Addiction." MSG: 67359.4. Diana Gabaldon. *Books and Writers Community*. Compuserve. Online posting. 12 May 2010. 14 Sept. 2015. http://forums.compuserve.com/discussions/Books_and_Writers_Community/_/_/ws-books/67359.4?nav=messages

"How Many Times Have You Read the Books?" Thread. MSG. 65431. Diana Gabaldon. *Books and Writers Community*. Compuserve. Online posting. 4 Oct. 2009–5 Oct. 2009. 27 Sept. 2015. http://forums.compuserve.com/discussions/Books_and_Writers_Community/_/_/ws-books/65431.1

"mommio2000." "Rank and Title." MSG. 56707.4. Research and Craft. *Books and Writers Community*. Compuserve. Online posting. 16 July 2007. 27 Sept. 2015. http://forums.compuserve.com/discussions/Books_and_Writers_Community/_/_/ws-books/56707.4?nav=messages

Pera, Mariam. "An Interview with Diana Gabaldon." *American Libraries*. Web. 8 Jan. 2015. 27 Sept. 2015. http://americanlibrariesmagazine.org/2015/01/08/an-interview-with-diana-gabaldon/

"Riverlady" (rgrassa). "ECHO (spoiler!)." MSG. 58919.61. Diana Gabaldon. *Books and Writers Community*. Compuserve. Online posting. 17 Feb. 2008. 27 Sept. 2015. http://forums.compuserve.com/discussions/Books_and_Writers_Community/_/_/ws-books/58919.61?nav=messages

"Sabine." "Do You Read #DailyLines, or Not?" MSG. 80417.1. Diana Gabaldon. *Books and Writers Community*. Compuserve. Online posting. 23 Apr. 2014. 27 Sept.

2015. http://forums.compuserve.com/discussions/Books_and_Writers_Commu nity/_/_/ws-books/80417.1?nav=messages

"Sally." "Read or Not Read—That Is the Question." MSG: 69195.23. Diana Gabaldon. *Books and Writers Community*. Compuserve. Online posting. 13 Nov. 2010. 27 Sept. 2015. http://forums.compuserve.com/discussions/Books_and_Writers_ Community/_/_/ws-books/69195.23?nav=messages

Skidmore, Elise. "Rank and Title." MSG. 56707.52. Research and Craft. *Books and Writers Community*. Compuserve. Online posting. 22 July 2007. 27 Sept. 2015. http://forums.compuserve.com/discussions/Books_and_Writers_Community/_/ _/ws-books/56707.52?nav=messages

"Symptoms of Outlander Addiction" Thread. MSG. 67359. Diana Gabaldon. *Books and Writers Community*. Compuserve. Online posting. 11 May 2010 to 4 Jan. 2012. 27 Sept. 2015. http://forums.compuserve.com/discussions/Books_and_ Writers_Community/_/Symptoms_of_Outlander_Addiction/ws-books/67359.1? nav=messages

"wynnleaf." "Read or Not Read—That Is the Question." MSG: 69195.38. Diana Gabaldon. *Books and Writers Community*. Compuserve. Online Posting. 13 Nov 2011. 27 Sept. 2015. http://forums.compuserve.com/discussions/Books_and_Writers_ Community/_/_/ws-books/69195.38?nav=messages

Melodrama, Gender and Nostalgia

The Appeal of Outlander

ELEANOR TY

In a somewhat tongue-in-cheek article in *Business Insider*, Jethro Nede-dog writes that Starz's *Outlander* is a show mainly watched by women (64 percent), and more specifically by soccer moms who have become hooked by reading Diana Gabaldon's novels, who like the characters' family values, and also find inspiration in Claire and Jamie's marriage, the strong female point of view, and the good-looking lead actor, Sam Heughan. While these reasons explain some of fandom, they fail to adequately explain the obsession readers and more recently, audiences have with the books and the TV series. Gabaldon's books have sold 26 million worldwide, and Ron D. Moore's production has averaged 5.1 million viewers each episode in the first half of Season 1 (Kondolojy).

Gabaldon's books offer multiple levels of intellectual, emotional, aesthetic psychic engagement, and Ronald D. Moore's production has been careful to replicate this experience on screen. Above all, there are five clear reasons why *Outlander,* the books and the TV series, has such a wide following and readership (and not necessarily just from soccer moms).

A Strong, Competent Heroine

Gabaldon presents a strong, intelligent heroine who is able to perform amazing feats of nurturing and healing because she has the advantage of 200 years of science and medicine. The first time Claire Beauchamp meets the Highlanders, her ability to fix Jamie's dislocated shoulder compels readers and makes us and Jamie fall in love with the heroine. In the tradition of Daniel Defoe's *Robinson Crusoe* or Stieg Larsson's *The Girl with the Dragon Tattoo* (2011), Gabaldon's *Outlander* provides us with "'competence porn,' the enjoyment derived from witnessing impressive feats of human capability" (Dartnell). Lewis Dartnell explains, "We're talking about men and women who succeed against expectations, either by their own wits and expertise or with the equipment and technology they wield. They inspire jaw-dropping awe by being far more proficient and accomplished than you at certain tasks" without making you feel inadequate or incompetent. In *Outlander*, Claire earns the love of Jamie when she "mended" him "twice in as many hours" (*Outlander*, ch. 27). Further, she earns Dougal's respect in that scene, and later when she helps ease another clansman's (Geordie's) pain when he is wounded during the boar hunt (ch. 10; Episode 104 "The Gathering").

Ron D. Moore understands our attraction to competent heroines and makes the most of Claire, and later, her sister-in-law, Jenny Murray, representing them as feisty, strong, and capable women at home in Lallybroch and on the road. Jenny Murray is as forceful as her brother. She defied Jack Randall when he tried to rape her by refusing to submit and laughing at him (Episode 112 "Lallybroch"). When Jamie is taken away by the Watch, she decides to go after them, even though she has given birth to Maggie, her second baby, only a day before. Claire is amazed at her intrepidity and skill. Like Claire, she knows how to do things that women of her time do not. Jenny tells her, "I used to make Jamie and Ian show me things, when they were young. How to build fires, and climb trees—even how to skin things. And how to track" (*Outlander*, ch. 33). In the Starz production, the scenes of two women, Claire and Jenny, riding off alone, capturing a Redcoat messenger and soldier, and torturing him for information, are some of the strongest feminist moments of the show which overturn expectations of what women could and could not do in the eighteenth century (Episode 114 "The Search").

In *Dragonfly in Amber* Claire uses her knowledge of eighteenth century history and twentieth century medicine to set up a nursing station at Prestonpans. Although she remembers that the "casualties of the Jacobite army were to be light" (*Dragonfly in Amber*, ch. 36), Claire takes charge of the Highlander wives, telling them, "We've done a lot, but there's a lot more to do. We shall be needing boiling water. Cauldrons for boiling, cream pans for soaking. Parritch for those who can eat; milk for those who can't. Tallow and garlic for dressings. Wood laths for splints. Bottles and jugs, cups and spoons. Sewing needles and stout thread" (*Dragonfly*, ch. 36). Claire's ability to use everyday, domestic objects, utensils, and kitchen herbs to heal is part of the magical technique Gabaldon uses to makes her powers believable. We admire her, yet the detailed catalog of her tools make it seem as if these are skills we too could have. Later, she uses mold to make homemade penicillin at Fraser

Ridge (*The Fiery Cross*). In the TV series, we catch glimpses of Claire's healing ability, but do not see her skills represented in as much detail. We do, however, see Claire sing and entertain (Episode 114 "The Search"), which reveal a more visual and aural spectacle of Claire's many talents. These scenes empower women who, in the eighteenth century literature, were usually praised more for their beauty and charm rather than their physical strength or organizational skills.

Melodrama

Nineteenth century melodrama is characterized by the clash between extremes of good and evil, strong and weak, rich and poor, but also by its use of archetypal, mythic beliefs. Martha Vicinus notes, "the focus on the family and its emotional conflicts gives melodrama its archetypal power ... familiar struggles become charged with intense feeling because of their psychosexual nature" (129). Gabaldon's novels are full of heart-wrenching scenes of emotional conflict. The flashback scenes of Black Jack Randall flogging Jamie work at a number of levels. The flogging, with Jamie's outstretched arms, is one of goodness and innocence at the hands of the wicked, suggestive of Christ at the hands of Roman soldiers. Sam Heughan called it an "epic battle of wills" between Jamie and Black Jack (Lutes). Diana Gabaldon describes Black Jack as a "pervert" and a "sadist" (Facebook post 28 April 2015), but the scene is also suggestive of the conflict between the English and the Scots. David Cameron appreciated the power of such these scenes when he supposedly requested that *Outlander* not be shown in Great Britain before the Scottish referendum.

In the eighteenth century, sentimental novels used stock characters and scenes to create affecting scenes for readers: a seduced maiden asking for forgiveness at her father's feet or the reunion between a father and his long, lost son. These affecting scenes are called "the sentimental tableau" or "frozen pathos" (Williams 465) because they rely on extensive literary description to create emotional scenes that readers remember. Different readers have their own list of favorite gut-wrenching scenes in *Outlander,* but for many, the scene at the standing stones hits hardest. After Claire tells Jamie her history, Jamie takes Claire to Craigh na Dun and tells her to go back to her "own time on the other side" because "There's nothing for ye on this side, lass!" (ch. 25). At the stones, they hold on to each other tightly, trying to do what is rational, but both are suffering unspeakable heartache and pain inside. Later, he admits that letting her go was the "hardest thing" he ever did. In the Starz production, the self-sacrifice is shown through dialogue and visual spectacle. At the camp where he waits for her, Jamie has cried himself to sleep, and then he weeps for joy upon her return. The camera zooms in on Sam Heughan's tearstained face, giving viewers a rarely-depicted scene of a man who has been crying. Interestingly, this scene was voted the most "courageous moment" by the Facebook users of *Outlander Starz* page on 27 June 2015.

A parallel scene between Jamie and Claire occurs in *Voyager* when Claire goes back to the eighteenth century Scotland after twenty years of separation. Like the scene at the standing stones, this scene works as a visual tableau, "a representation that captures a single-usually highly significant- moment of an action or a state. It is static.... It captures an act in a moment, and 'draws a frame around' it ... as if on a canvas or in a snapshot" (Williams 469). At this point, Claire has just entered into A. Malcolm, the printer's shop, and a shocked Jamie faints upon seeing her and realizing that she has really returned. They both collapse on the floor as she cradles his head:

> "God in heaven, you *are* real!"
> "So are you." I lifted my chin to look up at him. "I th-thought you were dead." I had meant to speak lightly, but my voice betrayed me. The tears spilled down my cheeks, only to soak into the rough cloth of his shirt as he pulled me hard against him.
> I shook so that it was some time before I realized that he was shaking too, and for the same reason. I don't know how long we sat there on the dusty floor, crying in each other's arms with the longing of twenty years spilling down our faces [*Voyager*, ch. 24].

Note that time is suspended momentarily in this important scene of melodrama. We are compelled to imagine their overwhelming emotions, "the longing of twenty years" and the way gestures, crying, embracing, shaking, become part of the physicalized emotions (Williams 472) that accompany their verbal expressions. These affecting scenes produce a sense of mourning for loss and for what might have been. As Tania Modleski writes, "one of the basic pleasures of melodrama ... is ... fundamentally about events that do not happen: the wedding that did not occur; the meeting in the park that was missed; and, above all, the word that was not spoken" (28). Here the poignancy comes from their regret and knowledge of the wasted years of separation between them.

In addition, melodramas often emphasize the weak and the unappreciated. "Melodrama always sides with the powerless" (Vicinus 130). Orphans were often vital figures in melodrama, as they were most likely to be neglected to be "helpless and unfriended" (Vicinus 130). Notably, Claire was orphaned at six, and brought up by her Uncle Lamb. Jamie's mother died when he was young, and his father died after witnessing his flogging. Claire and Jamie are both orphans, a fact which intensifies their isolation and need for each other. Promises of unconditional care become more critical. Early on in *Outlander*, after Claire dresses Jamie's shoulder in Castle Leoch, she begins to think of

Frank and starts to weep on his lap. He consoles her and promises, "You need not be scairt of me. Nor of anyone here, so long as I'm with ye" (ch. 4). Claire also receives care and comfort from Mistress Fitzgibbons who offers Claire a "kindly" welcome, dresses her and respects her as a healer. These scenes are important because Claire and Jamie have been itinerants or outlaws, without stable homes, and are emotionally starved. In the Starz production, when Claire imagines telling someone who she really is, it is to Mistress Fitzgibbons, a mother figure to Claire.

Reading scenes such as these sentimental ones arouses one's sensibility, a trait referring to an acute perception of or responsiveness toward something. While excessive sensibility was condemned by many writers, including Jane Austen in *Sense and Sensibility,* a certain degree of it in the eighteenth century was an indication of deeper perception. Individuals who were especially sensible were also those who were more aware of beauty, who tended to display virtuous feelings, especially those of pity, sympathy, and benevolence. Gabaldon's books and Moore's production allow modern day readers and viewers a way to cultivate and express our powers of sensibility through these emotionally expressive scenes.

The Renaissance Man as Hero

Even though actor Sam Heughan has been voted the "alpha male" of 2015 (Piester and Dos Santos), most women would agree that we are in love with the fictional character James Alexander Malcolm MacKenzie Fraser rather than Sam (though Heughan's looks certainly add to the charm). As well as being a brawny fighter and soldier, Jamie is a true Renaissance man, cultured and accomplished in the arts and sciences. He speaks English, Gaelic, French, Spanish, Hebrew, and German, and reads Latin. He quickly masters scatterings of Chinese, the pidgin slave language, and American Indian languages as well. His skill with horses translates to emotional intelligence, often understanding people's needs even before Claire. He is a born leader, and men respect and gravitate towards him whether he is in Ardsmuir prison (*Voyager*) or in the wilderness of North Carolina (*Drums of Autumn*). He can fix a mill wheel, knows how to run a farm, and later, can build log cabins with only an axe (*Drums of Autumn*). Well read, he becomes a printer and publishes his own book. He is a tender and passionate lover. The only thing he cannot do is sing because of an earlier head injury. Gabaldon has created a hero for all seasons, a combination of the kind of men we admire and fall in love with at various times of our lives: the brave warrior/soldier, the teacher/ intellectual, the superman who comes to the rescue of the weak, the strong leader, the caring father, the lord of the castle, the engineer and pioneer, the gentleman lover, and the reckless rebel. Describing the phenomenon as the "complex masculinity," Carly Lane writes in "The Complex Masculinity of *Outlander*'s Jamie Fraser": "what's most surprising about Jamie is that he encapsulates both the (fairly) innocent virgin and the male warrior in tandem, something that has almost been unheard of in fiction." She says, "It's a surprising twist on the trope" of the virgin, but after their first sexual encounter, Jamie shows himself willing to listen to Claire: "That thoughtfulness and willingness to reshape his worldview is not something that often goes hand-in-hand with an uber-manly man…. Jamie Fraser might seem like just your average hero—but he's a fascinating, layered character who doesn't simply fall prey to the typical traits of masculinity."

What is most attractive about the character of Jamie Fraser is his admirable devotion to and adoration of Claire. He is not only the strong, fiery, intelligent, handsome stranger, but he instinctively knows how to love, comfort, and make love. Taken to Castle Leoch by the Scottish Highlanders, Claire cleans Jamie's wounded shoulder, but suddenly remembers where she is and begins to weep bitterly. Even with his hurt shoulder, Jamie takes her into his arms. Claire notes:

> muttering soft Gaelic in my ear and smoothing my hair with one hand. I wept bitterly, surrendering momentarily to my fear and heartbroken confusion, but slowly I began to quiet a bit, as Jamie stroked my neck and back, offering me the comfort of his broad, warm chest. My sobs lessened and I began to calm myself, leaning tiredly into the curve of his shoulder. No wonder he was so good with horses, I thought blearily, feeling his fingers rubbing gently behind my ears, listening to the soothing, incomprehensible speech. If I were a horse, I'd let him ride my anywhere [*Outlander*, ch. 4].

Although it seems contradictory because modern women assert that they want to be strong and in control, there are times when we—yes, even feminists—also need comforting. In those circumstances, the prospect of giving oneself up to a stronger being, one with a "broad, warm chest" is extremely enticing.

Romance, Spirituality and Transgression

More than just an attractive male hero, what *Outlander* offers is elevation of earthly desires to the realm of the sublime and the spiritual. The sublime is associated with the noble, the awe-inspiring, magnificent, and almost heavenly or divine. In Gabaldon's books, love and passion are never just physical and sensual; they encompass a range of emotions that carry us from our mundane world to somewhere above the ordinary. Many of our favorite lines from *Outlander* are from this fertile mix of passion and spirituality (see Ty,

"Sex, Spirituality and Salvation"). For example, the marriage vows uttered in Gaelic translate: "Ye are Blood of my blood, and bone of my bone,/ I give ye my body, that we two might be one./ I give ye my spirit, 'til our life shall be done" (*Outlander*, ch. 14). The addition of the pagan vows adds another level of profundity and symbolism to Claire and Jamie's union, which harks back to a pre–Christian, mythic era in keeping with the trope of the stone circles.

Indeed, even Jamie and Claire's dialogue contains this mix of the sacred and the profane. Two days after their marriage, Jamie asks Claire if it is "usual" to feel so much desire for a partner: "Is it always so between a man and a woman?" (*Outlander,* ch. 17). He remarks, "I see why the Church says it is a sacrament…. I feel like God Himself when I'm in you" (*Outlander,* ch. 17). Gabaldon, like other romance writers, borrows from a number of discourses, such as those from women's fashion, Hollywood movies, classical and contemporary literature, pop songs, theology and religion, television, Freudian psychology, and others to create the "romance discourse" (Ty, "Desire and Temptation," 99). In romance novels, the sexual act is described using a combination of what Peter Stallybrass and Allon White call the "high" and the "low," where high discourses refer to literature, philosophy, statecraft, Church, and University, while low discourse refers to everyday speech, local dialects, the speech of folk and peasants (Stallybrass and White 4). Unlike pornography, which focuses on details of the body, the low forms, genitals, bodily fluids, and orifices, in romance novels, bodily pleasures are transformed into "distanced, spiritual, aesthetic expressions of beauty" (Ty, "Desire" 99). Orgasm is often described using lyrical prose, as in this example from a Harlequin romance: "He was wind and she was fire, he sweeping through her, touching her, marking her while she burned deep into the walls of his very soul" (Horton 156).

In the TV show, sexual acts are depicted in warm tones of gold and amber, sometimes with a soft focus lens, to create a dream-like effect. The camera moves slowly and deliberately, highlighting caresses and close-ups of hands, lips, shoulders, chests, to build to a crescendo where we imagine more than we actually see the sexual union (E107 "The Wedding"). Looks, sighs, whispers, short breaths, and undoing of garments suggest strong passion. In Gabaldon's books, we see the use of poetic language and metaphor, references to elements of wind, water, sky, and earth to describe sexual ecstasy. At the end of Gabaldon's *Outlander*, for instance, Jamie brings Claire to his "hot baths" in the abbey in France where they rekindle their passion after his traumatic experience at Wentworth.

> He held my hips firm against him, carrying me beyond myself with the force of an undertow. I crashed formless against him, like breakers on a rock, and he met me with the brutal force of granite, my anchor in the pounding chaos.
> Boneless and liquid as the water around us, contained only by the frame of his

hands, I cried out, and the soft, bubbling half-choked cry of a sailor sucked beneath the waves [*Outlander* ch. 41].

In these passages, we see passion represented using elements of water and earth. Jamie is a natural force, like an "undertow" or "granite," which powerfully pulls Claire into sexual sublimity.

While some see Claire and Jamie's marriage as the epitome of pure married love, it is also the embodiment of transgression and desire. All through the first two-thirds of *Outlander*, Claire's feelings for Jamie are ambivalently tinged with admiration and love, but also feelings of guilt, worry, and her sense of impropriety. She knows she is married to Frank, and the relationship with Jamie is that much more exciting because it is, in the back of Claire's mind, a forbidden one. Certainly, Jamie and Claire's relationship has been sanctified by marriage, but was she free to marry? There is nothing quite so exciting, romantically, as being reluctantly swept up into a passionate love affair, for once, letting one's body and soul judge what is right instead of following one's reason.

Nostalgia and Elegy

Outlander and *Dragonfly in Amber* are extended elegies for the Scottish clans, their kilts, and the Gaelic language. In the Starz production, Claire and Frank visit the battlefield of Culloden right at the beginning. In the novel, Claire warns Jamie not to participate in the Rising. She remembers "the clan stones, the grey boulders that would lie scattered on the field, each stone bearing the single clan name of the butchered men who lay under it" (ch. 25). We are reminded that the Highlanders and their way of life are doomed, and the impending destruction infuses the story with a sense of melancholia. Even though readers and viewers may not have been to Scotland, we feel nostalgia for the rolling green hills, the craigs, lochs, old castles, majestic mountains, and heather-covered fields. The Starz production makes the most of the pastoral beauty of Scotland by highlighting its magic and mystery. Terry Dresbach's meticulous and detailed costumes make even the drabbest wool and plaid come alive and look stunning. It is not surprising that tourism in Scotland has increased by 30 percent since the show started ("*Outlander* Boost to Scottish Tourism").

In *Prosthetic Memory*, Alison Landsberg argues that technologies of mass culture, such as films and television, make it possible for people today to share collective memories, to assimilate as personal experience historical events they themselves did not live. Landsberg points out that prosthetic memories are "derived from engagement with a mediated representation (seeing a film, visiting a museum, watching a television miniseries)" and "because they feel real, they help condition how a person thinks about the world and might be instrumental in articulating an ethical relation to the other" (20–21). While Landsberg talks mainly about the way films become "the basis for mediated collective identification," reading books as well as watching a TV series or film can also create "counterhegemonic public spheres" (Landsberg 21). We feel for those clansmen who died at Culloden, those Highland families who suffered starvation in the years following the 1746. Flowers frequently placed on the Fraser clan stone at Culloden by Gabaldon fans attest to the fact that readers and viewers "remember" and feel kinship with Highlanders whose tradition and way of life have been obliterated. Even if fans feel sorrow for fictional characters, the sense of loss for the Highland clans who perished is real.

Several scenes in the *Outlander* books series evoke the traditions of Scottish clans, creating a sense of wistfulness for a time gone by. In *Outlander*, the MacKenzie clans gather to pledge allegiance to their leader, Colum MacKenzie and the oath taking is marked with ceremony and honor (Episode 104 "The Gathering"). Even when they are no longer in Scotland, the Highlander tradition of pledging one's loyalty to a leader is practiced. At a Gathering of diasporic Scots in *The Fiery Cross*, Jamie calls together the Scottish settlers on Fraser Ridge and addresses them in Gaelic. His speech, using anaphora, the rhetorical technique of repetition of phrases, invokes their shared memories of the past in a formal manner: "We have all suffered much hardship on the road here…. Many of us died in battle…. Many died of burning. Many of us starved. Many died at sea, many died of wounds and illness…. Many died of sorrow" (*The Fiery Cross*, ch. 15). To Roger he says, "Stand by me in battle…. Be a shield for my family—and for yours, son of my house" (*The Fiery Cross*, ch. 15). The request and call are powerful reminders of pre-modern, almost mythic ways of asserting belonging, harking back to the oaths of fealty sworn by feudal tenants in medieval periods.

Through these techniques and themes, Gabaldon and Moore's *Outlander* series create an experience for readers and viewers that is at once contemporary and timeless, at once culturally specific and global. Although the books and the TV series are part-fantasy, part-science fiction, they offer an accurate glimpse of historical eighteenth-century Scotland. Gabaldon creates characters whom we admire and with whom we fall in love, and gives us the opportunity to share, albeit temporarily, in the daily lives of a pair of lovers whose days never seem to be without adventure and excitement, both physical and spiritual. The books and the TV series provide us with what the best art should provide, a bit of instruction and much delight, lifting us from the humdrum of our everyday existence to the evanescent realm of the marvelous.

Works Cited

Dartnell, Lewis. "Are You Hooked on Competence Porn?" *The Telegraph*. 09 April 2014. http://www.telegraph.co.uk/men/thinking-man/10744879/Are-you-hooked-on-competence-porn.html.

Gabaldon, Diana. "Black Jack Randall Is a Pervert." Facebook. Posted 28 April 2015. Accessed 1 May 2015. http://www.outlandertvnews.com/2015/04/diana-gabaldon-clarifies-black-jack-randalls-sexual-orientation.

_____. *Dragonfly in Amber*. New York: Random House, 1992. Kindle file.

_____. *Drums of Autumn*. New York: Random House, 1996. Kindle file.

_____. *The Fiery Cross*. New York: Random House, 2001. Kindle file.

_____. *Outlander*. New York: Bantam Dell, 1992. Kindle file.

_____. *Voyager*. New York: Random House, 1993. Kindle file.

Horton, Naomi. *The Ideal Man*. Silhouette Desire #518. New York: Silhouette Books, 1989.

Kondolojy, Amanda. "'Outlander' Midseason Premier Draws 1.2 Million Viewers at 9 p.m." *Zap2it*. 6 April 2015. http://tvbythenumbers.zap2it.com/2015/04/06/outlander-midseason-premiere-draws-1-2-million-viewers-at–9pm/385406.

Landsberg, Alison. *Prosthetic Memory: The Transformation of American Remembrance in the Age of Mass Culture*. New York: Columbia University Press, 2004.

Lane, Carly. "The Complex Masculinity of *Outlander's* Jamie Fraser." *Bitch Flicks*. 22 June 2015. Accessed 29 June 2015. http://www.btchflcks.com/2015/06/the-complex-masculinity-of-outlanders-jamie-fraser.html#.VZLyIedeFVR.

Modleski, Tania. "Time and Desire in the Woman's Film." *Cinema Journal* 23.3 (Spring 1984): 19–30. JSTOR. http://www.jstor.org/stable/1225094.

Nededog, Jethro. "5 Reasons So Many Moms Are Obsessed with Starz's Sexy New Historical Fantasy Show 'Outlander.'" *Business Insider*. 7 May 2015. http://www.businessinsider.com/starzs-outlander-mom-audience–2015-5

Newitz, Annalee. "What Makes *Outlander* so Similar to *Battlestar Galactica*?" *IO9: We Come from the Future*. 16 October 2014. http://io9.com/what-makes-outlander-so-similar-to-battlestar-galactica–1647292753.

Outlander. 16 Episodes. Prod. Ronald D. Moore. Based on *Outlander* series by Diana Gabaldon. Starz Tall Ship Productions, August 2014–May 2015. Television.

"*Outlander* Boost to Scottish Tourism." *The Scotsman*. Monday 06 April 2015. http://www.scotsman.com/lifestyle/travel/outlander-boost-to-scottish-tourism-1-3739460.

Outlander Starz TV Show. "Most Courageous Moment as Voted by You." Facebook. 27 June 2015. Accessed 29 June 2015. https://www.facebook.com/OutlanderTVSeries.starz.

Piester, Laura, and Kristin Dos Santos. "It's Official! The Most Beloved TV Actor Is…" *E! Online*. 6 May 2015. Accessed 29 June 2015. http://ca.eonline.com/news/653461/it-s-official-the-most-beloved-tv-actor-is

Stallybrass, Peter, and Allon White. *The Politics and Poetics of Transgression*. Ithaca, NY: Cornell University Press, 1986.

Ty, Eleanor. "Desire and Temptation: Dialogism and the Carnivalesque in Category Romances." *A Dialogue of Voices: Feminist Literary Theory and Bakhtin.*. Ed. Karen Hohne and Helen Wussow. Minneapolis: University of Minnesota Press, 1994. 97–113.

_____. "Sex, Spirituality, and Salvation in *Outlander: To Ransom a Man's Soul*." *Out-*

lander Idler. 3 June 2015. https://outlanderidler.wordpress.com/2015/06/03/sex-spirituality-and-salvation-in-outlander-to-ransom-a-mans-soul.

Vicinus, Martha. "'Helpless and Unfriended': Nineteenth-Century Domestic Melo-drama." *New Literary History* 13.1 (Autumn 1981): 127–143.

Williams, Anne Patricia. "Description and Tableau in the Eighteenth-Century British Sentimental Novel." *Eighteenth-Century Fiction* 8.4 (July 1996):465–484. DOI: 10.1353/ecf.1996.0046.

PART II

The Romance Question— Is It or Isn't It?

"Linked ... through the body of one man"
Black Jack Randall as a Non-Traditional Romance Villain

MICHELLE L. JONES

In Chapter 35 of Diana Gabaldon's *Outlander*, entitled "Wentworth Prison," the main character, Claire, attempts to rescue her husband, Jamie Fraser, from the villain of the story, Black Jack Randall. She says to herself in her interior monologue:

> Black Jack. A common name for rogues and scoundrels in the eighteenth century. A staple of romantic fiction, the name conjured up charming highwaymen, dashing blades in plumed hats. The reality walked at my side.
> One never stops to think what underlies romance. Tragedy and terror, transmuted by time. Add a little art in the telling, and voila! A stirring romance, to make the blood run fast and maidens sigh. My blood was running fast, all right, and never a maiden sighed like Jamie, cradling his mangled hand [*Outlander*, ch. 35].

In the first paragraph, the hero, Claire, is commenting almost as a speaker for Gabaldon that the story is only as "good" as its villain, and that Black Jack Randall is a "rogue and scoundrel," and that the "reality" she faces has all the characteristics of a traditional romance villain. In the next paragraph, Randall provides much of the "tragedy and terror" that Claire and her husband, Jamie, will face, except that there is a gender role reversal in the romance narrative where the maiden is Jamie himself and not a beautiful, young woman like Claire. The reference to Jamie's "mangled hand" represents the issue that interests us most in this essay, which is the way Gabaldon is able to take us out of romance into realism by exploring in excruciating detail the sadism of Black Jack Randall.

71

Gabaldon readers know that Claire's musings about Black Jack Randall as a larger-than-life romance villain reflects Gabaldon's literary practice in *Outlander*. However, few of the readers know how significant a role that the romance genre plays in the production of her texts. To familiarize ourselves with the conventions of romance, there is no better source than the Canadian critic, Northrop Frye. Frye is in fact renowned for his scholarship on the romance genre, for as Angus Fletcher states: "if we were to value Frye's writings for nothing else, it would be his penetrating analysis of the nature of romance that would perhaps most powerfully claim our attention" (756). Frye defines the romance genre as an adventure story, in which the "climacteric adventure … gives literary form to the romance," and that major adventure is "the quest" (*Anatomy of Criticism* 187). In typical romance narratives, the hero is a "mythical Messiah" (Frye, *AC* 187), and "the central form of quest-romance is the dragon-killing theme exemplified in the stories of St. George and Perseus" (*AC* 189). Traditionally, the romance narrative is so dominated by male heroes that even when Frye describes the typical narrative, he seldom acknowledges a female romance heroine. Gabaldon innovates romance tradition by reversing the gender roles, making the male the sexual object, a much more passive figure, and the prize of the quest. For instance, Frye talks about the romance narrative in terms of dreams, saying that the quest-romance "is the search of the libido or desiring self for a fulfillment that will deliver it from the anxieties of reality but will still contain that reality" (*AC* 193). What is non-traditional is not only that we must identify ourselves with the *female* hero's, Claire's, desires, but also that the villain, Black Jack Randall, obstructs the quest and the hero's desires by introducing a bisexual love triangle. However, what is even more non-traditional is that Black Jack Randall's sadistic tendencies take the narrative out of the mode of romance toward realism, or out of the dreamlike quality that reflects the hero's desires toward the reality of pain and suffering.

In order to understand Black Jack Randall in his role in *Outlander*, we must consider Frye's argument that the "characterization of romance is dialectical: characters tend to be either for or against the quest" (*AC* 195). Gabaldon emphasizes Black Jack Randall's loathsome character by pitting him against Claire's quest, which is establishing a romantic relationship, and ultimately marriage, with Jamie Fraser, while also converting her from her English identity and sympathies to the Scottish political cause, represented by the historic Battle of Culloden. We hate Jack Randall because he attempts to rape Jamie's sister, Jenny, he repeatedly attempts to rape Claire, and, surprisingly, he succeeds in raping and torturing Jamie. Jamie is the central love interest, and he is the main reason that Claire converts to the Scottish political cause. Given Claire's Scottish sympathies, Black Jack Randall's role as an English captain in His Majesty's Dragoons will inevitably make them political enemies anyway, despite Claire's English cultural identity. The fact that Black Jack Randall is the "six-times-great-grandfather" (*Outlander*, ch. 3) of Frank Randall, Claire's twentieth-century husband, complicates the personal and political conflict enormously. But the resentment toward Black Jack Randall, even after his death, continues to linger through Jamie's continuing trauma from Randall's sexual sadism.

It is not difficult at all to show how Jack Randall epitomizes the "moral antithesis of heroism and villainy" (*AC* 196). What makes *Outlander* both fascinating and difficult to read is the complexity that Gabaldon gives to Randall while maintaining this moral antithesis. Like Shakespeare's Shylock in *The Merchant of Venice*, we both sympathize with their feeling of vulnerability and fear their inclination to violence. Whether we read the book or watch the television series, we are deeply affected by Randall's sadistic tendencies, especially because they are repeatedly directed at Jamie. The realism with which she pursues these tendencies is evidence of Gabaldon's novelistic mode writing, not romance. Northrop Frye argues that the typical hero in the mode of romance has a power of action that is "superior in *degree* to other men and his environment" (*AC* 33). In *Outlander* this degree of Claire's superiority over other "men" and her environment is represented by her capacity to time travel. If "the hero of romance moves in a world which ordinary laws of nature are slightly suspended: prodigies of courage and endurance, unnatural to us, are natural to him [or her], and enchanted weapons, talking animals, terrifying ogres and witches, and talismans of miraculous power violate no rule of probability once the postulates of romance have been established" (*AC* 33). Her identity as a witch also confirms Claire's ability to go beyond the laws of nature as they are understood in the eighteenth century. As a person from the twentieth century, she has knowledge of future events, and advanced medical knowledge, so she is superior in degree to her eighteenth-century counterparts.

The problem with Black Jack Randall is that his gender identity complicates the characterization of the villain in romance, yet serves to enhance it. For example, in a recent Facebook post, Gabaldon states that "Black Jack Randall is *not* a homosexual. He's a pervert. He's a sadist. He derives sexual pleasure from hurting people, but he's not particular about the gender of a victim (Personality, yes—gender, no.)" (Gabaldon, *Facebook*). On face value, the claim that Jack is not a homosexual is belied by the abundant textual evidence throughout the first three novels of the series. Jack Randall is clearly bisexual, but his homosexual identity not only shocks the reader given the eighteenth-century context, when sodomy is considered a crime, but also because he is competing with the hero, Claire, for the object of her desire, Jamie. Jack Randall's attempts to rape Claire and Jenny are violent, but in Jenny's case, he is rendered impotent by her laughter, and Claire is rescued on two separate occasions.

However after several failed attempts, Randall finally succeeds in raping Jamie in the dungeon of Wentworth Prison. What is significantly different between the rapes of Claire, Jenny and Jamie is that the word "love" keeps surfacing only with Jamie, and suggests that he craves the love of his male victims. Randall's love for Jamie makes him an even greater threat to Claire because it suggests a bond that goes beyond a physical, sexual level toward the unification of their identities. If the ultimate goal of Claire's love for Jamie is marriage, it is because the two identities become one at a level beyond the merely physical, what we normally refer to as the spiritual. The marriage vow, spoken by both Claire and Jamie, represents this spiritual unity: "Ye are Blood of my Blood, and Bone of my Bone. / I give ye my body, that we Two might be One. / I give ye my Spirit, 'til our Life shall be Done" (*Outlander,* ch. 14). However, as Frye says at one point regarding the mixture of the romance genre with the genre of the novel, of which *Outlander* is an example, there is always a demand for "a romantic novel just romantic enough for the reader to project his libido on the hero and his anima on the heroine, and just novel enough to keep these projections in a familiar world" (*AC* 305). In his efforts to distinguish the novel from romance, Frye states, "The romancer does not attempt to create 'real people' so much as stylized figures which expand into psychological archetypes" (*AC* 304).

A prime example of this identification between the main characters is Catherine's declaration in *Wuthering Heights* "I *am* Heathcliff" (Bronte 60). Caught in a conflict between loving Edgar Linton and Heathcliff, Catherine tells her servant, Nelly, that she identifies completely with Heathcliff despite their continued separation. Catherine's love triangle mirrors Claire's love triangle, but with obvious gender differences of Randall's bisexual nature. The point is that Claire has made Jamie a part of her identity and Randall threatens to destroy that identity. It is the breakdowns of the individual identities in favor of the spiritual union between them that gives romance, Frye says, "a glow of subjective intensity" (*AC* 304). As Frye states, "it is in the romance that we find Jung's libido, anima, and shadow reflected in the hero, heroine, and villain respectively" (*AC* 304). In Jungian psychology, Jung himself states that "the feelings of a man are so to speak a woman's and appear as such in dreams. I designate this figure by the term *anima*.... To a woman it appears in masculine form, and then I call it the *animus*" (Jung 99). Jamie, as Claire's animus, therefore, represents the heroic side of Claire that is largely unconscious to her, especially Claire's need to fight for fairness and justice, to say nothing of her courage in battle expressed so often by Jamie's frequent acts of courage. Symbolically, and from a more negative point of view, Jack Randall's desire to possess and control Jamie is the same as Claire's, even though the method of achieving that goal is the difference between love and sadistic control.

As the "structural core of all fiction," romance is, according to Frye, the "loss and regaining of identity" (*SS* 15). In *Outlander* the struggle between Claire and Randall is really a struggle for Jamie's identity, especially his gender identity. Black Jack Randall is trying to break down Jamie's resistance to his sexual advances, but there is a political advantage as well, given the uprising of the Scottish against the English. During the rape at Wentworth, Jamie says of Randall, "He did not just hurt me, or use me. He made love to me, Claire. He hurt me—hurt me badly—while he did it, but it was an act of love to him" (*Outlander*, ch. 39). It should also be noted that in the episode of the television series entitled "To Ransom a Man's Soul" that Jamie is heard saying, "He made love to me, Claire" (Moore and Behr). After Randall is finished raping Jamie, Jamie tells Claire that "he had his arms round my neck, and he pulled on me, and buried his face in my shoulder, and I could feel he was crying ... he was saying 'I love you, I love you,' over and over, with his tears and his spittle running down my chest" (*Outlander*, ch. 40). If Randall is only a sadist and not homosexual, or bisexual, there would be no explicit declarations of love. Randall is emotionally vulnerable at this moment, and seems to want Jamie to reciprocate his love. When Jamie refuses, Randall begins "cursing and shouting" saying, "You know you love me! Tell me so! I know it's true!" (*Outlander*, ch. 40). What is so disturbing to the audience and the reader is not only that we are made to momentarily sympathize with the villain, despite the fact that he takes possession of Jamie, but also that he obstructs Claire, the hero, from gaining the object of her desire.

The sadistic nature of Black Jack Randall is what makes him such an intriguing and complex villain—he poses a unique menace to the very identity of Jamie Fraser. A threat to both men and women, Randall gets aroused by the pain and terror that he inflicts upon his victims, though this treatment varies depending on their gender. According to psychiatrist Stephen J. Hucker, "Sexual sadism refers to the derivation of sexual pleasure from the infliction of pain, suffering and/or humiliation upon another person. The pain and suffering of the victim, which may be both physical and psychological, is pivotal to the sexual arousal and pleasure" (Hucker).

The only time Randall is able to perform sexually is when he is raping and torturing Jamie, showing that while he is a sexual sadist, he seems to prefer men. He attempts to rape both Jenny and Claire, but fails each time. Actor Tobias Menzies, who portrays Randall in the Starz television series, says, "That character, I would argue, is a study of sadism.... He's interested in people's boundaries, their pain thresholds, what they can handle. It's a rather sickening investigation." This violent character is not out of place in the series, however. As Laura Mulvey states in her book, *Visual and Other Pleasures*, "sadism ... depends on making something happen, forcing a change in another person, a battle of will and strength, victory/defeat" (22). We see this battle whenever Jamie and/or Claire encounter Randall, but the battle of will and strength is seen most in the scene at Wentworth Prison. Randall uses Claire's image as a way to arouse Jamie by asking him things like "Does *she* do this for you? Can your woman [rouse] you like this?" (*Outlander*, ch. 39). Randall wants to defeat Jamie psychologically by breaking down his sense of loyalty to Claire, and indirectly, the Scottish cause, by using his body against him. The body is the means by which Randall attempts to destroy Jamie's sense of self, his identity. Jamie resists Randall by saying, "You can't take me alone, one-handed or no…. No, I'm bigger, and far the better fighter, hand to hand" (*Outlander*, ch. 35). Randall, however, is most successful when he goes after what Jamie values most, which is Claire herself. Jamie makes a deal with Randall for Claire's life by saying, "Let the woman go, and ye can have me…. Do what ye wish to me. I'll not struggle, though I'll allow you to bind me if ye think it needful. And I'll not speak of it come tomorrow. But first you'll see the woman safe from the prison" (*Outlander*, ch. 35). Randall is getting what he desires and taking Claire's sexual prize from her.

As Frye states, "Most of what goes on in the night world of romance is cruelty and horror" (*SS* 113). The night world for Frye is the world into which the hero descends, for a time, where he has less power than the audience does. As Frye describes it, "If inferior in power or intelligence to ourselves, so that we have the sense of looking down on a scene of bondage, frustration or absurdity, the hero belongs to the *ironic* mode" (*AC* 34). This descent to the night world is seen when Randall punishes Jamie for Claire's botched rescue attempt. He allows Claire to live, if Jamie sacrifices himself to save her. Jamie knows that he may one day have to sacrifice his identity in order to save her: "Seems I canna possess your soul without losing my own" (*Outlander*, ch. 23). To test the sincerity of Jamie's willing sacrifice, Randall nails his hand to a table. Since Randall cannot defeat Jamie "hand to hand," he is wise to weaken Jamie. However, more importantly, Randall breaks down his will to resist:

> Randall leaned past Jamie to pluck a ha'penny nail delicately from the reed basket. He positioned the point with care and brought the mallet down, driving the nail through Jamie's right hand into the table with four solid blows. The broken fingers twitched and sprang straight, like the legs of a spider pinned to a collection board.
> Jamie groaned, his eyes wide and blank with shock. Randall set the mallet down with care. He took Jamie's chin in his hand and turned his face up. "Now kiss me," he said softly, and lowered his face to Jamie's unresisting mouth [*Outlander*, ch. 35].

Randall is trying to break down Jamie's resistance to him and his sexual advances, but he is really trying to break down his heterosexual gender identity and thereby, to a large extent, his hyper-masculine Scottish clan identity.

The realistic detail evokes feelings of disgust in the reader and the television audience that breaks the romantic mood, which is based on the analogy of romance to the dream, the search of the libido in search of fulfillment.

Satisfied with the outcome, Randall escorts Claire out of the prison, throwing her out the door and into a "ditch of sorts.... At least a dozen [dead] men lay here, waiting either for a thaw that would make their burial easier, or for a cruder disposal by the beasts of the nearby forest" (*Outlander,* ch. 35). The beasts are not far off, either. There is a pack of hungry wolves scavenging the area, meaning that Randall literally throws Claire to the wolves, making Jamie the sacrificial lamb. Claire, nevertheless, turns the table on Randall by using her status as a witch to scare him when she attempts to rescue Jamie from Wentworth. Randall is mortified when she tells him the hour of his death:

> "You asked me, Captain, if I were a witch.... I'll answer you now. Witch I am. Witch and I curse you. You will marry, Captain, and your wife will bear a child, but you shall not live to see your firstborn. I curse you with knowledge, Jack Randall—I give you the hour of your death." His face was in shadow, but the gleam of his eyes told me he believed me [*Outlander,* ch. 35].

While women are unable to match Randall in strength, they use their intelligence to defeat him. Randall relies on fear to control his victims, and neither Jenny nor Claire are easily frightened by him. They are both quick to understand his vulnerabilities, and use them to their advantage. Jenny realizes that attacking Randall's pride cripples him so that he is unable to perform sexually. Claire preys on his superstitious belief that she is a witch, and gives him prophetic foreknowledge that people fear most: the moment he will die. Gabaldon flips the traditional romance by rendering the male (traditionally, the hero) helpless at the hands of the villain, and empowers her female hero with the ability to outsmart and defeat the villain.

The memories that Jamie has of the incident in the dungeon at Wentworth plague him for the rest of his life. Frye states in *The Secular Scripture* that, "the only companion who accompanies us to the end of the descent is the demonic accuser, who takes the form of the accusing memory. The memory is demonic here because it has forgotten only one thing, the original identity of what it accompanies" (*SS* 124). Randall destroys Jamie's identity. Jamie often wakes up "still trembling, and his face glossy with sweat ... [breathing] heavily with a hoarse, gasping sound" (*Outlander,* ch. 38) after having a nightmare about the trauma he experienced. Unlike popular romance, the hero is at the mercy of the villain and is too weak to save himself. Randall becomes a permanent memory, indicating that Jamie never fully escapes the situation, turning Randall into a metaphorical demon that threatens to terrorize Jamie for the rest of his life. After his escape, Jamie narrowly avoids death at the abbey in France. Jamie's soul has been completely destroyed by Randall to the point that he no longer wants to live. In order for Jamie to be saved, Claire must exorcise the demonic memory from him by drugging him with opium to induce hallucinations that she is Randall and to force Jamie to face him by invoking the extreme anger and hatred Jamie has for Randall. Even though Randall is thought to be dead after the escape from Wentworth, he is still very much alive to Jamie, making Randall an invincible villain that can never truly be beaten.

Going on the premise of Frye's Themes of Descent, specifically "the night world, often a dark and labyrinthine world of caves and shadows where the forest has turned subterranean" (SS 111), when Claire goes to Wentworth to find Jamie, she immediately looks for the dungeons, since "the dungeons in castles such as this were customarily underground, where tons of earth muffled any cries, and darkness hid all cruelty from the eyes of those responsible" (*Outlander*, ch. 35). Because Randall has descended underground to the dungeons with Jamie, we are looking down from middle earth, according to creation myths. And, as Frye states, "creation myths suggested by this would most naturally be sexual ones" (SS 112). This descent represents how, psychologically, Claire's desires are trapped where she does not want them to be.

The union between Randall and Jamie, which Frye describes as the demonic erotic relation, "becomes a fierce destructive passion that works against loyalty or frustrates the one who possesses it. The demonic parody of marriage, or the union of two souls in one flesh, may take the form of hermaphroditism, incest, or homosexuality" (AC 149). In the second book of the series, *Dragonfly in Amber*, when Randall comes looking for Claire at Holyrood to ask for medical help for his brother, Alex, he goes into detail about his unconventional union with Jamie. He tells Claire,

> I have had him as you could never have him. You are a woman; you cannot understand, even witch as you are. I have held the soul of his manhood, have taken from him what he has taken from me. I know him, as he now knows me. We are bound, he and I, by blood.... We are linked, you and I, through the body of one man [*Dragonfly in Amber*, ch. 38].

The bond that he and Claire now have after sharing the same man in such an intimate way leaves Claire bound to Jonathan Randall not just through Frank, but now through Jamie, as well. As Eve Kosofsky Sedgwick states in *Between Men: English Literature and Male Homosocial Desire*, "The bond that links the two rivals is as intense and potent as the bond that links either of the rivals to the beloved; that the bonds of 'rivalry' and 'love,' differently as they are experienced, are equally powerful and in many senses equivalent" (Sedgwick 21). This bond angers Randall because he knows Claire has what he will never have—Jamie's love. After Claire rescues Jamie from Wentworth, he tells her, "He was most terribly jealous of you, you know" (*Outlander*, ch. 39). Because of this, Randall tells Claire, "my feelings toward you are much as yours toward me must be" (*DIA* ch. 38). This peculiar focus on love makes Randall an unconventional villain, and Jamie's vulnerability at the hands of Jonathan Randall reverses the expectations of historical romance.

Jamie and Claire do not have the option to kill Jack Randall, because it would affect Frank's existence. However, Frank's lineage and existence are put into jeopardy when Jamie learns that Jack Randall is alive and in Paris at the same time as them. Jamie cannot kill him because if "[he] kills Jack Randall now, then Frank … won't exist. He won't be born" (*DIA,* ch. 21). Frank's lineage will be compromised, possibly ended completely, if Jamie kills Jack Randall, and it could potentially change his life, Claire's life, and risk their child's existence. If Jamie kills Jack Randall before the Battle of Culloden, Frank may not be born. If Frank is not born, Claire cannot marry him and go to Scotland on a second honeymoon, nor will she end up at Craigh na Dun where she travels through time, and therefore will not meet Jamie. However, Jamie is so focused on vengeance that he does not consider the implications of his actions, and argues, "Jesus God, Claire! You'd try to stop me from taking my vengeance on the man who made me play whore to him? Who forced me to my knees and made me suck his cock, smeared with my own blood?" (*DIA,* ch. 21). While Claire is actively trying to change history in some aspects by attempting to stop the Battle of Culloden from happening, she must fight to keep it the same in others, despite the violent nature of Jack Randall and all the harm he has brought to Jamie and her, because Jack Randall must have a child in order for history to remain unchanged.

Both the scene in Wentworth Prison with Jamie and the scene with Claire at Holyrood are extremely important to the series because, in Gabaldon's words, "[there] *has* to be a credible threat to the hero. Ergo, we have to have seen (and heard about) the real damage Randall has done to Jamie" (*Gabaldon Explains*). Randall is definitely a credible threat to both Jamie and Claire. He has raped and tortured Jamie nearly to death, and has attempted to rape, torture, and murder Claire on several occasions. The particular threat that Randall imposes on Jamie and Claire contrasts with other literary villains. The scene with Randall and Claire in the church at Holyrood shows a slightly different side of him. There is still no mistaking his sadistic side with the way he explains to Claire in detail what he shared with Jamie in the dungeon, but there is a hint of tenderness when he describes it. He also shows the love he has for his brother, Alex, by putting his feelings for Claire aside in order to ask for her help. Claire even questions whether "in different circumstances, might he have been like the great-grandson he resembled?" (*DIA,* ch. 38). Regardless of how he feels about her, he knows that she is a knowledgeable healer and can likely help his brother in ways that no other physician or healer can. The two work together, and even Jamie finds a way to tolerate Randall momentarily for his brother's sake. This compassion they both offer the villain grants him an extra dimension of reader sympathy.

Gabaldon allows men to be objectified in her series, both in positive, playful ways and in violent ways ending in assault. In her essay "Visual Pleasure and Narrative Cinema," Mulvey states that "the presence of woman is an indispensable element of spectacle in normal narrative film, yet her visual presence tends to work against the development of a story-line, to freeze the flow of action in moments of erotic contemplation" (Mulvey 19). Gabaldon is interested in breaking the traditional idea of female objectification by incorporating intense male vulnerability and violent physical assaults on masculinity in her series. As Lisa Fletcher states, "Historical fictions of heterosexual love are performative to the extent that they participate in the establishment and maintenance of prevailing ideas about the links between sex, gender, and sexuality" (L. Fletcher 15) within film and literature. Gabaldon breaks this tradition of the female gaze by introducing both heterosexual and homosexual objectification of men—positively in the case of the Duke of Sandringham, who also pardons Jamie, and negatively through Jamie's encounter with Jack Randall. Similarly, many female characters fawn over Jamie, from Laoghaire's eager stares to Claire's admiring him on their wedding night and after. As Anne Helen Petersen points out, "sex is almost always about gratifying the male gaze" (Petersen) both on television and in literature, but Gabaldon turns this around and gratifies the female gaze by objectifying Jamie through Jack Randall's violent assaults on Jamie at Wentworth Prison, both with the rape and torture, and with the brutal flogging. Jamie's body is also objectified when Randall says to Claire in the church at Holyrood, "You know, as I do, the touch of his skin—so warm, is he not? Almost as though he burned from within. You know the smell of his sweat and the roughness of the hairs on his thighs. You know the sound that he makes at the last, when he has lost himself. So do I" (*DIA*, ch. 38). The reference to Jamie having "lost himself" is a double entendre, meaning that he had a sexual orgasm with Randall and simultaneously lost his identity.

Jonathan Randall is what keeps Claire from fulfilling her libido. Randall's sadistic sexual appetite makes him an extraordinarily sinister antagonist that poses a deadly threat to both Jamie and Claire, but also blocks Claire from getting what she wants, which is Jamie. However, if Claire or Jamie were to kill Randall, it could alter history and Frank might not be born, which could dramatically change their very identities. Gabaldon does not use sexuality cosmetically in the series, and each of the sexual encounters found within the series will later affect the plot in some way. Randall's sexually sadistic impulses destroy Jamie's identity, turning Randall into a demonic accuser that haunts Jamie for the rest of his life. The fact that Gabaldon is not afraid to use sexual orientation, both heterosexual and homosexual, in positive and negative ways, shows that she is not afraid to take risks in her writing, and this allows sexuality to be a major driving force behind the *Outlander* series.

Works Cited

Cocks, H. G. "Homosexuality Between Men in Britain Since the Eighteenth Century." *History Compass* 5.3 (2007): 865–889.

Fletcher, Angus. "Northrop Frye: The Critical Passion." *Critical Inquiry* 1.4 (1975): 741–756.

Fletcher, Lisa. *Historical Romance Fiction: Heterosexuality and Performativity.* Burlington, VT: Ashgate Publishing Company, 2008.

Frye, Northrop. *Anatomy of Criticism.* Princeton: Princeton University Press, 2000.

_____. *The Secular Scripture: A Study of the Structure of Romance.* Cambridge, MA: Harvard University Press, 1976.

Gabaldon, Diana. "Diana Gabaldon Explains the 'Why' of the Wentworth Prison Scene in *Outlander*." March 2013. *Tumblr.* 20 October 2014 http://awyissout lander.tumblr.com/post/79566217462/diana-gabaldon-explains-the-why-of-the-wentworth.

_____. "Diana Gabaldon Facebook Fan Group." 28 April 2015. *Facebook.* 28 April 2015 https://www.facebook.com/AuthorDianaGabaldon/posts/893317154044455

_____. *Dragonfly in Amber.* New York: Dell Publishing, 1992.

_____. *Outlander.* Canada: Random House of Canada Limited, 2001.

_____. *The Outlandish Companion.* New York: Delacorte Press, 1999.

Hucker, Stephen. "Sexual Sadism." 2011. *Forensic Psychiatry.* 15 January 2015 http://www.forensicpsychiatry.ca/paraphilia/sadism.htm.

Jung, C. G. *Analytical Psychology: Its Theory and Practice.* New York: Pantheon Books, 1968.

Kosofsky Sedgwick, Eve. *Between Men: English Literature and Male Homosocial Desire.* New York: Columbia University Press, 1985.

Menzies, Tobias. "Things Get Disturbing." *16 Fascinating Facts About Outlander.* E! Entertainment Television, LLC. 2014.

Moore, Ronald D., and Ira Steven Behr. "To Ransom a Man's Soul." *Outlander.* Dir. Anna Foerster. Perf. Sam Heughan. Prod. David Brown. Starz Entertainment, LLC. 2015.

Mulvey, Laura. *Visual and Other Pleasures.* Bloomington: Indiana University Press, 1989.

Petersen, Anne Helen. *Outlander Is the Feminist Answer to Game of Thrones and Men Should Be Watching It.* 4 August 2014.*Buzzfeed.* 9 August 2014.

The Good, the Bad and Lord John Grey

Observations on Desire, Sex, Violence, Lust and Love

SANDI SOLIS

Introduction

Desire wears many faces in the pages of the *Outlander* books—an element that it shares with the "typical" Romance genre novel. As readers know, however, *Outlander* is anything but typical, and the three characters who are the focus of this essay illustrate that point. As my center of focus, I've chosen to examine the "higher" or loftier elements of love, power and honor against their "earthier"—or baser, if you will—counterparts of sex, perversion and lust respectively.

These characteristics will serve as a means to begin to investigate the subjects of desire and the men in this series. The characters of Jamie Fraser, Black Jack Randall and Lord John Grey offer distinctively different interwoven personality traits and elements that act as a lens with which to begin a discussion on societally defined notions and expectations of male sexual behavior in eighteenth-century Europe. By using these elements as a means with which to view a few key events and relationships in the life of one Jamie Fraser. I am, in essence, using his life and experiences as a fulcrum for my observations. I am using several universally recognizable conventions that define "what it means to be a man" as they apply to Jamie Fraser, Black Jack Randall and Lord John Grey. Specifically, Jamie is easily recognizable as the Hero or Good Man while Black Jack is the Villain. Lord John Grey is not so easily categorized as either and as such is something of a Chameleon or Shapeshifter. He's a complex, charismatic and nuanced character who weaves in and out of Jamie's life. Regardless of the guise he wears, he is always quick to adapt to the challenges he faces.

Jamie is the Hero because "he's so perfect in so many ways" (Moore) and is the embodiment of the traditional romance novel hero; he is a leader, lover and honorable man of action. Black Jack is the perfectly evil Villain possessed of power and position who hunts the hero and unjustly preys on him on multiple levels; he threatens the hero's loved ones, those dependent upon him and the very land which defines him. I refer to Lord John as the Shapeshifter because like Jamie and Claire themselves, his character adapts to ever-changing life situations in the context of Jamie's life. He is at times Jamie's friend, his prisoner, his jailer, a brother-in-arms, co-conspirator, enemy and ally.[1] One thing all three of these men have in common is that no matter what the situation, each remains true to his nature; Jamie always strives for that which he understands to be the best that he can be, Black Jack is the captain of occupying forces unafraid to wield his power and Lord John is always, always aware of honor and duty.

Jamie's interactions and relationships with both of these Englishmen give shape to his life as well as our own feelings for Jamie as readers who come to care deeply about the character. Why focus on Black Jack and Lord John? In large part because whether by accident or design, Gabaldon has given us opposite ends of the spectrum of male-on-male attraction in this era and provides insights into same-sex attraction/desire in a time before the word "homosexual" even existed, during a time when sodomy was a crime punishable by death. In a straightforward and (admittedly) incredibly over-simplified attempt to examine male sexuality of the time, I've attributed the elements of love and sex to Jamie, power and perversion to Black Jack and honor and lust to Lord John. While love and sex, desire and lust are all inter-related dynamics in most human relationships, the added element of violence fueled by personal (and political) power then wielded as domination, humil-iation and sexual perversion by Black Jack Randall creates a moment in time that resonates throughout Jamie's life. This horrific situation in Wentworth prison brings a depth of complication and angst to *Outlander* that simply does not exist in most Romance novels. As we say out in the street: This is where the shit gets real.

And this is one of the graphic and key elements that make *Outlander* not a romance novel.

That the worst of the violence and depravity happens to Jamie—The Hero—makes it all the more shocking. That he gives his consent to the rape and torture in order to save Claire makes it heart wrenching. Yet it is also one of the most important reasons that Jamie is so beloved; he promises Claire she has the protection of his body on their wedding day and the sac-rifice of his body is him simply keeping that promise.[2] Despite the fact that

Jamie knows that Black Jack wants him and he knows what the man is capable of (Jamie's back and Jenny's assault offered as Exhibit A and Exhibit B), when he makes his bargain with Jack he is fully aware that he is in for a night of horrors. That alone is a large part of what makes him The Hero.

Desire and Jamie Fraser, Love (and Sex)

James Alexander Malcolm MacKenzie Fraser.

His name alone elicits deep heart-felt sighs among (mostly) women of all ages and hearing his name spoken aloud during "The Wedding" episode brought Jamie to life in a way many have only dreamed about for years.[3] For fans of Diana Gabaldon's *Outlander* series, his name alone reminds us of why we love the books as deeply as with do. Sure, we love Claire for being the strong-willed, independent and empowered female character that she is, but let's be honest; it's all about "the King of Men" here.[4]

Larger than Life and the perfect specimen of Manhood—in body, mind and spirit—everyone wants a piece of Jamie. What in The Name of All That is Holy is it about this fictional character that makes people desire him both in the pages of *Outlander and* among fans in the real world?

A partial explanation is Jamie's seemingly universal appeal as the quintessential Hero. It stems not only from his physical attractiveness (on the surface at least) which is described in detail so we know he's a strikingly handsome man but rather that that throughout this series of books we watch him evolve. Through the course of decades we see him struggle with a myriad of emotions and situations that often leave him feeling helpless and at times resentful, in the aftermath of Culloden. He sees his family, tenants and country endure great suffering through constant raids by British soldiers, frequent false imprisonment (in the case of his brother-in-law Ian) and the constant struggle to stave off starvation. We repeatedly observe that his sense of honor helps him find a way to sacrifice himself in order to provide for those to whom he knows he has an obligation despite his own loss of birthright, freedom and love.

In the hands of many writers, it would not be a stretch to show Jamie as a martyr given the challenges he faces. Gabaldon does not portray him as such so that she allows us to see instead a man—a good man—who understands the need to take care of his family and who willingly does whatever it takes to get the job done. Jamie doesn't see what he does as a sacrifice but instead, as a part of his obligation as son, husband, brother, uncle and Laird. This begs the question; what is it about that his sacrifice that *isn't* appealing to readers/viewers who are altogether much too familiar with absent and/or deadbeat dads and divorce rates topping fifty percent? Jamie's sense of loyalty and sense of responsibility to take care of his own is simply another element that adds to his desirability.

As Gabaldon writes him, Jamie is a complicated character study of What It Means to Be a Man—in the past as well as today. The character of Jamie embodies "The Good" in large part for the reason Moore's team refer to him as TKOM; he is human and fallible yet noble with firm morals, a strong sense of self without taking himself too seriously. And while he might sometimes be a little too cocksure (what twenty-three-year-old isn't?), he has an innate kindness that allows others to see his heart as well as his strong sense of self. But he is JAMMF, and that makes him Larger Than Life. Gabaldon's Jamie is more than just a good person—she imbues the character with a rugged and self-effacing sexuality that simply *is*. He knows that the lassies find him attractive and as a healthy young man isn't above spending time in an alcove or two as he does with Laoghaire. As he says to Claire on their wedding night, "I said I was a virgin, no a monk" (*Outlander*, ch. 15), but his psychological makeup is such that he understands that he needs to temper the temptations of the flesh against the obligation of duty he has to family, tenants, clan and his own personal honor. It is this balance between duty and his own personal desires that make this character so appealing to such a wide and varied audience.

A simple illustration of this is one I saw on Gabaldon's Facebook page amongst comments from one of her many fans. As readers eagerly awaited the release of *Written in My Own Heart's Blood*, Gabaldon's eight "Big, Enormous Book" (DianaGabaldon.com) and prior to the airing of the first season of the Starz! series, there was lots of talk about how much everyone loves Jamie.[5] One woman made the comment that she and her wife had been together for many years but that her wife had given her blessing for Jamie to be her "free pass." She went on to comment that it was his heart and spirit that she loved—that for her as a lesbian, it didn't matter that he is male. And it is the courage, honesty and vulnerability of the character that creates desire where Jamie is concerned; he embodies what most of us want as well as what we try to be.

Desiring Jamie Part 1: Black Jack Randall, Power (and Perversion)

Desire—we know it when we feel it but like love, it stems from many sources and has a myriad of intricate motivations; desire is a reflection of many of the influences that make up who we are as individual, sexual beings. Desire can spring from many places—out of the highest impulses of the human soul or it can be grounded in the basest of our animalistic urges.

Claire, Lord John Grey and Black Jack Randall all desire Jamie in their own way and for their own purposes; these purposes may often intersect but the motivations can be vastly different.

There are three individuals whose love and/or desire for Jamie come to define the man he becomes. It is understood that Claire is the center of his universe, his soul mate, his love and his balance; this paper moves beyond their relationship and focuses on his complicated and complex relationships with Black Jack and Lord John. Of the two of these characters, the motives of Black Jack Randall are in some respects the easier to grasp and also more difficult to accept and understand; we realize that they are dark and malevolent and that his end game is the total control, command and destruction of Jamie[6] It goes without saying (for book readers at least) that his are also the most disturbing. His desire is based on his need to possess, to own, to hurt, debase and ultimately break, Jamie—it is *not* strictly based on sexual attraction and includes an element of opportunism. Black Jack knows that power is having a thing, being able to control it; his psychopathic nature and innate perversion allow him to destroy the prey—Jamie—that he has sought and pursued. For him, the thrill is in the hunt and the acquisition of his quarry; his pleasure comes from the kill and the destruction. The total power that he holds over Jamie for the one night in Wentworth allows him to completely give in to his psychopathic perversion. While Jamie may be at his mercy during the one night, it's interesting to note that Black Jack isn't wearing any masks—he is himself physically and figuratively as naked and exposed as Jamie even though he holds all the power. There are implications for his exposure later on in Paris and Edinburgh (*Dragonfly in Amber*). Because he has Jamie's word that he will submit and go to the gallows without a word against him in the morning, Black Jack exposes the true depth of his sadistic nature and desire to Jamie in a way he has rarely been able to before and thus exposes his vulnerabilities. Specifically, wanting, *needing* to hear Jamie tell him that he loves him and retaliating when Jamie refuses to do so.

Their meeting in Paris leads to a duel with catastrophic repercussions for both of them even though Jamie spares him his life. Interestingly, when they encounter each other later in Edinburgh Jamie has the opportunity to literally "turn the other cheek" at Alex Randall's death[7] when he reaches out to Black Jack.

The night at Wentworth with its intersection of sadistic desire, sex and violence is so traumatic and vivid that it has haunted many book readers on a visceral level for years; now, with the airing of the Starz! series, we have visual proof that yes, it really was as horrible for Jamie as we have imagined. As Ron Moore has said in interviews, following the airing of "To Ransom a Man's Soul": "Claire made Jamie a man; Black Jack made him his bitch," and more heartrending words have never been spoken. Yet, it is Jamie's struggle to come to terms with his experience and his (and Claire's) ongoing struggle for the reclamation of his soul that comes to define him. Witnessing the process of his recovery of his sense of self serves dual purposes for us as readers; it both elevates him as a character making him worthy of the status as King of Men as it also exposes his clay feet which allow us to see that he is a flawed and struggling human being. Noble and wonderful yes, but not perfect by any means.

Black Jack Randall has been described by Gabaldon as a sadist, a pervert and a psychopath; his stock in trade is "power over" others, pain, humiliation and domination. He is a Captain of Dragoon in the British Army for pity's sake. He's stationed in the Highlands and his job is to keep the "Scottish rebels" in check; use any metaphor you like—wolf in sheep's clothing/pedophile working in the candy shop—but the bottom line is that Black Jack and the government he represents have the power of life and death over the people whose lands they occupy.

The question has been asked by readers for years (and now by viewers) as to why it is that his treatment of Jamie is so completely ruthless; the short answer is that in Jamie Fraser, he has met his match, which means that Black Jack Randall *must* break him as Jamie is the perfect prey—smart, strong, proud, elusive and unyielding. Gabaldon has addressed this several times since *Outlander* was first published (on her Facebook page and in the CompuServe writers' forum) that in essence, Jamie telling Black Jack that he can have him in order to save Claire is nothing but empty words unless he (Jamie) really *does* suffer by following through on the bargain.

In other words, talk is cheap. It's actions that count.

Gabaldon has explained that in order for it to be a true sacrifice, Jamie cannot be rescued; his believing that he will hang in the morning gives him the strength he needs to endure what he understands will be a horrible night. In Jamie's mind, it is worth whatever he must endure if it guarantees that his Claire will survive. That he doesn't die and thus has to live with his scars and memories of knowing that Black Jack did indeed finally "break" him is just one more reason that the character of Black Jack is so universally hated. Claire's descriptions of finding Jamie awake and struggling with his nightmares of Black Jack Randall and Wentworth prison illustrate just how great a sacrifice Jamie made for her. While book readers have despised him for over two decades now, the television series has given rise to a new generation of *Outlander* fans to join the ranks of the Black Jack Randall haters. In fact, the character was recently voted Number One among "Seventeen Characters We Will Never Forgive" by eonline.com.

It isn't hard to hate the character of Black Jack Randall. His ongoing pursuit of Jamie and his actions towards him are so utterly shocking that it would be easy to fixate solely on the vicious nature of Jamie's rape and torture.

Much has been written about Season One episodes fifteen and sixteen by entertainment industry bloggers and television sites as well as casual bloggers; there has also been much discussion on *Outlander* fan pages (some Public pages and some belonging to Closed groups).[8]

If we can look beyond the horror of Jack's abuse of Jamie, however, we can begin to see that the power struggle that they are engaged in personally is a metaphor for the political situation in the Highlands between the Risings of 1715 and 1745 as well as immediately post–Culloden. In that vein, the body of Jamie can be seen to stand in for Scotland itself; he represents the traditional life patterns and culture of the land. Thus, the treatment of Jamie is, metaphorically speaking, a powerful indication of the brutal treatment of the Highlanders at the hand of the British government. After Culloden, they were robbed of their identity—forbidden to wear tartan or keep their lands. Many were physically tortured: shot, imprisoned, or left to starve. Utilizing Jamie's body as illustration makes it possible to put a face to the historical record.[9]

Black Jack is absolutely The Villain of the story and even though he is a soldier, he is not the kind of soldier and guardian that we recognize Jamie and Lord John to be. Instead of working for the good of the community he commands, he is instead warped by his own need to possess and destroy. His obsession with Jamie and seizing ultimate "power over" him strips him of any room we might give him as a human being; his actions toward Jamie (and Claire) prove him to be The Monster.

Given the complicated and warped nature of Black Jack Randall's motivations where Jamie is concerned, it would be easy to assume that Lord John Grey's motives are much less complicated. As we will see, that would be an erroneous assumption.

Desiring Jamie Part 2: Lord John Grey, Honor (and Lust)

Soldier/Diplomat/Spy. Loyal Friend. Husband/Father/Brother/Son. Man of Honor. Sodomite. These words can all be used to describe Lord John Grey and, with the exception of "sodomite," they can also be used to describe Jamie Fraser. That makes this a good place to begin to understand the long-standing and complicated friendship between these two men.

The character of Lord John Grey is what Gabaldon refers to in her work as "a mushroom"—"one of those unplanned people who pops up out of nowhere and walks off with any scene he's in—and he talks to me easily (and wittily)" (DianaGabaldon.com).[10]

As a chameleon, Lord John has the ability to adapt and become what is needed in any given situation; he can go from being a good Soldier to a good

Friend to a Lover and back to Regimental Colonel and does so all whilst maintaining his sense of dignity and honor. To this point, it's important to recognize that just because he can adapt does not mean that he is duplicitous. To the contrary, throughout his adventures in the Lord John novellas he is constantly looking for justice or trying to protect those around him as in *Lord John and the Private Matter* where his quest is to find out what his cousin's fiancé is hiding from everyone. Lord John adapts to an ever-changing environment yet does so without ever sacrificing his sense of self or honor and always living up to a code of personal conduct and decency that helps him make order of his world. He is willing to make the hard decisions based not on his own desires but on what may be needed in any particular situation with a firm understanding of the differences between right and wrong, justice and mercy and the realistic self-knowledge of himself as a less-than-perfect human being who has specific social roles and expectations to fulfill. Evidence of this can be seen throughout the *Outlander* series but most especially in the storyline of *The Scottish Prisoner*. Lord John and Jamie are forced to come to terms with a very emotionally messy aspect of their convicted traitor/parole officer relationship in order to work cooperatively to gain military justice in a situation that has great meaning for John but (initially) none for Jamie. Within the context of a reluctantly shared quest each has to acknowledge the strengths as well as the foibles of the other; while John has always recognized the warrior, natural-born leader and generosity of spirit within Jamie, until this point Jamie has not acknowledged the same or any other positive attributes in John.

Situations arise in which Jamie has to acknowledge that John's sense of honor, duty and obligation to family, friends and his regiment is not that different from his own similar feelings and connections to family, friends, his tenants and the men under him at Ardsmuir prison.

It is during this period of sometimes forced and often tense interaction between the two that we see John's struggle to balance his desire for Jamie against the man he knows Jamie to be. As he says to his sister-in-law, "If you mean, is he a man of honor, then, yes, he is. Certainly a man of his word … he has … a sense of himself that is quite separate from what society demands. He is inclined to make his own rules" (*The Scottish Prisoner*, ch. 11). When encountering Lord John after an absence of several years, Claire describes him thus: "I had to admit that I had seen no trace of either recklessness or cruelty in his character. On the contrary, he had struck me as a sensitive, kindly, and honorable man…" (*Drums of Autumn*, ch. 25).

Lord John may have started out as an "important minor character," but I would argue that in many respects he is as important as Black Jack Randall if not more so. As discussed earlier, for Black Jack Randall, Jamie's rape despite being a sexual act, was not an act of attraction so much as one of power, perversion and control. In other words, what we recognize as the classic definition of rape. Lord John desires Jamie as his equal despite their current differences of social or legal position (John *does* after all hold Jamie's parole). John sees Jamie as a gentleman and fellow soldier instead of his prisoner and as such presents an important counterpoint to the "refined and intelligent malice" (*Written in My Own Heart's Blood*, ch. 112) of Black Jack while also being his inverse despite his—Lord John's—desire for Jamie. John's attraction to Jamie is one that values him as a man of worth and honor and as well as a fellow soldier. John may indeed desire and even love Jamie, but his own sense of honor makes his respect for Jamie a driving force in their relationship. It is John's desire tempered by love, personal honor and respect for Jamie that defines him as the inverse of Black Jack.

In order to truly understand how Lord John differs from Black Jack it is helpful to begin with a quick look at both men's physical attraction (for lack of a better term in Black Jack Randall's case) to Jamie. The term "homosexual" itself did not exist until the late nineteenth-century and readers who try to understand Lord John through modern notions of "gay" or "homosexual" often fail to understand his true nature and his place in the world of *Outlander*. Gabaldon does offer a few glimpses into what we think of as stereotypical behavior when John overhears conversation between "Mollies" on a "molly walk"—they are easily recognizable as forerunners to today's drag queens but we quickly realize that this is a predilection John himself does not share. It is a huge disservice to think that he doesn't "like" women (which is a characteristic sometimes attributed to modern gay men) as he explains to a certain problematical young woman trying to blackmail him into marriage:

> "I do like women," he said exasperated. "I admire and honor them, and for several of the sex I feel considerable affection…. I do not, however, seek pleasure in their beds. Do I speak plainly enough?" [*Drums of Autumn*, ch. 59].

John's self-acceptance of who and what he is offers further proof of his character, strength and honor; he refuses to lie to himself despite living in a time and place where the crime of sodomy was punishable by hanging. To be convicted of the crime was a disgrace and would leave a stain on one's family; John's family honor is at stake as much as his own reputation. Despite all this, for John Grey, one of the tenants of personal honor is honesty.

While his desire for Jamie does indeed have a carnal element to it, his desire is not nefarious and is based on Jamie the man; not Jamie as Object or Prey. John recognizes Jamie as an equal and upon (re)meeting him at Ardsmuir he sees beyond the prisoner in iron fetters to the gentleman, Warrior and Laird. They are also connected by their shared experiences and tragedies on the battlefield of Culloden even if on opposite sides; John's loss of his first love and Jamie's loss of Claire as well as home and culture. As a soldier himself, he is attracted to Jamie's strength of character, his intelligence and his own strong sense of self and the code of honor that they have in common despite the extremes in their positions—they are both men of blood, iron and action. Because it is based on his own sense of himself as a soldier and the governor of the prison as well as his understanding that despite being his prisoner, Jamie is still a man of honor and worth, Lord John's desire for Jamie is different from that of Black Jack. Chief among those reasons is that John accepts his desire for other men and only rarely thinks of himself as "deviant."

While Black Jack ends up as a recurring nightmare for Jamie, Lord John becomes a welcome, often important and frequently returning friend who, through time and circumstance, comes to have very close ties to Jamie's life and his family. His psychological makeup is such that he values the person and life of Jamie so much that he willingly rises above his own sense of desire for him in order to call him "friend." John's sensibilities and values allow him to move beyond feelings of simple lustful desire for Jamie to that point of deep unspoken love for friends and family that at its core defines both of them.

In the end, Gabaldon has given us two very different men who desire Jamie for vastly different reasons, one destructive and the other (while not unproblematical) more affirming. Perhaps one of the best reasons for looking at the differences among these two characters is to understand where this leaves Jamie Fraser himself.

While it would be understandable that he might not have anything to do with men he knows or suspects to be "sodomites," Jamie ends up having one of the most important friendships of his life with Lord John. Their relationship is close despite a few missteps and misunderstandings, yet they both come back to the solidity of a friendship that always, always manages to survive the challenges that life puts in their path.

Their friendship is the opposite of Jamie's relationship/interactions with Black Jack. Jamie's interactions with one man leave him scarred physically, mentally and emotionally, yet they are an integral part of the man he will eventually become. John challenges Jamie to move beyond his narrow view of men who are attracted to other men; their interactions force Jamie to see the man beyond his (well-earned yet limiting) bias. In the end, each of these characters provides insight into the varying notions of masculinity in the eighteenth century and we begin to see that while there might have been proscriptions for what it meant to be a man, there were wide variations of definition depending on one's social status and political standing.

Lord John is not Black Jack Randall, and Jamie knows that. He may struggle for years to come to terms with his experience at Wentworth Prison at the hands of Black Jack, yet despite that challenge he still has the generosity of spirit and grace to allow Lord John to be a part of his life. Jamie's friendship with John speaks to his inner strength, his faith and his capacity to forgive and move on. His ability to see the good and the possible despite the dark place he has been are just one more reason that Jamie deserves the title as The King of Men.

NOTES

1. While evidence of this interconnectedness can be seen throughout the *Outlander* series, the storyline of *The Scottish Prisoner* illustrates the back-and-forth nature of John and Jamie's friendship.

2. This is one of many examples of a Christ-like sacrifice by one character or another. Gabaldon has acknowledged that there is a fair amount of religious iconography and references, her typical response has been, "it was my first book." That may be true but the religious aspect of *Outlander* seems to be an important character/element on its own and has consequently engendered a work in progress that looks at religiosity within the storyline.

3. Of course, this is due in large part to actor Sam Heughan who manages to embody the spirit of Jamie Fraser.

4. Moore has stated in many interviews that this is how they refer to the character of Jamie in the television production's Writer's Room. I first heard him use it in 2013 during a press junket while the production was in its early days.

5. I'm paraphrasing here; at the time this comment was posted-over a year ago—I had no idea I would be referencing it in an essay. My apologies to the poster for not being able to refer to her by name.

6. Black Jack is a true sexual sadist as well as a psychopath. In another day and age he might be considered a Dominant with sadistic tendencies in search of a pain-slut submissive. Born 250 years too early, he preys on the population on hand and at his mercy.

7. In the first case, Jamie's knowledge of what Black Jack is capable of when he tries to purchase the services of brothel-born Fergus and later on when Alex Randall dies. In the first instance Jamie displays the depth of his rage yet tempers it with mercy (he didn't after all kill him) and in the second he shows true compassion to Alex's brother Black Jack and escorts him back to his barracks despite how he feels about him. Perhaps one day Gabaldon will fill us in on what was said during that walk.

8. Interestingly the focus of some discussions—especially on some closed group pages—are centered on the impact the episodes had on male *and* female survivors of sexual assault.

9. Little wonder Prime Minister David Cameron put pressure on Sony pictures to stall the *Outlander* airing before the 2014 Scottish Independence Referendum. The English didn't look so good in Jamie's story. Wikileaks is the source of the leaked internal Sony memos as reported by *International Business Times*, 21 April 2015. www.ibt.co.uk/david-cameron-v-outlander-pm-met-sony-execs.

10. Gabaldon has said that she likes this character very much and in a Twitter Author's Chat in August 2015 noted that of all her characters, his sense of humor is most like her own. While Lord John is not universally loved (why not is beyond my comprehension!) he does have a loyal following within the *Outlander* fandom as evi-

denced by Facebook pages dedicated to the character including that of *The Lord John Grey Society* where I can at times be found lurking.

Works Cited

Gabaldon, Diana. Author Diana Gabaldon. *Facebook.com* April 2014. https://www.facebook.com/AuthorDianaGabaldon. Website.
_____. "DianaGabaldon.com." Books. Lord John Grey Series. DianaGabaldonwww. 7 July 2015. http://www.dianagabaldon.com. Website.
_____. *Dragonfly in Amber.* New York: Delacorte Press, 1992. Print.
_____. *Drums of Autumn.* New York: Delacorte Press, 1997. Print.
_____. *Lord John and the Private Matter.* New York: Delacorte Press, 2003. Print.
_____. *Outlander.* New York: Delacorte Press, 1991. Print.
_____. *The Scottish Prisoner.* New York: Delacorte Press, 2011. Print.
_____. *Written In My Own Heart's Blood.* New York: Delacorte Press, 2014. Print.
The Lord John Grey Society. Public Group. *Facebook.com* July 2015. https://www.facebook.com/groups/5684783954.
Moore, Ronald D. "An Inside Look: Casting Outlander." *Outlander: Season One—Volume One: Collector's Edition.* Sony Pictures Home Entertainment, 2015. Bluray.
"Seventeen Characters We Will Never Forgive." *Eonline.com* 30 May 2015. http://www.eonline.com/photos/16222/17-tv-characters-we-will-never-forgive-ranked/491709.
"To Ransom a Man's Soul." *Outlander.* Writ. Ronald D. Moore and Ira Steven Behr. Dir. Anna Forrester. Starz! Sony. 30 May 2015. Television.
"Wentworth Prison." *Outlander.* Writ. Ronald D. Moore and Ira Steven Behr. Dir. Anna Forrester. Starz! Sony. 16 May 2015. Television.

Traveling Through Time and Genre

Are the Outlander *Books Romance Novels?*

Jodi McAlister

"The big romance question—are they or aren't they?" reads one of the frequently asked questions on Diana Gabaldon's website. This is a question that has surrounded the *Outlander* books since the publication of the first installment in 1991. Are the *Outlander* books romance novels, or are they something else?

Author Gabaldon, in her response to this frequently asked question, asserts that her novels are not romance fiction, writing,

> my books don't fit the standard conventions of the modern romance at all. *Outlander* alone has some elements of a standard romance—enough to make it appealing to romance readers in general—but none of the other books do.... I don't object at all to romances, but I don't write them. I don't observe the conventions of the genre—or of any other, for that matter ["About the Books"].

However, Gabaldon's thoughts on the matter have not stopped readers from categorizing the novels as romances (which we might potentially read as evidence of Roland Barthes' oft-quoted theory that the author is dead, and their opinions have no relevance to the reading experience). The first book, *Outlander* (also published in some regions as *Cross-Stitch*), won the Romance Writers' of America RITA Award for Best Romance of 1991. The most recent instalment, *Written in My Own Heart's Blood*, won the Goodreads Best Romance of 2014 Award, as well as the Romantic Times Booklovers' award for historical fiction. *Outlander* regularly appears in the top ten of the All About Romance Top 100 Romances, appearing at #3 in 1998, #2 in 2000, #7 in 2004, #4 in 2007, #5 in 2010, and #5 in 2013. *Outlander* appeared at #2 on a 2015 Goodreads list of the top 100 romance novels of all time, and also appeared at #2 on a 2011 list aggregated from Amazon bestsellers and various other top ten lists. On the same list, *Dragonfly in Amber* appeared at #6 and *Voyager* at #8.

This clearly indicates that, despite Gabaldon's assertion that her books—particularly the later books in the series—do not follow the conventions of the romance, romance readers are reading them as such. "It [the *Outlander* cycle] is primarily an adventure story, in which history is as important a player as any of the individuals," Gabaldon writes ("About the Books"); however, the way in which the series is read as a romance suggests that the greatest appeal of the book is the romance at its center: the pairing of Jamie and Claire. This is something we also see evident in the reactions to the recent adaptation of *Outlander* for the screen: not only are fans hungry for more of the romance between the two protagonists, but also between the actors who play them, Caitriona Balfe and Sam Heughan.

In this essay, I read *Outlander* alongside several scholarly definitions of the romance novel in order to see whether an answer to "the big romance question" can be provided. Does Gabaldon's series uphold, contrary to her assertions, the conventions of the genre, or is it a series in which the romantic elements have simply been extraordinarily popular with fans?

Defining the Romance Novel: Do the Outlander Books Fit?

Before I begin to examine *Outlander* against some of the most popular and accepted definitions of a romance novel, it is worth noting the way that Gabaldon herself thinks about the genre. In her answer to "the big romance question," she repeats several times that her books do not meet generic conventions. She argues that while *Outlander* itself contains many of the elements of a romance, the other books do not, because they focus on the already established romance of Jamie and Claire. She reports being told, after *Outlander* won the RITA award in 1991, that it ought not to have won on the grounds that it did not adequately meet the conventions of the romance genre, because,

there wasn't enough concentration on the relationship between the hero and heroine, she was older than him (hey, everybody knows you can't do *that*! You want to know how many times I've heard "You can't do THAT in a romance!"—from romance writers at romance conventions?) they didn't meet until page 69, you didn't know he was the hero until much later, it was *much* too long, and it had all that HIStory, it was *in the first person!!* (an utterly heinous crime in that

genre, apparently), and as for what I did to Jamie...!! ["About the Books,"
emphasis in original]

But most importantly, Gabaldon contends that because the books in the series
do not have guaranteed happy endings—and, indeed, some, such as *Dragonfly
in Amber*, end with Jamie and Claire parted, seemingly never to meet again—
they do not meet the genre requirements for romance fiction: "I don't have
guaranteed happy endings—which you really *must* have in a romance," she
writes ("About the Books," emphasis in original).

On reading the *Outlander* series against some of the various ways
romance fiction has been defined, we can see that some of Gabaldon's claims
have more merit than others. Heroines who are older than the heroes are
certainly rarer in romance than the other way around, but it is by no means
a requirement of the genre that the hero be older: for example, Jennifer Crusie,
a romance author Gabaldon cites as being one of her favorites, paired a forty-
year-old heroine with a thirty-year-old hero in *Anyone but You* (1996)—a far
more substantial age gap than that which separates twenty-seven-year-old
Claire from twenty-three year-old Jamie. Likewise, historical romance is a
very popular subgenre of the romance novel, and novels are regularly set
against real historical events using real historical characters, just as the *Outlander* books are set against, among other events, the Highland rising and
the American War of Independence. For example, Isolde Martyn's *The Lady
and the Unicorn* (1998) is set against the backdrop of the Wars of the Roses
and includes historical figures such as Edward IV and Richard III as characters. The torture and rape of Jamie is indeed extreme, but the tortured hero
is a relatively common trope in many subgenres of romance, and is particularly obvious in paranormal romance, where the characters' supernatural
abilities allow them to endure superhuman levels of pain. Likewise, first person romance novels are not especially common, but are not proscribed—
and, indeed, the emerging "new adult" romance trend often uses first person.
Therefore, these elements might be unusual for a romance novel, but are not
unheard of, and certainly do not preclude the *Outlander* books from belonging to the romance genre. However, some of Gabaldon's other assertions—
such as the fact that the books cannot be romance because they deal with the
adventures of an established couple and because there is no guaranteed happy
ending—carry more weight.

There is no single authoritative definition of a romance novel. However,
there are several definitions which have achieved considerable levels of
acceptance, against which I read the *Outlander* series in order to ascertain
whether the books can be said to uphold the genre's conventions.

The first of these comes from the Romance Writers of America (RWA),
and is perhaps the most often quoted definition of the modern romance

novel. RWA contends that romance novels may be set in any time, any place, and can have any degree of seriousness and/or level of sensuality. This is thus a flexible framework, but a romance novel must contain two key elements:

> *A Central Love Story:* The main plot centers around individuals falling in love and struggling to make the relationship work. A writer can include as many sub-plots as he/she wants as long as the love story is the main focus of the novel.
> *An Emotionally Satisfying and Optimistic Ending:* In a romance, the lovers who risk and struggle for each other and their relationship are rewarded with emotional justice and unconditional love [RWA, "About The Romance Genre"].

The *Outlander* series clearly meets the first of these requirements. While considerable attention is placed on the historical setting of the novels, the central relationship between Jamie and Claire (and, to a lesser extent, the "next generation" romance between Roger and Brianna) is the focus. Certainly, a new romance is not constructed in every book—that is, not every book contains the "falling in love" element—but there is a strong focus on "struggling to make the relationship work." Jamie and Claire and Roger and Brianna all have to overcome considerable obstacles to manage their respective romantic relationships, not the least of which is the problem of time travel.

The second requirement is more problematic. How does one assess whether the *Outlander* series has an emotionally satisfying and optimistic ending when the series has not yet ended? However, I contend that the individual books in the series do meet this requirement—especially if we note that this ending does not necessarily have to be what we might call a "happy" ending, which features hero and heroine together. Author Jennifer Crusie, who was part of the RWA committee tasked with developing this definition, notes that, "I knew we had it [an appropriate definition] when *Gone with the Wind* and *Pride and Prejudice* made the cut, and *Madame Bovary* and *Message in a Bottle* didn't" ("I Know What It Is When I Read It"). *Gone with the Wind* does not have a happy ending, in that the book does not conclude with Scarlett and Rhett in a happy, established romantic relationship. However, it does have an optimistic ending, concluding with the line "tomorrow was another day," which seems to signify Scarlett's determination to win Rhett back or build some similarly satisfying future for herself: the "emotional justice" referred to in the definition. This emotionally satisfying, if not necessarily "happy," ending is also something that appears regularly in the time-travel romance, a subgenre to which *Outlander* clearly belongs: for example, in Jude Devereaux's iconic 1989 romance novel *A Knight in Shining Armor*, the primary romance is between modern heroine Dougless and sixteenth-century hero Nicholas, but Dougless' romantic ending takes place with Nicholas' modern reincarnation, whom she meets at the novel's conclusion. In this sense, we can argue that while they do not feature happy endings, most, if not all, of the *Outlander* books do feature an "emotionally satisfying and optimistic ending"—*Dragonfly in Amber*, for example, concludes with Jamie and Claire having been apart for twenty years, marooned in different centuries, but ends with Roger revealing to Claire that Jamie lived through the Battle of Culloden, thus signifying that there is hope for them to be together once more. Presently, it is impossible to say whether the entire cycle will meet the RWA requirement for an optimistic ending, but it is relatively clear that as it stands, the *Outlander* books fulfil the definition, even if they do contain some unusual and/or marginal elements.

The second definition of the romance I will turn to now is the one most commonly cited by scholars of romance fiction: that given by Pamela Regis in her seminal 2003 work *A Natural History of the Romance Novel*. Regis provides two definitions in this book. The first is a concise definition: "a romance novel is a work of prose fiction that tells the story of the courtship and betrothal of one or more heroines" (14).[1] While, as Gabaldon has noted, the *Outlander* series arguably focuses more on the adventures of established couples, the establishment of those couples—Jamie and Claire and Roger and Brianna—is a key part of the text. The *Outlander* books perhaps do not sit easily within Regis' shorter definition, but we could certainly make the case that they meet its requirements (especially when looked at as a series rather than as individual texts).

Regis' second definition is longer, and contains eight structural elements which she contends are present in every romance novel:

- Society defined (that is, the society in which the protagonists will conduct their courtship is outlined)
- The meeting between hero and heroine
- The attraction between hero and heroine
- The barrier between hero and heroine
- The declaration of love
- "Point of ritual death" (that is, the point where it seems that the hero and heroine can never be together)
- The recognition of the means by which the barrier can be overcome
- The betrothal [30]

Interestingly, Regis' definition does not include the happy ending (where protagonists end the novel in an established romantic relationship with each other), nor any reference to an "optimistic" ending, although it is relatively clear from the rest of her work that this is the kind of novel to which she refers, something supported by the inclusion of the element where the means are recognized by which the barrier between the protagonists can be overcome. Regis notes that while these elements are structural, they are also flexible: some may occur off stage, some may occur more than once, and some may be emphasised or de-emphasised, depending on the individual text (30).

It is relatively easy to see how the first book of the *Outlander* cycle meets these requirements:

- Society defined: we are introduced to the world of 1743 Scotland, the backdrop against which Jamie and Claire's romance will take place.
- The meeting between hero and heroine: Claire meets Jamie soon after she travels back in time, encountering him with Dougal's men.
- The attraction between hero and heroine: this attraction appears in several small ways in the establishment of Jamie and Claire's friendship before their marriage, and is certainly made evident after it.
- The barrier between hero and heroine: Claire is married to and in love with her twentieth-century husband Frank, and Jamie, an outlaw, does not have the ability to adequately support a wife.
- The recognition of the means by which the barrier is overcome: a de-emphasized element. Claire is compelled to marry against her wishes, and her need outweighs Jamie's economic and social situation.
- The betrothal: Jamie and Claire are compelled to wed to save her from Black Jack Randall.
- The declaration of love: Jamie's love for Claire becomes swiftly evident, and Claire effectively declares her love for Jamie when she chooses to remain with him instead of returning back to Frank via the standing stones. At Lallybroch, they say it to each other.
- The "point of ritual death": Jamie is tortured and raped brutally by Black Jack Randall, leaving him barely alive, desperate for death, and feeling unable to be a husband to Claire. With her love for him, Claire drags him through his suffering and back to life.

This would seem to support Gabaldon's contention that while the first *Outlander* book meets the generic conventions of the romance genre, the rest of the series do not. Both Regis' shorter and longer definitions include an emphasis on courtship and the nascent beginnings of romance that are not evident in the majority of the later *Outlander* novels. However, if we treat the cycle as a series, a different picture emerges. As noted above, Regis' elements can appear more than once. If we read the series in this way, we see several of the elements being recycled: for example, a second point of ritual death occurs in *Dragonfly in Amber*, when Claire returns to 1948 and believes for twenty years that Jamie is dead, and another in *An Echo in the Bone*, when Claire believes the ship Jamie is on has sunk and marries someone else in her grief. The barrier of time is one which regularly causes problems in Jamie and Claire's relationship. We see a second key meeting between hero and heroine in *Voyager*, when Claire returns to the eighteenth century and finds Jamie in his printer shop in Edinburgh. Likewise, Brianna and Roger work through these elements, and many of them are repeated in their romantic relationship. Thus, we can argue that, if we read the series as a whole, the repetition of Regis' eight structural elements position the *Outlander* books as romance novels, even though they focus more on established relationships than on their establishment.

One of the major problems we find when trying to position the *Outlander* books as definitively within or without the romance genre is the problem of an ending. While it is not technically encoded in either of the definitions I have discussed here, there certainly are strong reader expectations in the romance community that books will end happily: that is, with the hero and heroine in a strong, committed, romantic relationship. After the establishment of their relationship, the love between Jamie and Claire is never in doubt; however, circumstances—such as the exigencies of time travel—often mean that they are separated, and, indeed, they spend twenty years apart. This clearly presents a problem for categorizing the *Outlander* series as romance, one which Gabaldon notes in her answer to the "happily ever after" question: how can we be sure that Jamie and Claire will end up together (or, at least, receive the "emotional justice" of the RWA definition)?

Belgian scholar An Goris tackles this question insightfully, noting that serialization has become an increasingly popular practice in the romance genre—while in 1982, none of the novels which won the RWA's highest award belonged to a series, in 2012, nine of twelve did ("Happily Ever After ... And After"). This represents a significant change in generic conventions. (Indeed, it is possible to argue that the *Outlander* cycle is one of the series that triggered this evolution in the romance genre, given its popularity.) Goris notes that the rise in serialization raises questions around how romance is typically defined:

> Romance is a generic form defined by its happy ending, stakeholders across the board have argued. In a romance novel, the protagonists who meet, fall in love, and struggle to overcome the barriers between them are always rewarded with true love in the end. If this ending is a necessary feature of the genre, what does narrative serialization in a romance novel look like? ... Are there limits to the degree of serialization that the genre can handle, and if so what are they? ["Happily Ever After ... And After"]

These are useful questions to be asking when examining *Outlander*. What are the limits of serialisation within romance, and does the *Outlander* cycle fit within them? "Serialization has the potential to destabilize the romance form by subverting one of the genre's defining narrative features, the happy end," Goris writes ("Happily Ever After ... And After")—but given that serialization is becoming increasingly more popular in romance fiction, this destabilization does not appear to be enough to disrupt the romantic form altogether. There are, however, limits—and the fact that, as Gabaldon herself has written, the *Outlander* cycle does not have a guaranteed happy (or optimistic) ending makes it difficult to tell whether it falls within these limits or not.

Goris goes on to define several different kinds of romance serial. One is what she refers to as a "romance-based series": that is, it focuses on a single couple, developing their courtship and romance over multiple instalments, with their committed romantic relationship usually not concretely established until well into the series. This establishment does not herald the end of the series, however: rather, additional installments can go on to explore the couple's further adventures ("Happily Ever After … And After"). Perhaps the most well-known example is J.D. Robb's *In Death* series, which focus on the adventures of policewoman heroine Eve and billionaire Roarke. The series now has over fifty installments and is still ongoing, even though Eve and Roarke get married (signaling the formal establishment of their relationship) between the third and fourth installments.

Although the *Outlander* cycle does not fit this definition precisely— Jamie and Claire do not have a long ongoing courtship characterized by sexual tension and their relationship is formalized relatively early on, for example— it clearly fits into this category, and shares many of the problems Goris notes in regards to the romance genre's requirement for a happy ending: "The happy end is postponed beyond the material boundaries of the single narrative, which is highly problematic for a romance novel," Goris writes ("Happily Ever After … And After"). Despite this, she goes on to discuss the ways in which, although they are—like *Outlander*—often placed in a genre outside romance, such as fantasy, such books are read widely by romance readers, reviewed by major romance outlets like *RT Book Review*, and nominated for romance awards (of which, as I noted in my introduction, the *Outlander* cycle has won many). Goris claims:

> Institutional recognition inscribes these novels in the romance genre even though the individual narratives frequently lack a crucial ingredient of the genre. Romance-based serialization is then pushing the definitional boundaries of the romance genre and represents the conceptual limits of what romance novels can handle in terms of serialization ["Happily Ever After … And After"].

Thus, in this sense, it is entirely valid to claim that, while the *Outlander* series contains many elements which are unusual, it is still positioned within the romance genre. This is perhaps doubly true of the *Outlander* television series, which serializes an already serialized narrative. This allows for the creation of a slightly longer arc we might describe as "courtship," and, increasingly, moves from a focus on Claire and her experiences of 1743 Scotland toward a focus on Jamie and Claire as a couple, their relationship, and their shared experiences. While the show was not initially marketed as romance per se, the fan response to the show has focused very strongly on the central couple—

for example, some fan responses to the eighth episode, "Both Sides Now," noted disappointment in the fact that so much of the episode was devoted to Frank when it could have been devoted to Jamie and Claire's "honeymoon" period.[2] In addition, actors Caitriona Balfe and Sam Heughan appear regularly in interviews together, and it seems clear that the show is also trading on their chemistry as friends and potential romantic partners: something in which some fans are very invested, as even the most cursory glance at the "SamCait" tag on Tumblr will demonstrate. In this sense, it is both the emphasis on the romance in the *Outlander* series—that is, the "central love story" as described by RWA—and the way romance is read into the *Outlander* cycle that position it as romance.

What Is Romantic? The Alleles of Outlander

The definitions of romance discussed hitherto have been largely structural. In particular, Regis' elements represent plot points or "beats" that romance novels must hit. However, there is another way to define the romance novel, which focuses less on structure. To elucidate this, I turn to two other eminent romance scholars: Jayashree Kamble and Catherine Roach.

In her excellent 2014 book *Making Meaning in Popular Romance Fiction: An Epistemology,* Kamble subjects the term "romance novel" to scrutiny, and contends that it is "analogous to the structure of DNA, with 'romance' and 'novel' being two distinct yet intertwined strands in its double helix" (2). The "novel" strand refers here largely to form, and is of less interest in this instance than the "romance" strand. Kamble defines "romance" not as structural, but as "the adjective 'romantic' used to describe an element that is 'conducive to feelings of romance' ... that which codes for the traits of the erotic, the desirable, the pleasurable—for what is 'romantic' to the reader/apprehender under modernity and postmodernity" (15).

What is most appealing about Kamble's definition is its flexibility and historical specificity. The alleles that make up the "romance" strand of the double helix are not fixed: rather, they change and adapt depending on what is considered romantic in that time, place, culture, or other factor. Kamble writes that "the 'romantic' strand adapts itself to the environment, acquiring versions of traits that are favorable to its survival and discarding ones that are not, aided by the way authors code for them in a new sociopolitical environment" (15). In this sense, to determine whether the *Outlander* books are romance novels or not, we should examine what the series encodes as "romantic": is it in line with the way the romantic is generally portrayed in the romance genre?

The work of Catherine Roach gives us some insight here. At the International Association for the Study of Popular Romance conference in Thessaloniki in 2014, Roach (following Regis) outlined a further nine elements of the romance novel. Unlike Regis, who uses structural elements, Roach uses thematic elements, which explore the portrayal of romantic love:

- It's hard to be alone.
- Women are in a man's world.
- Love is a risk.
- Love is a religion (that is, one must have or come to have faith in love).
- Love is hard work.
- Love heals.
- Love brings the promise of great sex.
- Love brings happiness.
- Love levels the playing field for women (that is, women win, and gain power) ["(Another) Eight Essential Elements of the Romance Novel"]

An examination of the *Outlander* cycle allows us to see all of these elements present in the relationship of Jamie and Claire (and also arguably in the secondary romance of Roger and Brianna). It is difficult for Claire to be alone in the "man's world" of the eighteenth century, where she is repeatedly threatened with violence, sexual and otherwise. Still, it is the love she and Jamie share that causes her to remain in this unfriendly world: love is, in this sense, a great risk. It is something in which she must have faith and believe, evidenced perhaps nowhere as strongly as in *Voyager*, when she risks a second passage through the stones to be with Jamie once more. That said, love is not necessarily always easy for Jamie and Claire: their relationship is hard work—for example, Claire in particularly must work hard to help Jamie past his suicidal despair after his torture and rape at the hands of Black Jack. Their love is also—as evidenced in the same incident—healing, and, indeed, we see the healing power of love is literalized in Claire's medical abilities, as she brings Jamie back from the brink of death on multiple occasions. Their love brings them great happiness, which appears regularly over the series. Finally, Claire's romantic partnership with Jamie allows her to access power in a way that would otherwise be very difficult for women in the eighteenth century. A key moment in this sense is the infamous spanking sequence: Jamie's resolution that he will never lift a hand to Claire again signals a new kind of relationship, a kind of modern love out of step with eighteenth-century norms. In many ways—such as saving her from accusations of spying and witchcraft—Jamie protects Claire from the harshness of the historical setting, signalling the modernity of their two-person romantic world.

Conclusion

In her answer to "the big romance question" on her website, Gabaldon mentions one more way of defining romance: paratext. She explains:

> When we sold *Outlander*, the publisher held onto the book for 18 months, trying to figure out *what* to sell it as. They finally decided that—of all the different classifications the books could fit in—"Romance" was by far the largest single market. I agreed that they could market the paperback that way—provided that we had dignified covers (no Fabio, no mad bosoms), and provided that if and when the books became "visible" (which is publisherese for "hit the *New York Times* list"), they would reposition them as Fiction ["About the Books"].

In this way, we can see Gabaldon and her publishers attempting to leverage the romance market—something in which they were clearly quite successful—despite Gabaldon's firm belief that she was not part of it. Indeed, the *Outlander* books are not "standard" romance novels (if such a thing can be said to exist). However, the fact that the books appealed to and were recognized as romance by so much of the romance readership speaks to the fact that they do meet many of the genre's structural requirements and conventions, particularly in a market where serialized romance is so increasingly popular. Nevertheless, it is perhaps the *Outlander* series' romantic alleles that have ensured that readers (and, now, viewers) approach the text as romance: the relationship between Jamie and Claire is expressive of a modern—and, to the romance reader and viewer, recognizable—love. Many different genre labels may be applied to the *Outlander* cycle—fantasy, science fiction, historical fiction, military fiction, or even simply, as Gabaldon desired, fiction. However, what this chapter has made clear is that romance cannot be excluded from this list.

Notes

1. Regis has since revised this definition to include the word "protagonists" instead of "heroines," recognising that this gendered word excluded many queer romance texts.

2. See, for example, this comment in an article about "Both Sides Now":
that was too much Frank time for me. If this had been a two hour episode I'd have been fine with that amount of Frankfiction, but in a one hour episode it didn't leave enough time for all the Jamie/Claire scenes I felt were needed for us to start seeing the strong bond they formed post-wedding—and not just a sexual bond, which is pretty much all we've gotten so far on the show [Melissa, comment, "My Top Ten Moments of the *Outlander* Midseason Finale: 'Both Sides Now'"].

Works Cited

"About the Romance Genre." *Romance Writers of America*. Web.

Barthes, Roland. "The Death of the Author." *Image-Music-Text*. Ed. and trans. Stephen Heath. London: Fontana, 1977. 142–148. Print.

"Best Romance of 2014." *Goodreads*. Web.

"Best Top Romances of All Time." *Goodreads,* May 4, 2011. Web.

Crusie, Jennifer. 'I Know What It Is When I Read It: Defining the Romance Genre.' *Romance Writers' Report,* March 2000. JennyCrusie.com. Web.

Crusie, Jennifer. *Anyone but You.* New York: Harper Collins, 1996. Print.

Devereaux, Jude. *A Knight in Shining Armor.* New York: Simon & Schuster, 1989. Print.

Gabaldon, Diana. "About the Books." DianaGabaldonwww, n.d. Web.

_____. *A Breath of Snow and Ashes.* London: Arrow, 2005. Print.

_____. *An Echo in the Bone.* London: Arrow, 2010. Print.

_____. *Dragonfly in Amber.* London: Arrow, 1992. Print.

_____. *Drums of Autumn.* London: Arrow, 1997. Print.

_____. *The Fiery Cross.* London: Arrow, 2001. Print.

_____. *Outlander.* London: Arrow, 1991. Print.

_____. *Written in My Own Heart's Blood.* London: Arrow, 2014. Print.

Goris, An. "Happily Ever After ... And After: Serialization and the Popular Romance Novel." *Americana: The Journal of American Popular Culture 1900–Present* 12.1 (2013). Web.

Kamble, Jayashree. *Making Meaning in Popular Romance Fiction: An Epistemology.* New York: Palgrave Macmillan, 2014. Print.

Martyn, Isolde. *The Lady and the Unicorn.* Sydney: Bantam, 1998. Print.

Melissa. Comment on "My Top Ten Moments from *Outlander* Midseason Finale: 'Both Sides Now.'" *That's Normal.* 27 September 2014. Web.

Mitchell, Margaret. *Gone With the Wind.* New York: Macmillan, 1936. Print.

Outlander. Created by Ron Moore. Starz, 2014. DVD.

Regis, Pamela. *A Natural History of the Romance Novel.* Philadelphia: University of Pennsylvania Press, 2003. Print.

"RITA Winners." *Romance Writers of America.* Web.

Roach, Catherine. "(Another) Eight Essential Elements of the Romance Novel." Paper delivered at 5th International Conference on Popular Romance Studies: *Rethinking Love, Rereading the Romance.* Held at Makedonia Palace Hotel, Thessaloniki, Greece, 19–21 June 2014.

Robb, J.D. *Glory in Death.* New York: Penguin, 1995. Print.

Robb, J.D. *Immortal in Death.* New York: Penguin, 1996. Print.

Robb, J.D. *Naked in Death.* New York: Penguin, 1995. Print.

Robb, J.D. *Rapture in Death.* New York: Penguin, 1996. Print.

"Top 100 Romance Novels on Goodreads." *Goodreads.* February 9, 2015. Web.

"Top 100 Romances—1998." *All About Romance.* October 1998. Web.

"Top 100 Romances—2000." *All About Romance.* November 2000. Web.

"Top 100 Romances—2004." *All About Romance.* November 2004. Web.

"Top 100 Romances—2007." *All About Romance.* November 2007. Web.

"Top 100 Romances—2010." *All About Romance.* November 2010. Web.

"Top 100 Romances—2013." *All About Romance.* November 2013. Web.

"2014 RT Award Winners." *Locus Magazine.* April 17, 2015. Web.

Gabaldon and the
Practice of Gay Male
Homoerotic Reading

ANTHONY GUY PATRICIA

In August 2005, Bantam Dell, a division of Random House Publishing Group, reissued Diana Gabaldon's best-selling 1991 novel, *Outlander*, in mass market paperback form complete with a striking navy blue jacket featuring elegant bronze lettering and an elaborate illumination of a fiery royal crown. The text on the back cover of this edition reveals that the story's central character is former World War II combat nurse Claire Randall, who suddenly finds herself thrown some 200 years into the past after inadvertently walking through a portal in a set of ancient standing stones atop a hill in Scotland near the city of Inverness. The copy continues with: "Hurled back in time by forces she cannot understand, Claire is catapulted into the intrigues of lairds and spies that may threaten her life ... and shatter her heart. For here James Fraser, a gallant young Scots warrior, shows her a love so absolute that Claire becomes a woman torn between fidelity and desire ... and between two vastly different men in two irreconcilable lives" (*Outlander*, back cover). In the main, this rather hyperbolic description of *Outlander* emphasizes the romance aspect of the book, almost to the exclusion of all others, and it does so despite the fact that Gabaldon has insisted from the first that she does not write romance, at least not in what is now considered its conventional form.[1]

Pamela Regis traces the historical beginnings of the modern romance novel to Samuel Richardson's 1740 bestseller, *Pamela; or, Virtue Rewarded*, a book she describes as "the story of the courtship, betrothal, wedding, and triumph of lady's maid Pamela Andrews to Mr. B, the master for whom she works" (63). She adds that this overarching kind of "courtship story would become a major force shaping the novel in English, and with *Pamela* Richardson brings the courtship plot, which is to say the romance novel, into more than prominence. He makes it famous" (63). That fame has now lasted for some 275 years and shows no signs of abating. "I've probably read a couple of hundred 'real' romance novels," Gabaldon explains in the FAQ section of her website, "ranging from traditional category romances to F/F/P (Futuristic/Fantasy/ Paranormal). That's why I say I don't write romance; because I don't.... I don't observe the conventions of the genre—or of any other [genre] for that matter" ("FAQ: About the Books"). For a (stereo)typical academic definition of romances—with a lower-case "r"—*The Book of Literary Terms* describes them as:

> novels of sexual love between stereotypical adults set in idealized situations, usually written in purple prose—a breathless, gushy, overwritten style.... These sorts of novels are often called *escape literature* because they take readers away from the cares of the workaday world for a little while. They are also *formula stories* with plots that are virtually indistinguishable from one another [Turco 66].

Although there are, of course, countless others, Danielle Steel and Nora Roberts are two well-known contemporary authors of the kinds of romance novels as they are depicted in the above passage.[2] "My books," Gabaldon writes, "don't fit the standard conventions of the modern romance at all. OUTLANDER alone has some elements of a standard romance—enough to make it appealing to romance readers in general—but none of the other books [in the series] do" ("FAQ: About the Books"). She goes on to characterize *Outlander* and its sequels as "primarily an adventure story, in which history is as important a player as any of the individuals. To say nothing of which, I don't have guaranteed happy endings—which you really must have in a romance" ("FAQ: About the Books"). Indeed, for a variety of reasons, the HEA (Happily Ever After) ending is obligatory or a romance is just not a romance. Noted romance author Laura Kinsale claims that romances "have happy endings and the hero never dies in them because literature as represented by the romance genre expresses integration, not fractionalization, of the self" as that integration is symbolized by the union of the hero and heroine (40). Baldly put, no other type of conclusion is possible in romance fiction.

With this information in play, *Outlander* would be more correctly categorized as a Romance—with an upper-case "R"—or, a "fictional story in verse or prose that relates improbable adventures of idealized characters in some remote or enchanted setting; or, more generally, a tendency in fiction opposite to that of realism," according to *The Oxford Dictionary of Literary Terms* (Baldick 291). Romances trace their roots to the quest narratives and tales of chivalry that became enormously popular during the Middle Ages in Europe. The anonymous *Sir Gawain and the Green Knight* (ca. 1375–1400), Thomas Malory's *Le Morte D'Arthur* (1485), Miguel de Cervantes's *Don*

Quixote (1705), Sir Walter Scott's *Ivanhoe* (1819), Nathaniel Hawthorne's *The House of the Seven Gables* (1851), Marion Zimmer Bradley's *The Mists of Avalon* (1982), and A.S. Byatt's *Possession* (1990) are only a few descendant examples out of thousands of Romances that may be familiar to many readers of this chapter. As such, *Outlander* is in very good company in terms of its generic pedigree.

Genre distinctions aside, though, it seems that, at least in the minds of the general public and some critics, Gabaldon's *Outlander* and its sequels have been categorized as romances—stories that deal with women and men who meet, fall in love with one another and, by the time all is said and done, get married and set about the business of procreating the next generation in an implied, perpetually-unfolding, happily-ever-after.[3] In light of this over-whelmingly heteronormative narrative ethos, and the fact that, as statistical evidence has shown repeatedly, romance readers are, by far, female,[4] *Outlander* should not have had any kind of appeal whatsoever to someone like me—a gay man. But the fact of the matter is, as I read *Outlander* for the first time in the early 1990s, I found myself falling in love with its hero, Jamie Fraser, not unlike Claire did shortly after she found herself violently trans-ported back in time to eighteenth century Scotland during the Jacobite rising of the mid–1740s. Though now tempered by twenty-five years' more real life experience, that feeling of love for Jamie persists. Given these circumstances—in tandem with the resounding success of the STARZ® cable and satellite channel's television adaptation of Season One of *Outlander*, which has brought the book that started it all a great deal of new attention since it aired in two parts of eight episodes each in the Summer of 2014 and the Spring of 2015—using the insights and interpretive strategies made available in the fields of reader-response, gay and lesbian, and queer theory, this chapter will craft a principled analytical account of my idiosyncratic reaction to *Outlander* that will, I hope, contribute something of particular critical and cultural value to the ongoing discussion of Gabaldon's work. I seek, in other words, to explore as thoroughly and as rigorously as I can, how a gay male homoerotic reading of a heteronormative text like *Outlander* is even possible.

Though the period was already well underway on the Continent, par-ticularly in Germany where the early writing of Goethe was the progenitor and, thus, the exemplar, *Lyrical Ballads* (1798), a collection of poems by William Wordsworth and Samuel Taylor Coleridge, was one of the first works of the literary movement known as Romanticism[5] to be published in England. To produce *Lyrical Ballads*, Coleridge explains in his *Biographia Literaria*, the two poets decided that Coleridge's "endeavours should be directed to per-sons and characters supernatural, or at least romantic; yet so as to transfer from our inward nature a human interest and a semblance of truth sufficient to procure for these shadows of imagination that willing suspension of disbelief for the moment, which constitutes poetic faith" (677). The enigmatic phrase "willing suspension of disbelief" has proven useful for describing readers' experiences as far as fiction—especially when such fictions deal with fantastical elements of any kind, like the spirits, the nightmarish life-in-death female figure, and the dead bodies of the ship's crew reanimated by some unknown force that populate Coleridge's "Rime of the Ancient Mariner"— is concerned. In order for a fiction like "Mariner" to work as intended, readers, as active, rather than passive, participants in the reception of literature, must be able to surrender their instinctive disbelief—after all, rational people know that things like spirits and resurrected bodies of dead men do not exist in the material world—and temporarily accept that whatever is being presented to them in narrative form is truthful to the point of having the ability to affect them psychologically and emotionally as they experience imaginative works.

Many, if not all, readers of *Outlander* would likely consider Claire's time traveling from 1945 to mid-eighteenth century Scotland to be the most fantastical, or supernatural/romantic in Wordsworth and Coleridge's terminology, aspect of the novel. The way Gabaldon describes Claire's movement from the present to the past follows a logic that makes that transition seem entirely plausible (*Outlander*, ch. 2 and 3). This, in turn, makes it relatively easy for her readers to suspend their disbelief willingly. Indeed, readers may well be inclined to think that, if it was an actuality, traveling through time would likely feel for them exactly as it did for Claire. Hence, because the character of Claire is a fictional representation of a human being who encounters the extraordinary in a wholly believable way, Gabaldon's readers, regardless of their gender or orientation, can empathize with her to the point that they do not question the sheer impossibilities inherent in her initial story. However, as will be seen below, empathy is not quite the same thing as the cognitive experience of literary identification.

Laura Green defines the concept of literary identification as the "elaboration of bonds between and among readers, characters, and authors," of which one factor is a "reader's recognition of aspects of her- or himself in a fictional character" (1). The phrase literary identification, then, signals "an occurrence emerging from the encounter of the psyche of a reader and the rhetorical construction of a narrative by its author" (9). Interestingly, Green uses an assertion of no less a man of letters and the arts than William Hazlitt in support of her definition of literary identification. Hazlitt, in his late eighteenth/early nineteenth century criticism of French tragic drama, insists that the "true [dramatic] poet identifies the reader with the characters he represents; the French poet only identifies him [the reader] with himself.... We never get that something more, which is what we are in search of, namely, *what we ourselves should feel in the same situation*" (qtd. in Green 28; her italics) as the characters encounter within a dramatic fiction. Because of their interpretive potentialities, I will begin by using Green's notions about a reader's ability to recognize him- or herself in fictional characters and his or her ability to discover what he or she would do in their place as the basis from which to begin elaborating further on my response as a gay man to Gabaldon's *Outlander*.

As I revealed above, a significant part of my response to *Outlander* involves the fact that I am as attracted as Claire Randall is to Jamie Fraser. Put in other terms, insofar as it is possible for a human being to love a fictional character, I, just like Claire, love Jamie. This admission suggests, of course, that, in terms of literary identification, I identify fully with the character of Claire. According to noted romance author Laura Kinsale, the kind of reader identification at work here "is subjective: the reader *becomes* the character, feeling what she or he feels, experiencing the sensation of being *under control* of the character's awareness" (32). I am also convinced that Gabaldon's use of Claire's first-person point-of-view to drive the narrative facilitates both my ability and my willingness to identify with Claire and her feelings for Jamie as their story evolves throughout the novel. Despite their rather hasty marriage, Gabaldon allows Claire to fall in love with Jamie over time; her readers are given the same chance. As far as particulars are concerned, though, my response to Jamie centers on the character's repeated need for healing and rescue; his physical attributes; his penchant for self-sacrifice; his gallantry and protectiveness; and, finally, his instincts and skills in lovemaking. These elements combine to make what, for me, is a totally irresistible Jamie.

Starting with his physical attributes, Jamie cuts a particularly dashing figure the day he marries Claire, at Dougal's insistence, in order to save her from Randall. "A Highlander," Claire notes as she muses on the subject, "in full regalia is an impressive sight—any Highlander, no matter how old, ill-favored, or crabbed in appearance. A tall, straight-bodied, and by no means ill-favored young Highlander at close range is breathtaking" (*Outlander*, ch. 14). With his red hair neatly combed for once, clean garments, and an eye-catching crimson and black tartan, Jamie is quite handsome. Beyond the outer trappings of fine clothing and accessories, at "[w]ell over six feet tall, broad in proportion, and striking of feature, he was a far cry from the grubby horse-handler I was accustomed to—and he knew it" (*Outlander*, ch.14). In startling contrast to the "thoroughly disreputable" Jamie who had been "shirt-less, scarred and blood-smeared, with stubbled cheeks and reddened eyelids" (*Outlander*, ch. 4) after the MacKenzie party's arrival at Castle Leoch with Claire, this Jamie is a masculine sight to behold, for both Claire and myself as a gay male reader. As it is for Claire, a good-looking kilted Scot dressed otherwise to the nines is not likely to escape my appreciative attention.[6]

Beyond looks, the first time Claire meets Jamie—not long after traveling through the stones at Craigh na Dun and into the eighteenth century—she is obliged to heal him by treating his dislocated shoulder. Given the fact that the Scots are in some danger from the English if they linger too long, Claire must make quick work of fixing Jamie so that he can ride to safety with the rest of the MacKenzie party. That is exactly what she does, as "the shoulder gave a soft, crunching *pop!* and the joint was back in place" (*Outlander*, ch. 3), much to the astonishment of everyone but Claire. Once Claire has dressed Jamie's other more superficial wounds and improvised a sling meant to help him keep his shoulder immobile, the MacKenzie men are off, with Claire literally in Jamie's hands. That Jamie is grateful for Claire's efforts on his behalf becomes poignantly clear when, after they have ridden some distance, Jamie slows their horse and endearingly loosens his plaid so that he can wrap it around her, too. Instead of scolding Jamie for risking his shoulder as she is more than tempted to do, Claire helps him in this chore and is, shortly thereafter, comforted by the warmth of his body and his clothing (*Outlander*, ch. 3).

Claire sees to Jamie's medical needs again and again. This motif of healing reaches its climax in the novel's denouement, which takes place at the Abbey of Ste. Anne de Beaupré in France following Claire's daring and desperate rescue of Jamie from Captain Black Jack Randall at Wentworth Prison. Jamie has fallen into a dangerous fever. He begs Claire to just let him die, to which she says: "Damned if I will" (*Outlander*, ch. 39). Given my attachment to Jamie, I would have said the same words and felt the same way as Claire does in this moment. Still, Claire looks on in despair as Jamie's condition worsens and the monks give him the last rites of the Catholic faith. Though she, too, commends him to God, she continues searching for a way to save Jamie from death. The answer, which comes from the ghost of the dead witch Geillis Duncan, demands that Claire, at great risk to herself, exorcise the demon of Randall from Jamie's mind, body, and soul. Claire douses herself with liberal amounts of Randall's favorite lavender and valerian scents, drugs Jamie with opium, then makes herself the target of his rage, telling him: "Fight me! Fight back, you filthy scut" (*Outlander*, ch. 39). And fight back he does, in a way that he could not with Randall, almost killing both himself and his wife in the process. Nonetheless, Claire's gambit proves successful; Jamie's fever breaks and he is able to start, if not forgetting them completely, then at least making his peace with his experience insofar as he can.

My reactions to the scenes of healing and rescue discussed above exemplify Green's idea of literary identification being a phenomenon involving the "bonds between and among readers, characters, and authors" that extend "from the encounter of the psyche of a reader and the rhetorical construction of a narrative by its author." Beyond a rudimentary knowledge of first aid, I have no medical training. Although I am unlike Claire in that regard, I do nevertheless identify with her as regards her instincts to heal another person's hurts, minor and major. I would, in other words, want to take care of Jamie, or see that he is taken care of by others, in the same way as Claire. Furthermore, Gabaldon's rhetorical construction of these (and similar) scenes allows a gay male reader like me, one who identifies with Claire and loves Jamie just as much as she does, to really feel, at a highly visceral level, that Jamie is worthy of such attention and dedication. I have, in Kinsale's view, become Claire, and I am under the control of her character.

It is because of her abilities as a healer that Claire, along with *Outlander*'s readers, is first able to view Jamie's body. While she is changing his bandages early in the novel, the quilt Jamie is using to cover himself falls away, exposing his bare back to her eyes. "His upper back was covered with a criss-cross of faded white lines. He had been savagely flogged, and more than once. There were small lines of silvery scar tissue in some spots, where the welts had crossed, and irregular patches where several blows had struck the same spot, flaying off skin and gouging the muscle beneath" (*Outlander*, ch. 4). Claire is horrified by what she sees and what it signifies about the brutality that was inflicted on him. So was I as I read this scene. Indeed, my sympathy for and with Jamie increased exponentially following this visual revelation and, like Claire, I wanted to know how and why it came to be. Of course, Jamie incurred these wounds defending his sister Jenny from Randall and his men, without thought for himself. Despite his valiant efforts, he ended up being overpowered by the redcoats, arrested, and taken to Fort William without knowing what became of Jenny and where, as part of his punishment, he was flogged twice in less than a week by Randall who, according to Jamie, enjoyed every single moment of inflicting his sick brand of pain and torture upon Jamie's person.

Setting gender and sexual orientation aside, for any empathetic reader of *Outlander* there is no avoiding the fact that what Jamie suffers at the hands of Randall at Fort William (and later at Wentworth Prison) is horrific in the extreme. For this gay male reader, who feels a strong love attachment to Jamie, Randall's abuse of Jamie is beyond discomfiting because Randall is an equal opportunity sadist—he will indulge in tormenting others mentally, emotionally, and physically no matter their gender. At her website, Gabaldon says as much about Randall: "He's a pervert. He's a sadist. He derives sexual pleasure from hurting people, but he's not particular about the gender of a victim. (Personality, yes—gender, no.)" ("Other Projects/Outlander TV Series News"). Because sex, particularly anal penetration, is part and parcel of Randall's modus operandi, gay men are, if only by default, implicated in Randall's torture of Jamie. The fallacious logic here is that, since one of the activities gay men engage in for pleasure is anal penetration, they may all be just like Randall. The difference is, of course, the vast majority of gay men do not force themselves onto others as Randall does to Jamie in *Outlander*. But, nevertheless, the associative leap between what Randall does and what gay men do needs to be circumvented.[7] The only way that I can do so is by making it unequivocally clear that, unlike Randall, I as a gay man—and not a pervert or a sadist—have no wish to harm Jamie in any way. Quite the contrary. I am also self-possessed enough to know when to walk away when someone I am interested in is unable to return that interest. Unlike Randall, I could never force myself on anyone, least of all Jamie.

Meanwhile, Jamie's admirable willingness to sacrifice himself for the good of others is made plain when flirtatious Laoghaire must be punished by the MacKenzie for her willful disobedience. Quite unexpectedly, Jamie steps into the middle of these proceedings and offers to take Laoghaire's punishment on himself. Soon thereafter, Jamie is beaten ferociously by the MacKenzie's human agent of punishment until, at last, one of his eyes swells shut, blood starts to spurt from his mouth, and the assault is brought to an end. From the sidelines Claire watches—and Gabaldon's readers watch along with her—horrified as this spectacle unfolds. Then, when it is finally over, she rushes to Jamie's side so that she can, yet again, minister to his hurts. When she asks him why he did what he did for Laoghaire, Jamie tells her that he wanted to save the girl from shame and embarrassment and he was convinced that taking her punishment would be easier for him to do than for her. Claire is incredulous after hearing this and says as much to Jamie. She is left momentarily speechless when he asks her rhetorically: "Why not me?" (*Outlander*, ch. 6). He means, of course, that there is no reason for him to have done any differently for Laoghaire, even if she did not deserve his efforts—or his physical sufferings—on her behalf. In contrast, Claire thinks to herself that Jamie should not have done what he did because "you didn't know her, she was nothing to you. Because you were already hurt. Because it takes something rather special in the way of guts to stand up in front of a crowd and let someone hit you in the face, no matter what your motive" (*Outlander*, ch. 6). For those of us who are more than intrigued by Jamie's character and are watching over Claire's shoulder and listening to this exchange, Claire's observations about him resonate. He *is* a palpable representation of a man of strength and integrity; and he *is* worth a significant emotional investment. Alas, this is only one of a number of sacrifices that Jamie will make for others in *Outlander*.

Jamie's ultimate sacrifice in *Outlander* takes place at Wentworth Prison where, after once again being captured by the English, he has been sentenced to die shortly. As Claire is on the brink of rescuing him, Captain Black Jack Randall suddenly returns to the dungeon cell. With Claire held at knifepoint by Randall, and Jamie with seriously limited options, Jamie tells Randall: "Let the woman go, and ye can have me" (*Outlander*, ch. 35). He reminds a distraught

Claire that, since he is supposed to hang the following morning, what happens to him before then does not matter anymore—as long as he knows that she is safe (*Outlander*, ch. 35). Her safety, rather than her certain death, is ensured by this, what can be considered his sacrifice of sacrifices for the woman he loves despite its almost overwhelming fatalism.[8]

Jamie's numerous gallantries and protective efforts provide a welcome counterpoint to his increasingly extreme sacrifices for those he cares about and loves. These qualities emerge quite forcefully in the episode when Claire and the not unhappily newly-widowed Geillis Duncan are seized by an angry mob tried on charges of witchcraft (*Outlander*, ch. 25). When Claire, horrified by the barbarity, refuses trial by water, in which only near-drowning could prove her innocence, one of the angry judges commands: "Strip her and skelp her" (*Outlander*, ch. 25).[9] Claire is tied to an oak tree, her bare back being lashed with a cruel whip, much to the delight of the gathered observers. And then, suddenly, Jamie calls out her name.

Jamie pushes his way through the unruly crowd, knocking those who would stop him out of his way with a carefully aimed fist or elbow. When he gets close enough, Jamie cleverly uses his "showmanship" for the superstitious crowd and throws a jet rosary over her neck, demonstrating she's unmarked by holy symbols. This accomplished, he demands of the authorities that they "Cut her down" (*Outlander*, ch. 25). Free from the bonds, Claire's "arms dropped like bolsters, aching with released strain." Though she staggers, Jamie lifts her up. As the book adds, "Then my face was against Jamie's chest, and nothing mattered to me anymore" (*Outlander*, ch. 25). When the examiners challenge Jamie, he, with one hand on his dirk, the other on his sword, retorts: "'I swore an oath before the altar of God to protect this woman. And if you're tellin' me that ye consider your own authority to be greater than that of the Almighty, then I must inform ye that I'm no of that opinion, myself'" (*Outlander*, ch. 25). Jamie grabs Claire and they finally make their escape.

The Jamie Fraser that emerges from the interpretive pressure I have put him under so far in this chapter epitomizes the romantic hero. Although, like Claire, I too sometimes lose patience with Jamie given how often he finds himself caught up in circumstances in which he is mangled physically and psychologically, I also see the good he tries to accomplish—usually for the sake of others—by repeatedly stepping into harm's way. A character with less grit and less integrity would be nowhere near as attractive or sympathetic. In addition, Claire's descriptions of Jamie's physicality—from his well-muscled but horrifically scarred back to his person in full Highlander regalia—provide me with the means, as a gay man, to observe and to appreciate the good looks of another man. In comments on the appeal of romance heroes like Jamie to female readers of romance novels, Kinsale writes it is "fairly obvious that the bottom line is sexual admiration: to me, a large part of it feels like a simple, erotic, and free-hearted female joy in the very existence of desirable maleness. Hey, women *like* men" (36–7, her italics). Of course, some men *like* men, too, and are similarly able to indulge in equal sexual admiration of them. Finally, Jamie's derring-do elevates him into the top tier of romantic heroes, particularly when Jamie swoops into Cranesmuir on his horse and rescues Claire from the witch trial. If I were in such danger as a gay man, I would hope that the man I loved would save me in the same (melo)dramatic way. As I suspect it is for many, the fantasy of being as important to another human being as Claire is to Jamie is, for me, intensely provocative and satisfying. No matter where they fall on the spectrum of sexual identity, there are few who would not want to be both the object as well as the subject of such attention, commitment, and devotion from a love partner.

Thus far, though, my response as a gay man to *Outlander* and its hero has been, more or less, chaste. But, according to at least one critic, reading and responding to literature can be a mentally if not a physically (homo)erotic experience. Lara Farina writes that to "read erotically is to be moved by a text. It requires the reader to feel, emotionally and physically, a written work's affective pull. To read erotically is also, then, to become *implicated* in sexualized relations performed by and with reading material" (49, italics in the original). She elaborates on this initial conception by stating that "erotic reading is a kind of affective meaning-making. Erotic response to language or imagery, I would argue, is inseparable from a reader's use of memory to frame the signifier and to connect it to other sexualized experiences" that is in itself a legitimate and too-often elided form of literary/critical interpretation (51). I would suggest that the kind of erotic reading Farina details here is made rather easier when the text involved features sex scenes as *Outlander* does.

Turning to the first of these, which—once again in complete defiance of romance novel conventions—occurs nearly 300 pages into the novel, we find Jamie and Claire spending a significant portion of their wedding night talking as a means of getting more comfortable with one another. This is a love scene, or rather, a falling in love scene. And, inevitably, the time wanes and Claire suggests that they go to bed; "To bed? Or to sleep?" Jamie asks with an inquiring grin (*Outlander*, ch. 15). When Claire hesitates, Jamie offers to help her unlace and slip out of her wedding finery. This task taken care of, Claire abruptly decides that she will help Jamie undress. Before long, she "reached up and unfastened his shirt, sliding my hands inside and across his shoulders. I brought my palms slowly down across his chest, feeling the springy hair and the soft indentations around his nipples" (*Outlander*, ch. 15). Moments later, Claire runs her "hands up the length of his thighs, hard and lean under his kilt" (*Outlander*, ch. 15). Then Jamie "pressed me firmly to him, and I could feel that he was more than ready to get on with the business at hand.

With some surprise, I realized that I was ready, too. In fact, whether it was the result of the late hour, the wine, or his own attractiveness, or simple deprivation, I wanted him quite badly" (*Outlander*, ch. 15). Borrowing from Charlotte Brontë's *Jane Eyre* (1847): Reader, I wanted him quite badly, too, in this moment. Thus, as Farina theorizes from a queer perspective, I can say that not only have I been moved by the text of *Outlander* as a whole but, in this case, by one of its sex scenes. In addition, through the imaginative power of memory, I am able to link Jamie and Claire's fictional lovemaking with my own experiences in that realm of human existence. I, like Claire, know what it is like to desire a man; I know what a man's body feels like to the touch; and I know what it is like to make love with a man. And that memorial knowledge combines in what I consider to be an alchemical way with Gabaldon's writing and characters to make my reading and responses to *Outlander* and Jamie fundamentally (homo)erotic as opposed to merely platonic.

At this point, it is imperative that I make it clear that, in the foregoing paragraphs of this chapter, I am *not* trying to argue that all gay men would read and respond to *Outlander* in exactly same way as I do. My personal and critical (or my personal/critical since, in this case, they are so intertwined) take on *Outlander* is as idiosyncratic as any other reader's would be irrespective of their gender or sexual identity. The problem that I face in terms of contextualizing the reading I am putting forth here is twofold. Firstly, men's responses to the romance novel are, for the most part, nonexistent in the archive of academic criticism of the genre. Secondly, formal study of *Outlander* is really in the incipient stages and, as with the romance genre itself, systematic considerations of men's responses to Gabaldon's work(s) are unavailable.[10] To navigate through this particular rhetorical dilemma in a productive and, hopefully, illuminating way, I will turn to two sources—one academic and one anecdotal—in what follows. Thus I seek to ground my homoerotic reading of *Outlander* in the realm of the comparative.

Norman N. Holland and Leona F. Sherman's responses to the modern gothic romance novel—of which Daphne du Maurier's *Rebecca* is considered to be the progenitor—form the subject of the article "Gothic Possibilities." "A gothic novel," they write in their discussion of the castle, one of the recurrent tropes of the genre, "combines the heroine's fantasies about the castle with her fears that her body will be violated" by sexual penetration (218). For Sherman, "imagining being penetrated (an experience of being 'filled') can be a pleasure" (220); for Holland, on the other hand, such a possibility is profoundly threatening. He explains that, for him, "both identifying with a female and imagining being penetrated [sexually] call into question my male identity" (220). In tandem, then, identifying as a reader with a modern gothic romance's female heroine and having to allow for even the imagined possibility of sexual penetration discomfit Holland to the point of raising the "threat posed by the castle and the gothic machinery to a pitch where I no longer wish them relevant to me, the male me, and I sense myself relegating gothic to an alienating category, 'women's fiction'" (220). Based on the evidence Sherman and Holland provide in their work, the differences in their responses to the genre of modern gothic romance seem to have a great deal, if not everything, to do with their respective genders and sexual identities.

A presumably heterosexual male, Holland is profoundly disconcerted by even the hint of a sexuality in which his body would be made to function as a receptor of another man's penis. Sherman, a presumably heterosexual female, betrays no such concerns. In accord with Pamela Regis's assertion that, "for most of its history, the romance novel did not *have* sex scenes" (55), the modern gothics discussed by Sherman and Holland, following their eighteenth and nineteenth century predecessors, do not feature such scenes. Sex in these books always remains a visceral, but nevertheless shadowy, menace. That being the case, readers might wonder how Holland would react to novels like Gabaldon's *Outlander* that contain repeated, relatively explicit descriptions of sex that are integral parts of the narrative. As a gay male reader of *Outlander*, I experience a great deal of enjoyment and pleasure in reading about the specifics of the lovemaking that occurs between Jamie and Claire. My (gay) male identity remains fully intact and unthreatened, if not enhanced and validated as a direct result of such encounters. In contrast, it is not difficult to intuit that Holland would, more than likely, be made distinctly uncomfortable by the sex scenes in *Outlander*. Still, whether or not, as a homogenous group, all straight male readers of *Outlander* react like Holland does to the sexual elements is an interesting question to which only provisional answers can be found in the vast archive of Amazon.com customer reviews.

There are just over 14,000 reviews of *Outlander* the novel at Amazon.com as of this writing. Of course, such a large number makes a systematic study of all of them impractical for the purposes of this chapter. Nevertheless, a random sampling that yields productive results is possible. Insofar as customers' names are able to reveal gender and/or sexual identity, a very small percentage of the 14,000 reviewer-readers of *Outlander* who have commented on the book at Amazon.com seem to be straight males. For example, Randy Bernstein writes: "I was first introduced to *Outlander* when I saw that it was a television series…. From the beginning, I became engrossed in the story to the point where I would read during every spare moment…. Though this is classified as a 'romance' (which I probably wouldn't like), it is really more of an adventure story, with a basic love component" (Bernstein). The key word in Bernstein's review is "adventure." By far, like Bernstein, most of the straight male readers of *Outlander* focus their remarks on the adventure aspects of the book; if they acknowledge it at all, the romance of Jamie and Claire is downplayed. For instance, John Miller insists: "I am a guy that likes reading fantasy, sci-phi [*sic*] and historical adventure novels. This book was recommended by my wife, and though it is referenced as a romance novel, it is way more than that" (Miller); while James Tepper claims: "I am not a romance novel reader and there's no way that this could not be considered a romance novel.... But the writing is excellent and the history (of the 1745 'Rising,' a failed attempt to restore the Catholic Stuarts to the throne of England) fascinating and well-researched" (Tepper); and Claude H. Feistel asserts: "The first book [*Outlander*] makes readers think it is an action adventure layered onto an intense romantic drama" (Feistel). It should be noted that they all perceive the book as being marketed to women as romance, though Gabaldon herself would agree with these men that it has a heavy adventure component, enough that it should be classified with general fiction. Thus far, I have come across only one straight male reviewer-reader, Robert Kall, who addresses the erotic sex scenes in *Outlander* in a direct way: "For me, it got kind of weird when the love-making is given graphic description. My other half asked me if it turned me on. 'It's from a woman's point of view!' I exclaimed. So it was not a turn on, but it was interesting" (Kall). Though a necessarily incomplete survey, the inference to be drawn here is that those straight men who have read *Outlander* read it for the history and the adventure; they emphatically did not read *Outlander* for the romance or the sex. In that respect, they are different from at least some of their gay male counterparts—the author of this essay being one of them—who read the book.

By way of conclusion, I want to start by pointing out that, beginning with *Gender and Reading: Essays on Readers, Texts, and Contexts*, edited by Elizabeth A. Flynn and Patrocinio P. Schweikart and published in 1986, scholars have attempted to reckon with the fact that men and women read differently specifically on account of their genders. Men, according to Patrocinio and Schweikart, tend to focus on the "cognitive aspects" of reading, or "reading as apprehending the meaning of the text," while women tend to focus on the "affective aspects" of reading, or "reading as experiencing the effects intended by the text" (ix). As both a trained literary critic and a (gay male) reader, my approach to texts encompasses both the cognitive and the affective, as I hope I have demonstrated sufficiently above. Meanwhile, in her contribution to *Gender and Reading*, "Ourself behind Ourself: A Theory for Lesbian Readers," Jean E. Kennard insists that not only do men and women read differently, but that, even though their biological genders are the same, heterosexual women and lesbian women read differently because of their respective sexual identities (77). Although I have been unable to locate any critical work that analyzes the reading practices and strategies of gay males in relation to heterosexual males, Kennard's essay, as well as the deliberations I have put forth in this chapter, suggest that gay men read differently from heterosexual men. In any case, I would argue that Diana Gabaldon's *Outlander* is a particularly good text around which to organize such a study in the future, between the adventure aspects, Jamie's platonically admirable qualities, and the qualities that lend themselves so well to the practice of gay male homoerotic reading.

NOTES

1. The author wishes to thank the Marsh Library staff—particularly Connie Shumate (director), Evangeline Painter (circulation supervisor), and Seth Caudill (reference librarian)—at Concord University for their assistance with acquiring, through additions to the permanent collection and Inter-Library Loan, the various materials needed to write this essay.

2. For a more measured—and expansive—definition of the romance novel, see "The Romance Novel Defined," Part II of Pamela Regis, *A Natural History of the Romance Novel* (Philadelphia: University of Pennsylvania Press, 2003), 19–45.

3. Gabaldon discusses the rather vexed issue of genre categorization in relation to *Outlander* and its sequels in the Prologue to *The Outlandish Companion*, Revised and Updated Edition (New York: Delacorte Press, 1999), esp. *xxvii–xxvii*, as well as in the "FAQ: About the Books" section of her website.

4. According to figures available at The Romance Writers of America® website, "[w]omen make up 84 percent of romance book buyers, and men make up 16 percent" ("The Romance Book Buyer").

5. As a literary, artistic, and cultural movement, Romanticism came into being in the late eighteenth and lasted well into the nineteenth century. Its chief characteristic was a strong emphasis on human emotions as the source of aesthetic experience. Romanticism arose in direct opposition to the cold reason and rationality demanded by Enlightenment thinkers, artists, philosophers, and so on.

6. On the need for such circumvention, see, for example, Laura Byrne-Cristiano, "*Outlander*'s Diana Gabaldon Clarifies Black Jack Randall's Sexual Orientation," Hypablewww, 28 April 2015, accessed 20 August 2015. In this piece, Byrne-Cristiano discusses fan reaction to Episode 12 of the STARZ® television adaptation of *Outlander* from which many viewers and critics leapt to the assumption that Randall is gay. The social media chatter on this subject was such that Gabaldon took the step of making it clear on her Facebook page that, in her conception of the character (which Executive Producer Ronald D. Moore followed), Randall is *not* a homosexual. Not surprisingly, Gabaldon's assertion has met with a fair amount of skepticism; as such, the dialog on this subject continues.

7. See the "Gender and Storytelling" section of Valerie Estelle Frankel, *Scots, Sassenachs, and Spankings: Feminism and Gender Roles in Outlander* (USA: LitCrit Press, 2015) for an excellent critical examination of the experience of looking at Jamie as he appears in the STARZ® television adaptation of *Outlander*.

8. On the physical and psychological extremes the character of Jamie is put through in *Outlander*, see "Jamie and the Rule of Three," in Diana Gabaldon, *The Outlandish Companion* (New York: Delacorte Press, 1999), 419–421.

9. The *Oxford English Dictionary* online defines "to skelp" as: to "strike, beat, slap, smack"; to "drive with blows"; and to "kick violently."

10. As an indication of the significant dearth of study in this area, my work on this essay led me to a total of only four articles: Eric Murphy Selinger, "How to Read a Romance Novel (and Fall in Love with Popular Romance)," in *New Approaches to Popular Romance Fiction: Critical Essays*, eds. Sarah S.G. Frantz and Eric Murphy

Selinger (Jefferson, NC: McFarland, 2012); Gavin McNett, "My 'Outlander' Thing: How a Brainy Guy like Me Wound Up Reading Historical Romance Novels," Salonwww, 12 Aug, 1999; Norman N. Holland and Leona F. Sherman, "Gothic Possibilities" in Gender and Reading: Essays on Readers, Texts, and Contexts, eds. Elizabeth A. Flynn and Patrocinio P. Schweickart (Baltimore: Johns Hopkins University Press, 1986 and 1992), 215–233; and Peter H. Mann, "The Romantic Novel and its Readers," Journal of Popular Culture 15.1 (Summer 1981): 9–18.

Works Cited

Baldick, Chris. The Oxford Dictionary of Literary Terms. Oxford: Oxford University Press, 2008. Print.

Bernstein, Randy. "Only Read if You Have the Time to Spare—You Won't Be Able to Put It Down." Rev. of Outlander, by Diana Gabaldon. Amazon.com. 27 July 2015. Accessed 28 July 2015. Web.

Byrne-Cristiano, Laura. "Outlander's Diana Gabaldon Clarifies Black Jack Randall's Sexual Orientation." Hypablewww. 28 April 2015. Accessed 20 August 2015. http://www.hypable.com/outlander-gabaldon-jack-randall-isnt-gay.

Coleridge, Samuel Taylor. Biographia Literaria. Selections. The Norton Anthology of Theory and Criticism. Ed. Vincent B. Leitch, et al. New York: W.W. Norton & Company, 2001. 674–82. Print.

Farina, Lara. "Lesbian History and Erotic Reading." Chapter 3. The Lesbian Premodern. Ed. Noreen Giffney, Michelle M. Sauer, and Diane Watt. New York: Palgrave Macmillan, 2011. 49–60. Print.

Feistel, Claude H. "Outlander Is More than a Story of 8+ Books." Rev. of Outlander, by Diana Gabaldon. Amazon.com. 9 May 2015. Accessed 28 July 2015. Web.

Gabaldon, Diana. "FAQ: About the Books." Diana Gabaldon's Official Webpage. http://www.dianagabaldon.com/resources/faq/faq-about-the-books. Web.

Gabaldon, Diana. "Other Projects/Outlander TV Series News." Diana Gabaldon's Official Webpage. http://www.dianagabaldon.com/other-projects/outlander-tv-series/news/episode–12-about-black-jack.

Gabaldon, Diana. Outlander. New York: Bantam Dell, 2005. Print.

Gabaldon, Diana. The Outlandish Companion. Revised and Updated. New York: Delacorte Press, 1999.

Green, Laura. Literary Identification: From Charlotte Brontë to Tsitsi Dangarembga. Columbus: The Ohio State University Press, 2012. Print.

Holland, Norman N., and Leona F. Sherman. "Gothic Possibilities." Gender and Reading: Essays on Readers, Texts, and Contexts. Ed. Elizabeth A. Flynn and Patrocinio P. Schweickart. Baltimore: Johns Hopkins University Press, 1986 and 1992. 215–233. Print.

Kall, Robert. "Don't Plan to Get Much Work Done 'til You Turn the Last Page." Rev. of Outlander, by Diana Gabaldon. Amazon.com. 17 Nov. 2001. Accessed 28 July 2015. Web.

Kennard, Jean E. "Ourself Behind Ourself: A Theory for Lesbian Readers." Gender and Reading: Essays on Readers, Texts, and Contexts. Baltimore: Johns Hopkins University Press, 1986. 63–80. Print.

Kinsale, Laura. "The Androgynous Reader: Point of View in the Romance." Dangerous Men and Adventurous Women: Romance Writers on the Appeal of Romance. Ed. Jayne Ann Krentz. Philadelphia: University of Pennsylvania Press, 1992. 31–44. Print.

Miller, John. "Great for Both Sexes!!!" Rev. of *Outlander*, by Diana Gabaldon. Amazon.com. 28 Nov. 2014. Accessed 28 July 2015. Web.

Regis, Pamela. *A Natural History of the Romance Novel*. Philadelphia: University of Pennsylvania Press, 2003 and 2007. Print.

"The Romance Book Buyer." *The Romance Writers of America* website. https://www.rwa.org/p/cm/ld/fid=582. Accessed 28 July 2015. Web.

Schweickart, Patrocinio P., and Elizabeth A. Flynn. "Introduction." *Gender and Reading: Essays on Readers, Texts, and Contexts*. Baltimore: Johns Hopkins University Press, 1986. ix–xxx. Print.

"Skelp." *Oxford English Dictionary*. Oxford: Oxford University Press, 2015. Web.

Tepper, James. "Addicting Historical Fiction (and Romance)." Rev. of *Outlander*, by Diana Gabaldon. Amazon.com. 23 Oct. 2014. Accessed 28 July 2015. Web.

Turco, Lewis. *The Book of Literary Terms: The Genres of Fiction, Drama, Nonfiction, Literary Criticism, and Scholarship*. Hanover, NH: University Press of New England, 1999. Print.

PART III

Putting the Speculative in Speculative Fiction

The Short Stories on the Science Fiction Shelf, or Lord John Grey Complicates Matters as Usual

VALERIE ESTELLE FRANKEL

> The *Outlander* series combines romance, historical fiction, science fiction, mystery and the supernatural, to wildly popular effect. But the conventions that once neatly delineated the relationships between genres are not the only ones lying shattered—Gabaldon also cheerfully violates the rules within genres.
>
> —Bethune

Certainly, the books are best described as cross-genre, appearing in the general fiction section as a way of emphasizing their uncategorizable nature. As Gabaldon describes the book's genre decisions: "The *Outlander* series has enough historical twists and highbrow touches to attract mainstream readers, which is why Delacorte and Gabaldon have tirelessly pressured bookstores to stock the books in the general-fiction section, rather than the romance aisle" (Koerner).

The series is not only a vast historical saga, with cameos from Bonnie Prince Charlie, King Louis XV, and smaller stars like Jenny Cameron, but military fiction as well: Jamie struggles with ethics and the price of command as he leads the men of Lallybroch to Culloden, even knowing their doom, then fights in the American Revolution under good commanders and bad. Meanwhile, there is high fantasy as Jamie meets the Wild Hunt. Geillis and Master Raymond do real magic, while Jamie has the sight and Mandy and Jem, a strange mystic bond. Beyond all this of course are the standing stones.

125

Science fiction appears in Gabaldon's complex rules of time travel: her article "The Gabaldon Theory of Time Travel," appeared in the *Journal of Transfigural Mathematics* in 2010, emphasizing its scientific thought and accuracy.

With so many genres, Gabaldon is correct that the series has a genre for everyone. This may in fact be fueling its popularity. One article on historical fiction with a touch of genre notes, "Mash-ups help spread this genre beyond its core base … mash-ups give readers a fresh look at genres that they might overlook, whether it is historical fiction, fantasy or science fiction" (Rabey 40–41).

On her website, Gabaldon flies into a passionate defense of the series' deserved place in the general fiction section. Other essays in this collection have tackled the romantic aspects of the books, which exist to the point where many fans consider them deserving of the romance classification (indeed, Gabaldon's fervent protests suggest she too has seen readers thus classify it). The books' position between romance and adventure/general fiction is well known, as are their obvious third classification of historical (typically sorted among general fiction, rather than separately). Still, another set of genres present themselves: mystery, science fiction, paranormal-gothic, fantasy, and military. While light in the adventure-romance *Outlander* books, these genres are far stronger in the Lord John spinoff stories.

The Lord John novels and short stories all take place during Jamie and Claire's separation in *Voyager* between 1756 and 1761. Jamie works at Helwater and Lord John lives in London near his family, though he also travels on military missions to Prussia, Ireland, Canada, and the West Indies, varying the setting beyond London society. Gabaldon explains, "These books are part of the overall series, but are focused for the most part on those times in Lord John's life when he's not 'onstage' in the main novels" (*The Scottish Prisoner*, Preface). He grows as a character, making friends and enemies as well as new in-laws, but all the stories are written to work on their own. Gabaldon adds: "The Lord John novellas and novels are sequential, but are built to stand alone; you don't need to read them in order" (*The Scottish Prisoner*, Preface). Lord John's family (brother, stepbrother, nephews and niece) return in *An Echo in the Bone* and *Written in My Own Heart's Blood*, further tying in the spinoffs. These short stories add a new list of genres to Gabaldon's already full-ranging series, creating stories that are certainly historical fiction but more paranormal mystery, overt fantasy/paranormal, or escapades of military and manners than epic time-travel romance.

Cozy Mystery and Society Stories

The first written novella "Lord John and the Hellfire Club" (1998) first appeared in the British anthology *Past Poisons: An Ellis Peters Memorial*

Anthology of Historical Crime. Gabaldon adds, "Lord John began his independent life apart from the *Outlander* books when a British editor and anthologist named Maxim Jukubowski invited me to write a short story for an anthology of historical crime" (*Hand of Devils*, xii). It is undoubtedly a mystery, as the story begins with a murder on the streets of London that Lord John attempts to solve. As he's not a police employee by any stretch of the imagination, this falls under the category of "cozy" mystery.

Peter Lovesey, Anne Perry, John Dickson Carr, Richard Falkirk, and Emily Brightwell all wrote historical mysteries set in the 1800s in England. As with the Lord John stories, most of the crimes are solved by amateur detectives. The historical element is central here, as are the characters. Jordan Foster of *Publishers Weekly* explains:

> Violence is never absent from these tales—they are, after all, murder mysteries—but there's a definite lack of gore and gratuitous carnage. Louise Penny, whose award-winning Chief Insp. Armand Gamache series is set in the tiny Quebec village of Three Pines, likens the suspense in her novels to that of famed director Alfred Hitchcock, who "knew that less is more." Says Penny, "My books aren't about murder—that's simply a catalyst to look at human nature. They aren't about blood but about the marrow, about what happens deep inside, in places we didn't even know existed."

While asking questions and seeking justice for a victim dead nearly in his arms, Lord John ventures into strange corners of London while facing dark truths about himself. Of course, its original appearance in an anthology of "Historical Crime" is significant for genre classification, though it's reprinted in *Lord John and the Hand of Devils*, a Gabaldon collection found in the general fiction section beside *Outlander*.

Lord John and the Private Matter (2003), published as a stand-alone novel, soon followed. (Gabaldon recounts in the foreword to *Lord John and the Hand of Devils* her humorous conversation with her publisher who told her that by normal, non–*Outlander* standards, it was novel length.) The title poses it as a novel of manners—of one's social standing and relationships, much in the tradition of Jane Austen or Oscar Wilde. A comedy of manners is most concerned with satirizing the customs of a social class, and as a comedy, it generally concludes with happy marriages. The plot often follows an illicit love affair or similarly scandalous matter, though this is subordinate to the play's commentary on human foibles. This story indeed begins in scandalous fashion, as Lord John discovers that his cousin Olivia's fiancé has syphilis and must find a socially-appropriate way to stop the wedding. As he investigates, his cousin bustles about choosing lace and floral arrangements, filling the house with all the accoutrements of a society wedding and oblivious to the upcoming danger. When John asks his mother how Olivia would feel to lose her fiancé, she replies, "She knows nothing of his character, nor of the real nature of marriage, and if she truly is in love with anything at the moment, it is with her wedding dress" (ch. 11). As such, she emphasizes the public, superficial nature of marriage, in contrast to Jamie and Claire's deep love and messy need for compromise. In keeping with the public nature of it all, John's mother warns him to keep any scandal to himself, as Olivia will have to ignore it after she weds. The book thus subverts the comedy of manners as John is trying to stop a wedding, not bring one about. Simultaneously, the ladies of town humorously see Lord John as something of a catch, and he struggles to avoid entanglements, insisting, "I have no estate or household that requires a mistress, and Hal [John's older brother] is making an adequate job of continuing the family name" (ch. 8).

Meanwhile, the Crown appoints him to investigate the brutal murder of a fellow officer who may have been a traitor. Solving both puzzles involves making smalltalk in fashionable drawing rooms and also visiting brothels where he finds surprising allies among the lower class. Finally, he must venture to the infamous Lavender House, a gentlemen's club "for gentlemen of a particular sort," trailing a cross-dresser in the height of the homosexual district of London. Once again, the upper class society world is subverted with telling explorations of what lurks below. The cozy mystery tradition also continues, albeit in startling venues. Foster adds of the genre: "From Holmes's flat at 221B Baker Street in Victorian London to the tiny English hamlet of St. Mary's Mead where Miss Marple spent her days, the setting and the surrounding community is integral to the story."

Much of the Lord John books take place at his club; Grey was enrolled in The Society for the Appreciation of the English Beefsteak at birth by his godfather, who began taking him there for lunch every Wednesday starting when he was seven. Other marks of society appear, not only in garden parties but in institutions and historic events as Lord John attends George III's coronation, while John's brother wagers on his father's innocence in the famous betting book at White's.

A subplot involves Tom Byrd getting himself hired as Lord John's valet—though it's soon revealed that he's really a boy who cleans boots, cleverly ingratiating himself while on a quest for his vanished brother. As John thinks, "the boy must plainly have been aware that he was sacrificing his position—and quite possibly his skin—by his actions, and yet he had not hesitated to act" (ch. 5). Lord John likes him and keeps him on, making this a success story of a servant's rise to valued member of the inner circle, another trope of the comedy of manners.

One critic already sees the show as a story of manners and society, or at least written to appeal to those fans. He explains:

> The "Outlander" books date to 1991, but it seems likely that TV executives looked at them and thought, oh, "Game of Thrones" meets "Downton Abbey."

> The series ... has some of ye-olde-time grimy violence and sex of "Games" and a little of the plummy accents and cozy Anglophilia of "Downton" [Hale].

Certainly, the books, show, and Lord John novels all have careful verbal sparring over tea or elegant dinners, as the protagonist tries to survive the shifting world of public disapproval and scandal.

Lord John and the Brotherhood of the Blade (2007), published as another novel, deals with the mysterious death of Lord John's father—murder or suicide—and the possible motivations behind it. Determined to publicly clear his family name, Lord John traces a long-dead Jacobite plot. The novel also focuses heavily on John's homosexual relationship with his new stepbrother, Percy Wainwright, even as John struggles with his feelings for Jamie. Here, Gabaldon does extensive research about Lavender House and the "Molly-walks" of London, considering how and where homosexual affairs would take place in Georgian London. In a poignant look into class and circumstance of the time, Percy tells John that he first lay with a man for three shillings—a fortune that prevented him and his mother from starving. As he adds, "It made the difference between poverty and outright hunger. And I discovered that my own tastes ... lay that way" (ch. 27). Thus Gabaldon balances the homosexual community with realism, and considers such a life for the less privileged.

The flirtation of a comedy of manners also appears, but subverted, in the byplay between Percy Wainwright and John Grey. Like Austen's Emma and Mr. Knightly, they are siblings of a sort, though still distant enough to make a relationship workable (privately, if not publicly). On entering a room where Percy is half-dressed, being fitted for the wedding, Lord John bows elaborately with the words "Your servant, sir." Percy can only say "I fear you take me at a disadvantage, sir" with "mock dignity" as he scrabbles for his trousers (ch. 9).

This aspect of the story fits well into the cozy mystery genre, adding humor and charm as well as character depth:

> Often, the focus in the cozy is the engaging—and often quirky—hero or heroine and his or her network of friends and enemies, rather than the nitty-gritty details of crime solving. The shift in emphasis from puzzles to characters and atmosphere is a key element in differentiating the cozier offshoots from their more traditional predecessors and contemporaries. Humor is also a cozy staple, helping to provide a counterbalance to the murders, as bloodless as they might be, that propel the stories [Foster].

"Lord John and the Haunted Soldier" introduces another mystery even while Lord John discovers that the soldier whose death he's investigating had run off with a paramour, now pregnant and in terrible straits. A romantic plot follows, as the scoundrel Marcus Fanshawe buys every piece of jewelry she pawns, planning to keep it for her and wed her "when she had reached a state of complete desperation" (297). However, he lets her degrade herself in a brothel to further her suffering, and she dies of a fever. This too echoes the cruelest of Austen's villains—Mr. Willoughby or Mr. Wickham, as they seduce the helpless and use marriage as a calculated bargaining chip. Lord John discovers all this in Vauxhall Pleasure Gardens, wearing a scarlet domino mask, in another moment of romanticism and intrigue. In his adventures, Lord John explores "the masks that most men wear in commerce with their fellows" (301), adding a certain emphasis to his own quiet detective work.

Military

The war novel hit a new level of popularity during the nineteenth century, with works like Leo Tolstoy's *War and Peace* (1869, Napoleonic Wars), and Stephen Crane's *The Red Badge of Courage* (1895, American Civil War). Historical military fiction thereafter includes such popular series as *Horatio Hornblower* by C.S. Forester (Napoleonic Wars), *Richard Sharpe's Adventures* by Bernard Cornwell (Napoleonic Wars), or *The Army of the Potomac* trilogy by Bruce Catton (American Civil War).

These stories focus on the realities of life at the time, as well as the excitement of battle and its strategies. Personal relationships, scenes of wartime atrocities, and questions of morality, duty, and honor also dominate. Certainly, plenty of this appears in the Jacobite Rebellion and especially the American Revolution that follows in the main series. This has aided in its popularity.

> "You have quite a large demographic potentially interested in things military," says Harley B. Patrick, publisher of L&R Publishing/Hellgate Press…. [More than this,] Patrick cites America's fascination with heroism and hero archetypes. He says readers are hard-pressed to find another topic that forces them to confront fundamentally human challenges like death, loss and survival as a matter of routine [Martinez].

Having a war in the story isn't enough to qualify it as military fiction— *Gone with the Wind* is a romance set during the Civil War, filled with historically true adventures, but it focuses far more on Scarlet's loves, and life for those who remain at home, than the battles. *Outlander* is closer to this than to most military fiction. By contrast, as they lack the romance and the mysteries, several Lord John stories could be categorized as historical military fiction beyond all else.

Casemate Publishers' managing editor Steven Smith believes increased interest in military fiction comes with people's modern uncertainty and desire to weigh questions of ethics and culpability in perilous times (Martinez). Besides its society/mystery elements, *Lord John and the Brotherhood of the*

Blade (2007) explores John's time in the military with a highly unusual plot for historical war fantasy. Percy, his stepbrother and lover, is arrested for homosexuality and is condemned to death—and John, who catches him cheating, is the sole witness. John runs to Jamie for advice as he struggles between public and private honor. His brother Hal heartlessly tells John that a trial would cause further scandal, so John should bring Percy a pistol and persuade him to shoot himself in a chapter called "The Honorable Thing" (ch. 27). As Hal adds, "It would be best for everyone … including him." Laws are swept under the rug in hopes that the scandal will vanish. In fact, when Hal investigates, he discovers the crime of sodomy has only rarely been persecuted. "The conclusion there was obvious and something Grey had also known for years; the military hierarchy had no appetite for that sort of scandal—save of course, when it might cover something worse" (ch. 28).

There is also much about day-to-day military work: In *Brotherhood of the Blade*, Lord John lectures Percy on how to act like an officer and reassure his men through confidence (ch. 10). The pair join the 46th Regiment, assigned to fight under Duke Ferdinand of Brunswick in the Rhine Valley during 1758, then Grey later fights at the Battle of Crefeld on June 23, 1758. As the book adds:

> Grey's days were a blur of activity, rushing from Whitehall offices to shipping offices, holding daily councils of war with the other officers, receiving and reviewing daily reports from the captains, writing daily summary reports for the colonels, reading orders, writing orders, hastily donning dress uniform and dashing out to leap on a horse in time to take his place at the head of a column to march through the London streets in a guildhall procession to the cheers of a crowd, then throwing the reins to a groom and brushing the horsehair from his uniform in a carriage on his way to a ball at Richard Joffrey's house, where he must dance with the ladies and confer in corners with the gentlemen, the ministers who ran the machine of war, and the merchants who greased its gears [ch. 16].

Building on this genre, "Lord John and the Haunted Soldier" (originally published in *Lord John and the Hand of Devils*) never appears in a fantasy anthology. In fact, it has basically no fantasy elements, beginning as it does with a military tribunal investigating a cannon accident. Lord John fired it and was severely wounded, while another man was killed. The horrors of military injury follow, as Lord John undergoes appalling surgery, sobbing with relief when the doctors stop hurting him. No opium is permitted—only a leather strap and his brother's hand (*Brotherhood of the Blade*, ch. 29). The doctors are unable to remove a metal fragment, which may pierce his heart and kill him at any time. With this ticking clock embedded in his body, Lord John investigates the man who died, while also investigating the reality of the explosion.

Gabaldon brings in military expertise with cannon types and constructions as Lord John investigates the reality behind this one's explosion. She also points out the hypocrisy of army life—when Lord John protests that the tribunal can't prove he's guilty, his friend Quarry replies, "I doubt they'd have to ... if they can raise enough doubt about your actions and get enough talk started" (197).

Eight more guns have exploded, and the mystery is finally solved with a scandal of stolen copper. The navy gives the culprit safe passage, aiding in helping him get away with a crime that has killed his fellow officers. As Lord John demands to know whether a sailor's life is worth more than a soldier's, the matter is quickly closed. Once more, military hypocrisy and wrongdoing take center stage, allowing readers to work through similar issues in their own lives.

Lord John remembers the battle, and especially the point at which "he had thrown all emotion and sense of self-preservation to the wind, and flung himself howling on the deserting gun crew, shouting and beating them with the flat of his sword, forcing them back to their duty by the power of his will." This with the heat of battle "had melted all the shattered bits of mind and heart and forged him anew—into something hard and adamant, incapable of being hurt" (204).

Many readers, in the military and outside it, can see themselves in such moments, leading to the series' popularity. Juan Martinez notes in *Publishers Weekly*:

> Despite the current challenges facing the publishing industry, war and military history titles continue to sell—the recession, a plethora of free online information and the declining number of living WWII veterans evidently have not affected books. Publishers offer many explanations for their success, but the most obvious reason the category continues to thrive might simply be the sheer number of Americans who are associated with the military. According to the Department of Defense, the number of people serving in the U.S. armed forces stood at 1,402,227 as of December 31, 2008. The U.S. Department of Veterans Affairs lists the number of living veterans at 23,442,000. Add family members and friends of current or retired military personnel, and it's no wonder publishers find a market for their titles.

"The Custom of the Army" (2010) was first published in the 2010 anthology *Warriors*, edited by George R.R. Martin and Gardner Dozois. Despite the title, the book lines up in the science fiction section, with stories by Peter S. Beagle, David Weber, Carrie Vaughn, S.M. Sterling, and other top science fiction/fantasy writers. There's also a new *Game of Thrones* short story included, possibly the book's biggest draw.

In contrast with these, Gabaldon's tale is pure military fiction, beginning with a trace of London society. At an electric eel party (a staple of the time), Lord John inadvertently insults a lady, duels with her suitor, and kills him. To escape the scandal, and the obligation to wed the lady, Lord John runs off to Canada. There, Captain Charles Carruthers has requested him as a character witness at his court-martial.

Details of a court-martial appear, as Captain Carruthers confides in Lord John about his predicament. His commanding officer, Lord Siverly, collected all his troops' plunder to allegedly sell it and split the proceeds. However, he never actually paid them. As Carruthers adds, "Worse—he began withholding the soldiers' pay. Paying later and later, stopping pay for petty offenses, claiming that the paychest hadn't been delivered—when several men had seen it unloaded from the coach with their own eyes" (252). When he stole food and rifles as well, his troops finally mutinied. In consequence, the mutineers were hanged and Major Siverly kept his rank and commission, emphasizing the corruption of the military institution. It's Carruthers who insisted on making matters public, and who is charged with failing to prevent the mutiny as a result. Gabaldon presents the unjust laws for readers to examine through moral Lord John's eyes—Carruthers has asked for him as the one just person he knows, adding, "If there is any order in the world, any peace—it's because of you, John, and those very few like you" (254).

"Customs of the army" follow, from plunder to savaging the countryside, to the officers who are horrified by the latter and drink heavily or take mistresses. Lord John discovers his cousin's wife has an illegitimate child, and while he confronts the man, furious, he is forced to accept that he has been scarred by the horrors of what he's seen, as he has killed farmers and tortured women and children on army orders. "The men, they don't mind. Half of them are brutes to begin with…. Think … nothing of shooting a man on his doorstep and taking his wife next to his body," his cousin-in-law explains brokenly (265). Gabaldon has clearly done immense research into the British army practices of the time, revealing a group rife with corruption as personal honor, morality, and the law were often in conflict.

At last, Lord John is caught in the Siege of Quebec beside Simon Fraser. As General Wolfe recites "Elegy Written in a Country Churchyard" as they row toward battle, he offers a poignant moment of beauty on the cusp of war. The poem concludes, "The paths of glory lead but to the grave," as they head into the fray, where he indeed is killed. The randomness of battle pervades the rest of the story as Lord John saves the life of his philandering cousin, and then is saved by Major Siverly, while Carruthers dies of illness before his trial. Lord John departs, marveling over the haphazardness and corruption of his world.

Paranormal-Gothic

Gabaldon calls "Lord John and the Succubus" (2003) "a supernatural murder mystery, with military flourishes" (42). The short story was originally published in the 2003 Del Rey anthology *Legends II: New Short Novels by the Masters of Modern Fantasy* (edited by Robert Silverberg). The subtitle, *Masters of Modern Fantasy*, is central here. This is an anthology of top fantasy writers each offering a story that takes place in the larger world of their epic novel series—Orson Scott Card has one from *The Tales of Alvin Maker*, Anne McCaffrey brings a new *Dragonriders of Pern* short story, Neil Gaiman has one from *American Gods*, Terry Brooks from *Shannara*, Raymond E. Feist has one from *The Riftwar Saga* and yes, George R.R. Martin has a short story from the world of *Game of Thrones*. Gabaldon certainly has an epic world, but hers is likely the least fantastical of the collection. Nonetheless, she happily took her place among them, tacitly acknowledging that her epics are fantasy enough, and reaching out to McCaffrey and Card's readers with her own work.

Here she continues a tack she started in "Hellfire Club"—the title is fantastical, promising a succubus. However, the solution to the mystery is that the ghost is in fact a hoax, though disturbing enough to frighten characters in the story. Of course, the debunked supernatural is a Gothic staple, as with Ann Radcliffe's novels, in which character and reader continue to question; Poe's stories, too, often leave the reader wondering whether a supernatural event has occurred. "The explained supernatural is a genre of the Gothic in which the laws of everyday reality remain intact and permit an explanation or even dismissal of allegedly supernatural phenomena" (Thomson 9). Most Lord John stories debunk the mysterious, but "Plague of Zombies" in particular is more nebulous. The main *Outlander* series also has these moments of deniable supernatural, particularly involving Claire's auras, Jamie and Brianna's sight, and Jem and Mandy's unique magic.

> According to Tsvetan Todorov, a certain hesitation exists throughout a Gothic tale: the hesitation of the reader in knowing what the rules are in the game of reading. Can our understanding of familiar perceptions of reality account for strange goings-on or do we have to appeal to the *extra*ordinary to account for the setting and circumstances of the mysterious story? [Thomson 16].

The Sookie Stackhouse world, more paranormal romantic cozy mystery than strict fantasy, also joins some of the collections. "Lord John and the Succubus" is another mystery, though there are other "paranormal mysteries" in these collections. Oddly, of course, Gabaldon's Lord John short stories can thus be found in the science fiction/fantasy section, while her Lord John books and *Outlander* series appear in general fiction. She appears the only author in the collections suffering from such a split.

"Hellfire Club," "Succubus," and an original novella, called "Lord John and the Haunted Soldier" are collected in the book *Lord John and the Hand of Devils*. (Gabaldon reveals in the foreword that she had planned on "And a Whiff of Brimstone" but this would have led to translation issues. Both book titles once again emphasize the paranormal element.) While "Haunted Soldier" does mention a local ghost story, the real haunted solider appears to be Lord John, tottering about on the edge of death and frantically investigating the thief who stole the necessary copper from the cannon that exploded on him. Once again, the circumstances are all realistic. Yet, gothic is more than the presence of magic—it is the spooky, creepy, and chilling, whatever the cause:

> Generally speaking, gothic literature delves into the macabre nature of humanity in its quest to satiate mankind's intrinsic desire to plumb the depths of terror. We offer seven descriptors that frequently appear in works called gothic: 1) the appearance of the supernatural, 2) the psychology of horror and/or terror, 3) the poetics of the sublime, 4) a sense of mystery and dread 5) the appealing hero/villain, 6) the distressed heroine, and 7) strong moral closure (usually at least). But expect us to revisit this contentious issue in the near future [Thomson 12–13].

"Supernatural," "paranormal," and "gothic" might be deemed somewhat equivalent, all referencing mildly unnerving stories of vampires, werewolves, ghosts, zombies, and other "creatures of the night." In the recent young adult paranormal romances, teens fall in love with the entire list, in *Twilight* and many similar novels filling the shelves with black covers. Gothic, too, hinges on the innocent lass falling for the monster, drawn to his darkness and bloodlust. Lord John stories mostly skip the romance and debunk the monster, discovering a rational explanation for the spookiness. Nonetheless, the stories contain enough of the staple elements to fit smoothly into the speculative fiction anthologies.

Identified elements of gothic include graveyards, ghosts, possession, and exorcism ("Succubus"), the haunted castle or house with an ancestral curse on the inhabitants ("Zombies"), anti–Catholic feeling (*The Scottish Prisoner*), body snatching ("The Custom of the Army"), the Devil ("Hellfire Club"), the Doppelgänger (Percy in *Brotherhood of the Blade*), nightmares ("Succubus"), supernatural tools and passages (the cup in *The Scottish Prisoner*, the Hellfire Club itself), masochism (Lord John's ongoing love for Jamie), superstition ("Succubus," "Zombies"), entrapment ("Hellfire Club"), revenge (*Brotherhood of the Blade*), the grotesque (Carruthers in "The Custom of the Army"), the pursued protagonist ("The Custom of the Army" or John's secret homosexuality), and strong emotion, mystery, and the uncanny (all of them). Basically, when the stories are combined, all the elements are represented.

"Lord John and the Hellfire Club" has particularly gothic elements, as the club members attempt to initiate John in horrific fashion. As "something warm and sticky cascaded over Grey's head" Sir Francis Dashwood says, "I baptize thee, child of Asmodeus, son of blood..." (34). They give him drugged wine and punch him into compliance. Finally, they fling him into a room with a dead girl, whom he's told he is supposed to murder as the price of admission. She appears to have died by accident, but the real threat comes from the instigator, George Everett, who attempts to murder Lord John. A duel to the death follows, as Lord John struggles for his life in their court of horrors. The Hellfire Club was real, more a society playacting at wickedness than a place of anything truly supernatural (though the men there did pray to the devil and various demons). The title suggests fantasy, though under the trappings no actually fantasy elements occur.

Even the more prosaic "The Custom of the Army" takes Lord John to the horrors of the battlefield in mysterious, savage Canada. The story begins with an electric eel party, which nearly kills Lord John and transports him to a strange state of being. As he fights a duel then travels across the world to visit a deformed friend, both incidents mention a doctor eager for pickled body parts, a Gothic trope. "Body-snatching came to represent a particularly horrid instance of sacrilege, an invasion of religious space by an aggressive and often commercially motivated science" (Thomson 2).

In "Lord John and the Succubus," Lord John's friend Stephan von Namtzen explains, "The succubus takes possession of the body of a dead person, and rests within it by day." It can hide within a churchyard and emerge to terrorize sleeping folk at night, as this one is rumored to do (59). A succubus in European myth is a demon that seduces human men at night. Succubae were known for tempting saints with dreams of naked women—consorting with succubae was a common accusation in sixteenth and seventeenth century witch trials. "The actual term nightmare seems to be a bastardization of the Old Norse and Anglo-Saxon term *mara*. A mara is defined as a demon which sits upon the chests of sleepers and brings bad dreams. Most cultures seemed to characterize nightmares as being caused by demons" (Thomson 7). In the story, the Prussian Princess Louisa calls it *Der Nachtmahr*, the Nightmare (110).

> The *mora* could be banished through certain charms, from turning the pillow and making a sign of cross on it to leaving a broom upside down behind the door, or putting a belt on top of the sheets. Lord John is told that riding a white stallion over the grave will lay the demon to rest. As it turns out, the succubus is a hoax. Nonetheless, as the story brushes against magic and superstition, John must involve himself in an extensive investigation amid bats and ethereal charms in the haunted outskirts of future Germany [Frankel 188–189].

As a ghost story in Eastern Europe, the tale is highly gothic. There are even fluttering, fainting women in pale nightdresses hoping to be carried off by a young lord (though Lord John isn't particularly interested).

Lord John and the Plague of Zombies (2011) was first published in the 2011 anthology *Down These Strange Streets*, edited by George R.R. Martin and Gardner Dozois. This is another of the fantasy anthologies, though the title and theme suggest urban fantasy of the city, and the word "strange" encourages paranormal and urban legend rather than the staples of fantasy. Gabaldon presents a tale of the West Indies and zombies, mixing British practicality with the haunting magic of the islands in imagery that touches on *Jane Eyre*. John reflects, "Having encountered German night hags and Indian ghosts, and having spent a year or two in the Scottish Highlands, he had more acquaintance than most with picturesque superstition" ("Lord John and the Plague of Zombies" 321).

In Jamaica, there is more than a trace of Southern Gothic, as the air is boiling hot and the slaves on the plantations seethe with rebellion. Smells of "sweat, seasickness, and sewage" linger (309). In every scene, the air is hot and oppressive. With ominous shadows and unexpected passageways, the story begins in the governor's "old wreck" of a mansion (309). There are even sheer muslin curtains and candles, with bats fluttering outside. A giant spider lands on John's head, and after he kills it, a slave tells him the spider's bite is invariably lethal. In the middle of the night, someone emerges from the dark to strangle Lord John in his sleep. He stabs. "It screamed, releasing a blast of foul breath directly into his face, then turned and rushed for the French doors, bursting them open in a shower of glass and flying cotton" (323). It smells of death and Lord John is chillingly sure his attacker "had almost certainly come from a recent grave" (324).

Zombies are a popular trend in young adult paranormal fiction, now that vampires and werewolves are played out. *Beautiful Creatures*, *Feed*, and *iZombie* head the list, though many others fill the shelves. They are, of course, the most well-known monsters of the West Indies tradition, so they fit in smoothly with the characters' travels there in *Voyager* and just beforehand.

As always, Lord John's story begins with a murder, this time of Geillis's latest husband. Lord John meets Geillis, who has made herself a zombie army, or so it appears. Geillis explains that a *houngan* has taught her to make zombies—she gives a person blowfish poison and partially buries them with a rotting corpse. When the victim awakes, he thinks he is dead, and will obey orders until he wastes away and actually dies ("Lord John and the Plague of Zombies" 337). "While this is a scientific experiment, done with drugs rather than magic, it contains the horror of having one's body co-opted and placed in a state of living death" (Frankel 174–175). A zombie bites Lord John, further filling the story with body horror.

In Haitian Vodou, zombies were corpses raised by a *bokor* (sorcerer) to be his slaves, as they lacked free will. In modern times, zombies have been rationalized as fanciful tales, as individuals with schizophrenia, or as a metaphor for the evils of slavery in Haiti. Wade Davis, a Harvard ethnobotanist, had a different theory with which Gabaldon is clearly familiar. As he published in *The Serpent and the Rainbow* (1985) and *Passage of Darkness: The Ethnobiology of the Haitian Zombie*

(1988), he believed a living person could be transformed into a zombie by introducing special powders into the bloodstream: The first included tetrodotoxin (TTX) from a blowfish and the second, dissociative drugs such as datura. These would unite to place a person at the sorcerer's mercy. The scientific community was doubtful of Davis's story, especially since tetrodotoxin produces paralysis and death but not a trance state. Nonetheless, the theory earned attention at the time and has been smoothly integrated into Gabaldon's fantasy novellas, in which magic is frequently revealed as science and hoax [Frankel 175].

The story still retains more than a touch of the inexplicable, with *loas* and the voudou religion. With skill with herbs and poisons, the historical Obeah man or shaman was said to be able to "render someone invincible, resuscitate the dead, cure all diseases, protect a man from the consequences of his crimes, and cause great harm to anyone he wished" (Giraldo). As Giraldo adds, "The practice of Obeah is the belief that one can use certain spirits or supernatural agents to work harm to the living, or to call them off from such mischief." In the short story, the local Obeah man has laid a curse on the governor and is protecting the escaped slaves of the island, leaving Lord John the touchy task of negotiating a peace.

The Obeah man tells Lord John that a snake is riding on his shoulders. Geillis adds that some of the *loas*, or angelic voudou spirits, are snakes and asks John if he's been dreaming of them. Later, in "The Space Between," Madame Fabienne describes her pet snake, possibly the same one, as a *mystere*, or *loa*, "a spirit, one who is an intermediary between the Bondye and us. Bondye is *le bon Dieu*, of course" (175–176). At the book's climax, John must pick up a deadly African krait. While this act should kill him, the *loa* on his shoulders appears to protect him. After he is seen to survive, the headman rewards him by taking the snake *loa* from his shoulders, adding, "You have carried him long enough, I think" (368). Once again, the paranormal elements abound, though this time they may be understood as real, if the reader desires.

Fantasy

Both fantasy and historical fiction are built upon the world the author creates for the reader: exploring its environment, explaining its rules, and introducing characters that fit within such a world. The only difference is that historical fiction uses the past as a starting point, while fantasy relies upon an author's imagination to create a new world or put a new spin on our own world. When the author reinvents the past with fantastical elements, it gives the novel more opportunities for creativity [Rabey 40].

If ghosts and succubae are paranormal, then high fantasy is the province of the glamorous, ethereal fairy court. *The Scottish Prisoner* novel (2011), unlike the others, is half-told from Jamie's perspective, making it more closely linked to the *Outlander* series (also indicated by its stand-out title and cover among the Lord John stories). It has a heavy fantasy component as Jamie beholds the Wild Hunt, vicious rogue fairies.

The Wild Hunt, in folklore, rode through the heavens, hunting animals and sometimes people. Gabaldon adds in her Author's Notes for the book: "In some forms of these stories, the horde consists of faeries, in others, the 'hunt' consists of the souls of the dead. Either way, it isn't something you want to meet on a dark night—or a moonlit one, either." Gabaldon then quotes Yeats' "The Hosting of the Sidhe":

> *The host is riding from Knocknarea*
> *And over the grave of Clooth-na-Bare;*
> *Caoilte tossing his burning hair,*
> *And Niamh calling Away, come away:*
> *Empty your heart of its mortal dream.*
> *The winds awaken, the leaves whirl round,*
> *Our cheeks are pale, our hair is unbound,*
> *Our breasts are heaving our eyes are agleam,*
> *Our arms are waving our lips are apart;*
> *And if any gaze on our rushing band,*
> *We come between him and the deed of his hand,*
> *We come between him and the hope of his heart.*
> *The host is rushing 'twixt night and day,*
> *And where is there hope or deed as fair?*
> *Caoilte tossing his burning hair,*
> *And Niamh calling Away, come away.*

This of course is as fantastical as it gets.

Later in the novel, Jamie tells the chilling story of seeing the Wild Hunt after he killed a deer but hadn't yet said the prayer. He jumped in the river and hid, explaining, "Ye dinna want to look upon them.... If ye do, they can call ye to them. Cast their glamour upon you. And then ye're lost" (ch. 28). In the morning, he found that someone had taken the head and entrails and a haunch—"the huntsman's share."

At the climax of the story, an Irish Jacobite kills himself and scribes the word *Teind* in his blood on the wall, offering the fairies his soul to pay their tribute for failing to put Prince Charlie on the throne. Gabaldon adds in her afterword, "The idea of the *teind*—the tithe to hell—is from 'Tam Lin,' and likely a word that would have resonance to people who lived by a code of honor, to whom betrayal and treason would carry a heavy price."

> Jamie buries the man but witnesses the Wild Hunt yet again. He hears Horns. Like the blowing of trumpets, but trumpets such as he had never heard, and the hair rippled on his body.
> *They're coming.* He didn't pause to ask himself who it was that was coming but

hastily put on his breeks and coat. It didn't occur to him to flee, and for an instant he wondered why not, for the very air around him quivered with strangeness. *Because they're not coming for you,* the calm voice within his mind replied. *Stand still.*

... They were closer now, close enough to make out faces and the details of their clothing. They were dressed plain, for the most part, dressed in drab and home-spun, save for one woman dressed in white—*why is her skirt no spattered wi' the mud?* And he saw with a little thrill of horror that her feet did not touch the ground; none of them did—who carried in one hand a knife with a long, curved blade and a glinting hilt [*The Scottish Prisoner,* ch. 37].

The *Outlander* main series has other moments of fantasy, as Claire stumbles upon the Loch Ness Monster. On the show, Claire insists witches, fairies, and demons can't exist. However, they were considered an accepted part of life in the Highlands at the time, as even Jamie, in the same episode, refuses to tempt fate "by making light of Old Nick in his very own kirkyard" (E103). Geillis adds, "Have you never found yourself in a situation that has no earthly explanation?" (E103). After the standing stones, Claire can say nothing. The stones themselves of course are the most fantastical element, transporting characters to far-distant times. The time travel borders on science fiction, with a heavy dollop of folklore, adding a multifaceted nature to the science fiction-fantasy nuances of the epic.

Along with all these other genres, there are traces of real science fiction in *Outlander.* The story was inspired from the first by *Doctor Who*—perhaps the most famous and longest running time travel show—and specifically the episode "War Games" with the Second Doctor (Patrick Troughton) and his beloved companion, Jamie MacCrimmon (Frazer Hines). While Jamie is a kilted young Highlander recruited from just after the Battle of Culloden, he spends the episode debating gender roles with a fiery English ambulance driver. Gabaldon explains:

In this particular scene, Jamie McCrimmon and Lady Jennifer, a WWI ambulance driver (hence demonstrably no one's delicate blossom), are somewhere with the TARDIS, but without the Doctor, who was presumably in considerable danger elsewhere/when. Jamie declares that he must go rescue the Doctor, tells Lady Jennifer to wait there, and heads for the TARDIS—followed closely by Lady Jennifer. When he perceives that she plans to come, too, he insists that she must stay behind, ostensibly because someone needs to tell their other companions what's going on. Lady Jennifer greets this piece of feeble persuasion with the scorn it deserves, demanding, "You just want me to stay behind because I'm a woman, isn't that right?" To which our courageous young Scotsman (who is considerably shorter than Lady Jennifer) replies, "Well, no, I—that is ... you.... I ... well ... yes!" Now, I found this demonstration of pig-headed male gallantry riveting ["The Doctor's Balls" Kindle Locations 334–349].

On the show, Frazer Hines plays a warden of Wentworth Prison in homage. In another nod, Brianna jokes with a family friend about how much she wishes she had a TARDIS instead of the standing stones (*Written in My Own Heart's Blood*, ch. 97).

However, the story has greater links to science fiction than the inspiration for a single character. Gabaldon went on to formulate complex rules of time travel, something rare in time travel histories or romances. Most often in similar series, a character steps through standing stones (a portal, a magic mirror…), arrives, and returns the same way. There are no pages of laws and exceptions, it's simply "one of those mysteries," an inexplicable moment needed to drive the character's predicament. Gabaldon's decision to lay out all the rules and theories of time travel, then have Roger and Brianna do it themselves in a journal, emphasizes the strategic thought needed for proper science fiction worldbuilding. Her article "The Gabaldon Theory of Time Travel," actually appeared in the *Journal of Transfigural Mathematics* in 2010, emphasizing its scientific validity.

She also keeps an eye on time travel in popular science fiction series, as she comments, "The most successful stories of this type most often involve either a resolution or a process in which the main character ends up as his or her own ancestor and/or descendant. The two best-known classics of this type are Robert Heinlein's *By His Bootstraps*, and David Gerrold's *The Man Who Folded Himself*" (*Outlandish Companion*, 335). Thus she writes her time travel adventures with full awareness of other works in her genre.

Final Thoughts

This survey, already quite long, has admittedly left out the other short stories in *Outlander*'s world. These are unquestionably worth a read, even more than the Lord John novels, as they're more firmly tied to the main characters and their adventures. "The Space Between" (2013) appeared in the speculative fiction anthology *The Mad Scientist's Guide to World Domination* and follows the further adventures of Master Raymond and St. Germain, while Joan McKimmie and Michael Murray decide their destinies apart or together. There's more than a trace of straight-up fantasy, as St. Germain returns from death, tracking Raymond amid his crystals, auras, and standing stones. "Virgins" (2013) published in *Dangerous Women*, is a straight-up buddy-comedy prequel of Jamie and Ian's mercenary days before the beginning of *Outlander*, in which a clever heroine gets the better of them both. "A Leaf on the Wind of All Hallows" (2010) in *Songs of Love and Death*, is a romance of course, blending time travel and gothic with the tragedy of Roger's parents. It also offers insight into Frank, the wartime spymaster. All bring additional genres into the main series as they spin off into secondary characters' lives.

So what are the Lord John novels? Speculative? Paranormal mysteries? Historical military fiction? As with the *Outlander* novels, it seems the best one can do is file them as multi-genre or genre mash-ups. And of course, wait eagerly for more.

WORKS CITED

Bethune, Brian. "*Outlander* Gives *Game of Thrones* a Run for Its Money." *Maclean's* 12 June 2014. http://www.macleans.ca/culture/books/outlander-gives-game-of-thrones-a-run-for-its-money.

Foster, Jordan. "Some Like It Mild: Cozy Mysteries." *Publishers Weekly* 4 May 2009. http://www.publishersweekly.com/pw/print/20090504/4567-some-like-it-mild-cozy-mysteries.html.

Frankel, Valerie Estelle. *The Symbolism and Sources of Outlander.* Jefferson, NC: McFarland, 2014.

Gabaldon, Diana. "The Custom of the Army." *Warriors.* Eds. George R.R. Martin and Gardner Dozois. New York: Tor, 2010. 225–284.

_____. "The Doctor's Balls." *Chicks Unravel Time: Women Journey Through Every Season of Doctor Who.* Eds. Deborah Stanish and L.M. Myles. USA: Mad Norwegian Press, 2012. Kindle Edition.

_____. "FAQ." *Diana Gabaldon's Official Webpage.* 2014. http://www.dianagabaldon.com/resources/faq.

_____. "A Leaf on the Wind of All Hallows." *Songs of Love and Death.* Eds. George R.R. Martin and Gardner Dozois, USA: Gallery Books, 2010. 429–468.

_____. *Lord John and the Brotherhood of the Blade.* New York: Random House, 2011.

_____. "Lord John and the Haunted Soldier." *Lord John and the Hand of Devils.* New York: Random House, 2007. 161–302.

_____. "Lord John and the Hellfire Club." *Lord John and the Hand of Devils.* New York: Random House, 2007. 3–39.

_____. "Lord John and the Plague of Zombies." *Down These Strange Streets.* Ed. George R.R. Martin and Gardner Dozois. New York: Penguin, 2011.

_____. *Lord John and the Private Matter.* New York: Random House, 2003.

_____. "Lord John and the Succubus." *Lord John and the Hand of Devils.* New York: Random House, 2007. 45–156.

_____. *Outlander.* New York: Bantam Dell, 1992.

_____. *The Outlandish Companion.* New York: Delacorte Press, 1999.

_____. *The Scottish Prisoner.* New York: Random House, 2011.

_____. "The Space Between." *The Mad Scientist's Guide to World Domination: Original Short Fiction for the Modern Evil Genius.* Ed. John Joseph Adams. New York: Tor, 2013. 161–243.

_____. "Virgins." *Dangerous Women.* Eds. George R.R. Martin and Gardner Dozois. New York: Tor, 2013. 459–532.

Giraldo, Alexander. "Obeah: The Ultimate Resistance." *Slave Resistance: A Caribbean Study.* University of Miami. http://scholar.library.miami.edu/slaves/Religion/religion.html.

Hale, Mike. "A Highland Fling Would Not Be Unexpected Here." *New York Times* 1 Aug 2014. http://www.nytimes.com/2014/08/02/arts/television/outlander-a-starz-series-adapted-from-the-novels.html?_r=0.

Koerner, Brendan. "*A Breath of Snow and Ashes*: The Romance Novel at the Top of the New York Times Best-Seller List." *Slate* 2005. http://www.slate.com/articles/arts/number_1/2005/10/a_breath_of_snow_and_ashes.html.

Martinez, Juan. "Words of War: Military History and Memoirs." *Publishers Weekly* 24 Aug 2009. http://www.publishersweekly.com/pw/by-topic/new-titles/adult-announcements/article/5092-words-of-war-military-history-and-memoirs.html.

Moore, Ronald D., and Anne Kenney. "The Way Out." *Outlander.* Dir. Brian Kelly. Starz Entertainment, LLC. 2014.

Rabey, Melissa. "Historical Fiction Mash-Ups: Broadening Appeal by Mixing Genres." *Young Adult Library Services* 9.1 (2010): 38–41. Academic Search Complete.

Thomson, Douglass H. *A Glossary of Literary Gothic Terms.* Saylor.org http://saylor.org/site/wp-content/uploads/2012/05/engl403-1.3.1-A-Glossary-of-Literary-Gothic-Terms.pdf.

Half-Ghosts and Their Legacy for Claire, Jamie and Roger

Stella Murillo

In *Drums of Autumn* there is a Cherokee concept introduced by Stephen Bonnet, that of an asgina ageli.

> Asgina ageli is a term that the red savages employ—the Cherokee of the mountains; I heard it from one I had as a guide one time. It means "half-ghost," one who should have died by right, but yet remains on the earth; a woman who survives a mortal illness, a man fallen into his enemies' hands who escapes. They say an asgina ageli has one foot on the earth and the other in the spirit world. He can talk to the spirits and see the Nunnahee—the Little People [*Drums of Autumn*, ch. 2].

In the *Outlander* series, three main characters match the description of a half-ghost. In some cases, there are certain animal associations with them that show their mystical and "ghostly" characteristics. However, it is not clear in the definition of a half-ghost how the communication with the spiritual realm is achieved. Furthermore, being in a dire situation could be a life-changing experience that could detrimentally affect the psyche. Jamie, Claire and Roger encounter ghosts throughout the series. However, most of the time the nature of the ghosts does not seem to be supernatural but psychological.

Claire has experienced several events in which she has been close to losing her life. Some of them are Malva's poisoning attempt, the miscarriage of her first daughter, Faith, and the injury on her arm inflicted by a pirate. The most prominent instance of Claire communicating with an actual ghostly entity is when she encounters Otter-Tooth's specter. His ghost is described as a fire-carrier, a nocturnal spirit that goes about with a light. The Cherokee avoid this entity since it is relatively unknown and considered dangerous. However, the fire-carrier moves away when approached. Claire is initially scared when meeting Otter-Tooth's ghost until she realizes that she has had some sort of communication with him.

> Nothing moved, no words were spoken. But quite clearly the thought formed in my mind, in a voice that was not my own.
> *That's enough,* it said [*Drums of Autumn,* ch. 23].

Otter-Tooth's ghost behaves in a totally unexpected manner. He is friendly as opposed to dangerous, and he also approaches her hideout instead of moving away from her. In fact, he is looking specifically for her. He has come to the realization that Claire is a time-traveler like he is, and even gives her his own opal talisman so that she can travel back to her time. Claire discovers Otter-Tooth's skull and gemstone before encountering his specter, and starts talking to him without realizing that she is actually giving away information about herself. She analyzes the skeletal remains and describes aloud her conclusions in a conversational manner, the decapitation of Otter-Tooth for being disliked. Forensic analysis was not a standard practice in the eighteenth century, emphasizing her displacement and thus kinship with the spirit. In a further anachronism, she proceeds with the recitation of poetry written by John Keats who was born in 1795. In fact the fire-carrier appears during her recitation of "Ode on a Grecian Urn."

Of interest is the mental communication that Claire establishes with the wisewoman Nayawenne when they meet for the very first time. "I had the odd feeling that she was talking to me—and I to her—without the exchange of a single spoken word," Claire thinks (*Drums of Autumn,* ch. 20). It resembles her subsequent communication with Otter-Tooth—the only difference is that Nayawenne is alive during this interaction. This resemblance foreshadows Nayawenne's death.

After losing her friend, Claire takes hold of her amulet. According to Pollyanne, a former slave adopted by the Tuscarora, Nayawenne's ghost walks with Claire since the amulet attracts the shaman's ghost (*Drums of Autumn,* ch. 53).

This ability to communicate with the spirit realm has become prominent in Claire with aging. In *Voyager,* Ishmael informs her that she will be able to perform magic successfully once her menstrual periods stop (ch. 61). Similarly Nayawenne confirms that Claire will find her full power once her whole hair is white (*Drums of Autumn,* ch. 20). However, not all of the ghosts that she encounters are real. In some of her interactions, Claire does not see their spectral forms. Everything is achieved via sensations, physical contact and thought processes. These interactions also share a particular commonality: they happen when Claire is about to fall asleep or about to wake. In fact, they seem to be hypnagogic or hypnopompic experiences, hallucinatory events that take place in the intermediate states of falling asleep or waking up respectively.

One of these hypnagogic experiences occurs when Claire communicates with her deceased husband, Frank, after the birth of her grandson. At the time, Jamie is concerned about Jemmy's parentage and cannot sleep. In order to quiet him down, Claire uses a phrase that Frank used to say for soothing her and Brianna when worried: "Sufficient unto the day is the evil thereof" (*Drums of Autumn*, ch. 64). This phrase comes as a thought to Claire and leads her to ask Frank whether he knows the baby's sex. Of course, there is no reply, but the end result is that Claire relaxes and falls asleep. Time is nonexistent in this form of communication. It is possible for a half-ghost to establish contact with any entity from the past or future since it seems to be all in the mind. Claire continues communicating with Frank prior to Brianna's wedding after waking up one morning at the Mount Helicon Gathering.

> *Shouldn't I come to see her married?*
> I couldn't tell whether the words had formed themselves in my thoughts, or whether they—and that kiss—were merely the product of my own subconscious [*The Fiery Cross*, ch. 1].

There is not only communication but also physical contact. Tactile phenomena associated with the hypnagogic or hypnopompic states include the feeling of being touched, buzzing in the head, sudden spasm and others (Mavromatis 36). Hypnagogia is usually characterized by vivid images, described as 3D movies (Mavromatis 29), which is probably one of the reasons why they are more like hallucinations. Claire's hypnagogic experiences do not consist of images most of the time as opposed to Jamie's. She seems to hear Frank's voice in her head, something brought up by a memory.

> [...] the transition from the waking to the dreaming state is effected through "the memory of sounds," such as when, while falling asleep, we think of a conversation between ourselves and some other person who then gradually takes on a vivid appearance and thus constitutes the first element of a dream [Mavromatis 92–93].

When Claire is locked at Sheriff Tolliver's jail in New Bern, she is worried about Jamie's fate so she cannot fall asleep. The phrase that Frank used to say to relax her comes all of a sudden as a thought, and then she starts having an imaginary conversation with him.

> Imagination or not, the thought had succeeded in wrenching my attention off the single-minded track of worry.... The urge to talk to him. The need to escape into conversation, even if one-sided ... and imaginary.
> *No. I won't use you that way*, I thought, a little sadly. *Not right that I should only think of you when I need distraction, and not for your own sake* [*A Breath of Snow and Ashes*, ch. 90].

In this interaction Claire acknowledges that her communication with Frank is in her mind, and that the ghost is not real. It also shows Claire's feelings of guilt in regards to him. She is basically using him in order to ease her concern about Jamie. Frank's continued presence in Claire's mind could be related to his sudden death. There were things in their relationship that required sincerity and clarification. However, there was never an opportunity for them to be reconciled. These hauntings are associated with guilt: "It might have been me—my fault, I mean," I said at last, into the silence. "I couldn't forget, you see. If I could … it might have been different" (*Drums of Autumn*, ch. 47).

Claire thinks she is to be blamed for the failure in her first marriage, if not fully at least partially. She basically stops loving Frank after falling in love with Jamie, whom she has been unable to forget after many years. She probably attributes Frank's infidelity and unhappiness in their relationship to being her fault even though she gave him the choice to leave her.

Frank is not the only one about whom Claire feels guilty. Tom Christie and his niece, Malva, are also some of the characters that Claire sees in one of her visions. She blames herself for Tom's confession of killing his niece, a lie he fabricated since he wanted Claire safe and free. In regards to Malva, Claire has mixed feelings. She sees her as a promiscuous girl but also as a smart apprentice. Her guilt seems more associated with being unable to help Malva or find the man responsible for her pregnancy and murder and with the inability to save her child. Of note is the fact that Tom Christie is not dead at the time in which this vision occurs. Claire also feels guilty about killing Geillis. This is probably associated to the fact that Geillis sacrifices herself by proclaiming Claire's innocence in the trial at Cranesmuir.

> Sometimes I thought of her, of Geillis, when I was alone in the forest. Sometimes I thought I heard her voice behind me, and turned around swiftly, but saw no more than the hemlock branches, soughing in the wind. But now and then I felt her eyes on me, green and bright as the springtime wood [*Drums of Autumn*, ch. 45].

These cases demonstrate that Claire is conscious and awake when having hypnagogic hallucinations, even though when she sees Tom, Malva and Frank she is extremely tired, lying in bed with Jamie. The case in which she experiences hearing Geillis' voice is puzzling but can still be attributed to hypnagogia. In fact, some subjects are able to perform complex fine motor acts and have a conversation while having a hypnagogic experience (Mavromatis 28).

Another entity that Claire perceives in the hypnagogic state is Faith. In *The Fiery Cross*, Claire tries to visualize how hard it has been for Jocasta to lose all her daughters while reading Dr. Rawlings' recordings. As a result, she starts thinking about Brianna and Jemmy, and her stillborn daughter, Faith.

> How did a woman bear such loss? I had done it, myself, and still had not idea. It had been long time, and yet still, now and then, I would wake in the night,

feeling a child's warm weight sleeping on my breast, her breath warm on my neck. My hand rose and touched my shoulder, curved as though the child's head lay there [ch. 96].

This is not the only case in which Claire perceives Faith's presence. The event in which Claire meets Adso is of special note. Claire is sleeping when she first experiences the gentle sensation of Adso's small paws on her body. She feels the cat kneading her breasts. While dreaming, she confuses this physical contact with that of nursing a child until the cat bites her.

This scene foreshadows her future encounter with the abandoned newborn Alicia Beardsley, who latches onto her nipple to nurse. Claire describes this experience as "shocking in its familiarity" (*The Fiery Cross*, ch. 31), which could refer to her remembering nursing Brianna as a baby or having frequent hypnagogic sensations. Claire's immediate body response to Alicia's hunger or search for comfort might be evidence that Faith has been connected to her for a long time regardless of the nature of the contact, real or not. Claire even acknowledges that Faith is real and that she perceives her nearness whenever she touches a baby (*The Fiery Cross*, ch. 32). Jamie establishes the association between Alicia and Faith when he offers Claire to raise the child as their own.

"I saw ye with the wean, Sassenach, riding. Ye've a great tenderness about ye always—but when I saw ye so, wi' the bairn tumbling about beneath your cloak, it—I remembered, how it was, how ye looked, when you carried Faith" [*The Fiery Cross*, ch. 32].

In regards to Jamie, the old lady who read his palm when he was a student in Paris revealed to him that he was going to have nine lives like a cat before dying. Significant and life-changing events include his escape from Wentworth Prison, the healing from a bayonet injury incurred at Culloden, and his recovery from a snakebite. To understand the nature of the ghosts that haunt Jamie, an analysis of his out-of-body experiences is required. In fact, the ghosts that haunt Jamie are not real but imaginary.

The way in which Jamie communicates is through visions and images based on memory, sometimes induced by certain "Places." The event in which Jamie meets Adso details one of these visions. While riding Gideon, he comes to a particular location that he refers to as the "Place." The author capitalizes this word to give a special meaning to it. Both Jamie and the horse are calm and charmed by this "Place." Jamie has also encountered similar "Places" before.

He thought of such places in a way that had no words, only recognizing one when he came to it. He might have called it holy, save that the feel of such a place had nothing to do with church or saint. It was simply a place he belonged to be, and that was sufficient, though he preferred to be alone when he found one. He let the reins go slack across the horse's neck. Not even a thrawn-minded creature like Gideon would give trouble here, he felt [*The Fiery Cross*, ch. 18].

It is at this location in which Jamie has "a vision of his mother, one of the small vivid portraits that his mind hoarded..." (*The Fiery Cross*, ch. 18). This is not the only portrait or image that Jamie has stored in his mind. In *Drums of Autumn*, Jamie takes his son to the Tuscarora to prevent him from getting measles. There is a scene in which he is watching Willie, and that particular moment gets stamped in his mind for the rest of his life.

But these—the still moments, as he called them to himself—they came with no warning, to print a random image of the most common things inside his brain, indelible. They were like the photographs that Claire had brought him, save that the moments carried with them more than vision [ch. 27].

He acknowledges that he has had moments like that in the past, images of loved ones "fixed in his mind like an insect in amber" (ch. 27). The different visions Jamie has are memory-based. When having the vision of his mother at the "Place," he feels contented. There is no physical contact or exchange of words in this communication though. Afterwards he says a prayer and spills some whiskey on the ground. Then he finds Adso, gets bitten by him, and his finger starts to bleed. He decides to do an offering of his blood to the spirits of this "Place" for the gift he has received. The whole scene is a mystical experience, and somehow ritualistic and syncretic. The offering is reminiscent of the Gaelic wedding vows in which blood is withdrawn, an old practice, "pagan" in the series but fictional in the real world. The gift given to him is most likely the cat, even though the vision of his mother cannot be disregarded. The new acquisition is eventually named after a monk whose writing his mother enjoyed reading, Adso of Melk. Overall the whole scene is a representation of what Jamie is, a Roman Catholic but with ingrained superstitions and old traditions. Due to the association between Adso and a young infant in Claire's hypnagogic experience, the cat could actually be Faith reincarnated in animal form. Jamie considers Adso a gift given to him and also one that he plans to give Claire. The cat represents a gift to both of them in exactly the same way their children are. In *Drums of Autumn*, he regards his living daughter as a gift: "Brianna was his blood, and his flesh as well. An unspoken promise kept to his own parents; his gift to Claire, and hers to him" (ch. 44).

Jamie performs a similar ritual later at the White Spring when invoking Dougal MacKenzie. This ritual consists of Jamie obsessively washing himself in preparation. This is followed by a blood offering that is dropped on the boulder at the head of the pool. The following description from Claire's point of view suggests that something supernatural is occurring due to the change in the state of nature:

Jamie said something aloud in Gaelic. It sounded like a challenge—or perhaps a greeting. The words seemed vaguely familiar—but there was no one there; the clearing was empty. The air felt colder, as though the light had dimmed; a cloud crossing the face of the sun, I thought, and looked up—but there were no clouds; the sky was clear. Jemmy moved suddenly in my arms, startled, and I clutched him tighter, willing to make no sound.

Then the air stirred, the cold faded, and my sense of apprehension passed. Jamie hadn't moved. Now the tension went out of him too, and his shoulder relaxed... [*The Fiery Cross*, ch. 22].

The White Spring is a "Place" to Jamie. There is a resemblance between the blood ritual performed at this location and the one done at the other "Place" where Adso was found. The only difference is that Jamie may consider the White Spring holy, since he carved a cross on the boulder, bringing to mind the mix of ancient practices with Christian ones. Another difference is that he does a blood offering to Dougal instead of unnamed or unknown spirits. It is a sort of a pact. The end result of this vision or interaction is a soothing moment for Jamie. Furthermore, he reveals to Claire that he has made peace with Dougal long time ago, implying that he has had some interaction with his uncle's ghost before. Since this event is described from Claire's point of view, it is hard to determine whether Jamie has a vision of Dougal or just some form of communication without actually seeing him. Since Jamie stores vivid images in his mind, it is possible that he saw and created an apparition of Dougal. What is conclusive at this stage is that pleasant visions or mental images based on memory seem to be induced by particular "Places."

Jamie uses his repertoire of vivid images stored in his memory for his out-of-body experiences.

it makes more sense to see the world of the OBE (out-of-body experience) as a world of the imagination, or cognitive map. And so to my mind this makes sense of all that has been said about the astral world. For it is a "thought-created world," a "world of images," "a world of illusion" [Blackmore 169].

However, research findings demonstrate that people who have out-of-body experiences have less vivid imagery than average (Blackmore 170). Exceptions to these findings do occur though. Blackmore details the case of a female subject whose experiences resemble Jamie's. She had a remarkable repertoire of imagery, and used to be troubled by vivid apparitions of her father, who had tried to rape her as a child. She used to perceive her father's smell, voice, and see the indentations left in the bed every time he sat on it. As a treatment, she was suggested to make her father appear for herself. After a while she was able to produce and control apparitions not only of her father, but also of her friends, relatives and of herself. She was able to go into this double or astral body and see things from that position. Once inside the double's body, she could revert to any time in her past. In this experiment, the out-of-body experience is induced, a case in which one's consciousness is transferred to the created image of oneself (171–172). Similarly Jamie is able to create not only images of loved ones but also of Jack Randall.

Distressing apparitions are associated with memory lapses, a characteristic that both Jamie and Claire share. At River Run, before meeting Flora MacDonald, Claire reminisces about the different historical figures that she has met. However, when she thinks about Louis of France, she has a vivid recollection of the intimate contact she had with him. She realizes that she has somehow repressed that unpleasant memory. However, this event has come back as a flashback, causing her to feel uncomfortable and have what looks like a panic attack. There is also an external factor bringing this vivid recollection to Claire's mind, a briar rose. The smell of this flower reminds her of the rose oil that Louis applied to her private parts before having intercourse. It seems that certain olfactory stimuli remind Claire of unpleasant events. The scent of lavender, Black Jack's signature scent, seems to have a similar effect on Jamie. Following her encounter with Louis's ghost, Jamie offers Claire whisky. The smell of it reminds her of the night she and Jamie got drunk after her rescue from Hodgepile and his band of criminals. In this particular case, the smell of any alcoholic beverage brings the memories back.

Jamie's memory lapses are associated with Culloden and a particular ghost, Black Jack. Events from Culloden resurface in Jamie's dreams. Claire explains:

> I knew that small scenes from that day came back to him now and again in his sleep, fragments of nightmare—but whether it was from trauma, injury or simple force of will, the Battle of Culloden was lost to him—or had been, until now [*The Fiery Cross*, ch. 7].

Culloden represents negativity to Jamie. It is one of the reasons why he had to send Claire back to the twentieth century besides the fact of her pregnancy. It marks the end of Highland culture and lifestyle—the clan system in which he grew up was basically eliminated. Furthermore, the battle ended in the slaughter of his own companions, including his godfather, Murtagh. As a result, he does not remember performing a heroic and noble act during the battle, the saving of young Archie Hayes from one of the Murchison twins. Unpleasant memories undermine positive ones.

Associated with Culloden is the ghost of Jack Randall. Jamie does not even remember whether he killed him or not. In *A Breath of Snow and Ashes*, Jamie has a dream in which Black Jack asks him to kill him. This dream is cryptic. While this is an out-of-character request from Black Jack, it is something that Jamie would have said after being rescued from Wentworth. Its possible meaning is Jamie's unsatisfied desire for revenge, transferred to the apparition of his deepest enemy. In *Drums of Autumn*, he tells Brianna that he meant to take back his honor, his manhood by killing Black Jack in the duel in Paris (ch. 48). After waking up after this dream, Jamie finds himself expecting to meet Jack Randall. However, he starts to ensure that the environment around him is real. The book relates, "He set his hand on the bedstead, comforted by the solid wood. Sometimes when he woke, the dream stayed with him, and he felt the real world ghostly, faint around him. Sometimes he feared he was a ghost" (*A Breath of Snow and Ashes*, ch. 31).

This passage implies that Jamie probably sees Black Jack while having false awakenings, a dream within a dream. In this scene he has an urge to wake Claire up to verify whether his body is tangible to her. This testing of the physical world is evidence that Jamie frequently has lucid dreams, those ones in which the conscious mind tells the dreamer that everything is fake; the subject becomes aware of the dream even though everything looks real. Jamie could also be having a spontaneous out-of-body experience in many of his dreams. It seems that sometimes he experiences dreams inside the astral projection of himself without being aware of it, probably the reason why he believes he is a ghost at certain times and unable to touch things. Blackmore explains the possibility that spontaneous out-of-body experiences tend to occur while a person is having a lucid dream (116). Experimental research has demonstrated that lucid dreams occur in REM sleep, which means they are true dreams. A person would not be able to talk or move anything since the muscles are paralyzed during dreaming sleep. This could be an explanation to why things cannot be moved in OBEs (118), and Jamie's reason for testing the world upon waking up. If Jamie is fully awake when seeing Black Jack's ghost, he could be in a hypnagogic or hypnopompic state. In fact, hypnagogic images may persist after awakening.

> On emerging from sleep a person sometimes opens his eyes to find that a dream he has been having continues, and that having shifted his attention to an object in the real world of his room the dream imagery is somewhat interrupted but resumes its full strength as his attention is removed from the immediate surroundings [Mavromatis 36–37].

The research literature reports cases of the hypnopompic variety in which a subject sees "ghostly" images after waking up. A particular report consists of a subject having a vivid dream about an acquaintance, and seeing this same person standing at bedside immediately after waking up (Mavromatis 37). Hypnagogic apparitions are not restricted to just one ghost. One can witness a party in a bedroom with people dancing and live music (Mavromatis 39). This is similar to Claire seeing the "ghosts" of Frank, Tom and Malva at the same time. Furthermore, out-of-body experiences are related to hypnagogia, initial dreams, lucid dreams, and false awakenings to the point that their distinction is blurry (Mavromatis 98).

Another way in which Jamie remembers the events at Culloden is by consumption of a psychoactive substance, tobacco. When Bird, a Cherokee chief, asks him about how many he killed at Culloden, he is unable to answer. The movement of his fingers is an indicator that he is sure of killing fourteen men whose faces he does not remember. His inability to answer is related to the fact that he does not know whether he killed Jack Randall. The possible inducer of memories in this scene could be the smoke of the pipe he is sharing with Bird and Alexander Cameron.

> The smoke burned in his chest, behind his eyes, and for an instant he tasted the bitter smoke of cannon fire, not sweet tobacco. He saw—he saw—Alistair MacAllister, dead at his feet among the red-clothed bodies... [*A Breath of Snow and Ashes*, ch. 44].

This vivid memory could be a hallucination caused by a combination of two factors, the inhalation of tobacco and Jamie's sensitive mind. The species of tobacco used by the Cherokee at that period of time is *Nicotiana rustica* (Winter 18), as opposed to *Nicotiana tabacum*, which is employed today for the production of cigarettes. Indeed, altered states of consciousness and hallucinations are attributed to *N. rustica* when ingested in high amounts. The preference for this particular species of tobacco is related to the spiritual beliefs of the Amerindian population, in which dissociative states or out-of-body experiences facilitate communication with the spirits (von Gernet 66). Furthermore, smoking to achieve spiritual powers was not restricted to shamans since pipes are a conspicuous feature in the archaeological record (von Gernet 66), and many aboriginals used to constantly have pipes in their mouths as noted by European observers (von Gernet 68).

After recalling the death of Alistair MacAllister at Culloden, Jamie has an out-of-body experience, in which he feels "somehow to rise a little way above his body..." (*A Breath of Snow and Ashes*, ch. 44). In this scene, Bird's mother, Calls-in-the-Forest, massages his head and encourages him to talk, creating a comforting atmosphere. Being probably still under the effect of tobacco, Jamie starts remembering Culloden and sees two shades of Black Jack. Jamie's comments at this stage are revealing: "I hold to no evil in my heart," he said, hearing his voice come slow, from a long ways off. "This evil does not touch me. More may come, but not this. Not here. Not now" (*A Breath of Snow and Ashes*, ch. 44). Jamie has probably come to the realization that Black Jack is only in his mind and that his hauntings could be associated with his unfulfilled desire for revenge. Instead of fighting Black Jack, he evades him.

Based on his mystical experiences at his "Places," Jamie likes to be in a serene state of mind. In order to be fully at peace he needs to forgive Jack Randall, which is terribly hard for him to do. There is a possibility that he might be able to do it since he was capable of forgiving and making peace with Dougal and worked briefly with Black Jack at the scene of Alex Randall's death. At the same time, the realization that Black Jack's ghost is his own creation could be a reason for Jamie to consciously start controlling the apparitions he produces. This OBE is drug-induced and it differs from those ones that take place in REM sleep while the subject might be having a lucid dream. Induced experimental OBEs occur in stage 1 sleep as opposed to REM sleep. They occur in either the hypnagogic or hypnopompic state (Blackmore 131). This makes sense since the scene between Jamie and Calls take place at the guesthouse when Jamie is tired. It is possible for Jamie to talk about his feelings while having an OBE. Hypnagogic imagers are able to have a conversation while having an imagery experience (Mavromatis 28).

Of interest are the hallucinations reported by subjects who were given marijuana or THC in an experiment:

> In the early stages simple geometric forms predominated. There was often a bright light in the centre of the field of vision which obscured central details but allowed images at the edges to be seen more clearly and the location of this light created a tunnel-like perspective.... At a later stage the geometric forms were replaced by complex imagery including recognizable scenes with people and objects, [...] Even in this stage there was much consistency, with images from memory playing a large part [Blackmore 173–174].

It seems that *N. rustica* causes similar hallucinations produced by cannabis. Jamie also naturally has a repertoire of images that facilitates the creation of complex imagery or apparitions in an altered state, such as a vivid double vision of Black Jack. Blackmore mentions that in drug-induced hallucinations "the subject becomes part of the imagery and it seems quite real to him, even though it comes from his memory" (175). Of interest is the description of the tunnel with a light in the hallucinations caused by marijuana, which are also common in near-death experiences (Blackmore 174). When Jamie recovers from snakebite, he describes having a near-death experience in which he sees a "passage way of some kind," and realizes that he could go through it if he wants. (*The Fiery Cross*, ch. 93). Blackmore attributes the imagery associated with near-death experiences to be the "products of the imagination or hallucinations of a dying brain" (134). The similarities of both experiences are associated to the fact that everybody has anatomically and physiologically the same brain and nervous systems (Blackmore 174).

The possibility of N. rustica producing a hallucinogenic effect on other characters cannot be disregarded. After meeting the Tuscarora for the first time, Claire also describes having a dream or what could be considered one in which she sees Jamie as a bear before engaging in sex. This dream is probably a hallucination since Jamie and Claire have not only smoked tobacco from a stone pipe but also shared whisky with the aboriginals.

Roger MacKenzie is another character who exhibits the characteristics of a half-ghost. After the incident in which he was hanged, Brianna dreams about Deborah, a university friend who used to make money doing Tarot readings. There is a description of the Hanged Man in her dream.

> "A man is suspended by one foot from a pole laid across two trees. His arms, folded behind his back, together with his head, form a triangle with the point downward; his legs form a cross. To an extent, the Hanged Man is still earth-bound, for his foot is attached to the pole."
> I could see the man on the card, suspended permanently halfway between heaven and earth. That card always looked odd to me—the man didn't seem to be at all concerned, in spite of being upside-down and blind-folded [*The Fiery Cross*, ch. 73].

Many factors delayed the timing of Roger's possible death, such as rope quality, the experience of the hangman, and Claire's twentieth century knowledge of surgery. However, this is not the only time in which Roger has been close to death. His mother has saved his life directly and indirectly in the past. Due to his young age, it takes Roger time to remember the events associated with the death of both his mother and maternal grandmother. As Claire and Jamie did, he had a lapse of memory. At a certain point, he remembers that she saved his life by throwing him into a lower level of the shelter during a German bombing. He could have perished in this event but he continued living. Intriguingly, this scene is revisited in the short story "A Leaf on the Wind of All Hallows," in which Roger's birth father time travels and returns to his old life only to discover that everyone believes him dead and that he has become a ghost to them. There, he helps to save his young son, giving Roger a true ghost encounter with his lost father.

Roger's mother also indirectly saves him when he tries to go through the stones for the first time. It is a failed attempt and what protects him from burning is a locket with garnets that his mother used to wear. Roger does not perceive her presence as a ghost but as memories:

> "Oh…. I do remember her," he said, slowly, digging the ball of his thumb into the place where her neck joined her shoulder. "Only, it's just in bits and pieces. Sometimes, when I'm dreaming, or thinking of something else, I get a quick glimpse of her, or some echo of her voice. A few things I recall clearly—like the locket she used to wear round her neck, with her initials on it in wee red stones. Garnets, they were" [*The Fiery Cross*, ch. 98].

Roger also has some interaction with his adoptive father, Reverend Wakefield. The way this interaction starts is reminiscent of how Claire's communication with Frank begins. It also resembles Jamie's since it is based on good memories.

> *Who makes a garden works with God.* That had been written on the edge of the old copper sundial in the garden of the manse in Inverness where he had grown

> up. Ironic, in view of the fact that the Reverend had neither time nor talent for gardening.... He smiled at the thought, and made his mental good-night to the Reverend's shade [*The Fiery Cross*, ch. 57].

He continues saying mental good-nights to several people, some of them dead. Roger does not perceive anything wrong with this ritual. He is at peace. This resembles Jamie's sensation after having contacts with the "ghostly" entities of loved ones. The only difference is that Roger does not require special "Places" to perform this ritual. In his meeting with Hermon Husband during the War of the Regulation, Roger experiences another interaction with Reverend Wakefield. The communication in this case is achieved by the Quaker practice of reflecting about events internally. As the Hanged Man, Roger must undergo a regeneration process and become a new person (*The Fiery Cross*, ch. 73). His interactions with the Reverend thus lead him to reflect about his life and follow the steps of his adoptive father. Reborn with a true purpose, he takes the initiative to help people like Amy McCallum, a widow who lives in poverty, and to keep peace between Catholics and Protestants at the Ridge by becoming a preacher and offering religious services. Peace is vital to him, and it is the reason why horrid acts, such as those violence done by Hodgepile and his comrades, shock him to the point of aggression. His reaction to Lionel Brown's comments blaming the Indians for the fate of the O'Brian family is likewise confrontational: "Indians didn't write that," he snapped, jerking a thumb at the note in Brown's hand. "And if it was revenge against O'Brian for being a Regulator, they wouldn't have taken the children" (*A Breath of Snow and Ashes*, ch. 25).

When Roger reveals his calling to be a minister to Jamie, he finds it difficult to explain the conversations he has with Reverend Wakefield late at night and the experience he had when convincing Hermon Husband to avoid bloodshed between the Regulators and the Loyalist troops (*A Breath of Snow and Ashes,* ch. 51). There is a possibility that these mystical experiences could be hypnagogic in nature. Mavromatis states that Tibetan yogis use hypnagogia for the induction of mystical experiences (153). Visions of saints are also attributed to hypnagogia (152).

Native Americans refer to both Claire and Jamie with specific animal names. Jamie is known as "Bear Killer" and Claire is called "White Raven." In regards to Jamie, there is something ritualistic in his name acquisition, an act that involves a symbolic interaction between humans and the spirit of an animal. During the fight with the bear, Claire hits the bear twice with a fish. Later, Jamie complains to Claire about her hitting him in the head with the same fish. Furthermore, Jamie kills the bear under some trees and crawls into a clearing to meet Claire on all fours. The fighting scene seems to be an assimilation in which Jamie acquires bear-like characteristics. This is further supported by the hallucinatory dream in which Claire sees Jamie as a bear.

Furthermore, some Tuscarora witness the fight, and the assimilation acquires a mystical nature. After taking the whisky offered by Jamie, Nacognaweto pours a small amount of whisky into the bear's mouth and also around the carcass. This deed shows that for the Tuscarora the value of whisky is very similar to that of tobacco.

> In much of eastern North America, tobacco was not only smoked but cast (as dried powder or compressed leaf mass) into fires, water, and rock crevices. The reason for this was linked to the widespread belief that even inanimate objects had souls, and that spirits inhabited virtually every realm.... Spirit beings were particularly fond of tobacco and, hence, were offered the precious substance at every opportunity [von Gernet 67].

Nacognaweto is basically sharing the whisky with the spirit of the bear. Jamie describes this deed as a charm similar to the pouring of "holy water to the four airs of the earth" to protect oneself from the spirit (*Drums of Autumn*, ch. 15). This ritual proceeds with Nacognaweto lighting a pipe with tobacco that he subsequently shares with the bear's carcass. "Then he knelt, and taking another deep lungful of smoke, carefully blew it up the nostrils of the dead bear. He repeated this process several times, muttering something under his breath as he exhaled" (*Drums of Autumn*, ch. 15).

After performing this small ritual, Nacognaweto gives the pipe to Jamie. According to von Gernet "blowing and sucking of smoke are perceived to be shamanistic metaphors for the transfer of spiritual power" (66). By sharing the pipe with Jamie, Nacognaweto is transferring to him the spirit of the bear. In this scene Nacognaweto is also showing reverence to the bear's spirit, and in this way respecting and befriending Jamie. This whole episode is a symbolic representation of Jamie acquiring characteristics of a bear, and that interaction with the spiritual realm is not restricted to the ghosts of people but open to various types of entities.

In *The Fiery Cross*, Jamie notes the resemblance between the Amerindian shamanistic system and the notion of the four airs among the Scottish Highlanders. He attributes this resemblance to a similar lifestyle (ch. 81). Color symbolism is an important aspect of the Cherokee shamanistic system. There is a spirit that lives in each of the four cardinal points, assigned with a particular color and meaning (Mooney 342). Jamie's color could simply be red due to his hair and good fighting skills, a possible reason why Bird sends women to his bed every time that Jamie visits his village. This decision seems to be associated with more than honoring the King's agent. Red hair is rare even among the European population, so Jamie's look is truly unusual to the Cherokee. The entity associated with the red color is known in the series as Michael of the Red Domain, whom Jamie invokes before every battle. By contrast, the Black Man of the West is death. Throughout the series there are some characters or folk creatures associated with the black color: the escaped slave with cannibalistic practices and the Nuckelavee. This table from Mooney's *Cherokee History, Myths and Sacred Formulas* illustrates the spread of colors (342):

Color Symbolism in the Shamanistic System

Direction	Color	Attributes
East	Red	Success; triumph
North	Blue	Defeat; trouble
West	Black	Death
South	White	Peace; happiness
Above?	Brown	Unascertained, but propitious
—	Yellow	About the same as blue

The color associated with Claire is white. Jamie refers to her as a White Lady from European myth, as well as a description of her coloring.

> "My wife was a healer. What they call in the Highlands a charmer, but more than that. She was a white lady—a wise-woman." He glanced up briefly. "The word in Gaelic is *ban-druidh*; it also means witch" [*Voyager*, ch. 10].

This description also matches how the Cherokee perceive white animals, "as being significant—and often sinister" (*The Fiery Cross*, ch. 81). Further, it reflects the duality of how people perceive a raven.

In a dream, Nayawenne sees Claire become a white raven and lay an egg in her hand. Inside the egg, there is a stone, which Nayawenne equates with great magic, the power to heal. The next day, she finds a sapphire, which she considers to be a gift from Claire, and claims to be a powerful aid in curing people in the village (*Drums of Autumn*, ch. 20). What the raven symbolizes is of dual character. In the Scottish Highland, positive things associated with the raven include the gift of Second Sight and knowledge. However, they also foreshadow trouble and death (Frankel 140). This dual meaning also applies to the white raven.

> White ravens in myth might mean hope or terrible doom—to the Native Americans of the Midwest, seeing one presaged the end of the world. In Celtic lore, ravens with white feathers were a good omen of blessing and spiritual cleansing, especially if they had white on the wings. While many animals can be born albino, there is a genetic possibility for a white raven—from an incredibly rare gene, even less likely to be found in both halves of a mated pair. Thus its uniqueness, like Claire's with her own genetic components, makes it a bird of great omen [Frankel 141].

Claire's association with the color white extends to include all types of white animals. According to the Cherokee, white animals are worthy of respect since they carry "messages from the otherworld." (*The Fiery Cross*, ch. 82). Worthy of note is the event in which the Cherokee enlist both Jamie and Claire to kill a ghost bear. Physically this ghost bear is white, and the

Cherokee think of it as a "kindred spirit" to Claire due to her pale skin tone (*The Fiery Cross*, ch. 81). As a result, another connection between her and the spirit realm is established. The fact that the animal is a bear also reflects Jamie's condition as a half-ghost. The ghost bear's behavior is erratic and malicious, especially for white animals. It attacks humans and domestic animals, and also steals crops; it also eludes its trackers. The natives believe that it is an evil spirit manifesting itself in the form of a bear (*The Fiery Cross*, ch. 82). However, the actual perpetrator of these crimes turns out to be a cannibalistic African belonging to a group of escaped slaves that have settled close to the Cherokee village. The fact that the aggressor is of color fulfills what is described in the shamanistic system.

Jamie's memorable dream at the opening of the fifth book, concerning the ritual in which the ancient Kings of Ireland were crowned, involves the candidate copulating with a white mare. At a certain point, Jamie's dream characters decide that the mare's legs need to be cut off to facilitate the process for a short candidate. Of course, Jamie objects to this action but suddenly the white mare becomes a black one. The candidates no longer want the mare, even though Jamie tries to convince them that the black mare is a better option. White mares, according to him, are weak and produce blind offspring. This white mare represents Claire. Jamie made a vow to protect Claire even with his body when he married her. This is the reason why he protects the white mare from having her legs fractured. The white mare being not good for reproduction may signify Claire's fertility and pregnancy problems. Furthermore, the candidates' rejection of the black mare is consistent to both the shamanistic system and the notion of the fours airs. The change in color of the mare may signify that Claire is a doctor or healer with good intentions but others might see her skills in a different light and regard her as a witch. The difference between a healer and a witch is not defined blurring Claire's real nature. At Jocasta's wedding shortly thereafter she dreams of herself being a white mare being seduced by a stallion that proclaims itself the King of Ireland. In this dream, the horse imagery is sexual. However, it is not Jamie who is the one dreaming but Claire. With this information, both Jamie's dream and Claire's hypnagogic communication with Frank can be interpreted since both are occurring at the same time.

There is something about control regarding Claire's hypnagogic experience in which she is communicating with Frank at the same time that Jamie is dreaming about becoming the King of Ireland. In fact they are associated with the scene in *Outlander* in which Jamie whips Claire. Frankel states that a black horse in dreams "signifies mystery, wildness, and the unknown," and that Claire is a wild horse that Jamie is trying to tame (40). This interpretation is further supported when Claire notifies Jamie about Tom Christie whipping Malva. In their argument Jamie confesses that he never cared about Laoghaire enough to whip her, a revelation that infuriates Claire.

"[…] I didna want to possess her. You, *mo nighean donn*—you, I would own."
"Own me? I said. "And what, exactly, do you mean by that?"
"What I say." There was still a gleam of humor in his eyes, but his voice was serious. "Ye're mine, Sassenach. And I would do anything I thought I must to make that clear" [*A Breath of Snow and Ashes*, ch. 47].

Claire got lashed by Jamie because of her failed attempt to go back to Frank, which caused a series of complications such as Jamie risking his life to save her and endangering members of Clan MacKenzie. Jamie trying to control Claire is a constant struggle throughout the series. Her dreams and Jamie's reflect their hidden desires and quarrels, as well as a search for higher wisdom.

Through all the books, Claire, Jamie and Roger share characteristics of what the Cherokee define as an Asgina ageli, a half-ghost. They all have experienced events in which they have escaped from enemies and death several times. However, most of the ghosts they encounter are not real. The ghosts that haunt them exist mostly in dreams and in hallucinations, and are the result of both good memories and traumatic ones. However, a distinction between an imagined or an actual ghost is not a requirement for these characters to be half-ghosts. In fact Amerindians do not make a distinction between what is hallucinatory or real since they use psychoactive substances to achieve out-of-body experiences in order to communicate with spirit beings. Furthermore, two of these characters, Jamie and Claire are associated with animals that reflect their ghostly status. All are questing for purpose and wisdom after their many brushes with death. This will likely conclude by coming full circle, as ghost–Jamie will return to Claire in *Outlander* chapter one, emphasizing the metaphysical aspects of the journey they will take together.

WORKS CITED

Blackmore, Susan J. *Beyond the Body*. 1982. Chicago: Academy Chicago Publishers, 1992. Print.

Frankel, Valerie Estelle. *The Symbolism and Sources of Outlander*. Jefferson, NC: McFarland. 2015. Print.

Gabaldon, Diana. *A Breath of Snow and Ashes*. 2005. New York: Bantam Dell. 2006. Print.

_____. *Drums of Autumn*. 1997. New York: Dell Publishing. 2002. Print.

_____. *The Fiery Cross*. 2001. New York: Bantam Dell. 2005. Print.

_____. "A Leaf on the Wind of All Hallows." *Songs of Love and Death*. Eds. George R.R. Martin and Gardner Dozois, USA: Gallery Books, 2010. 429–468.

_____. *Voyager*. 1994. New York: Bantam Dell. 2002. Print

Mavromatis, Andreas. *Hypnagogia*. 1987. London: Thyrsos Press, 2010. Print.

Mooney, James. *Cherokee History, Myths and Sacred Formulas*. 1891. Cherokee: Cherokee Publications, 2006. Print.

von Gernet, Alexander. "Nicotian Dreams." *Consuming Habits: Drugs in History and*

Anthropology. 2d ed. Eds. Jordan Goodman, Paul E. Lovejoy, and Andrew Sherratt. Abingdon: Routledge, 1995. 65–85. Print.
Winter, Joseph C. "Traditional Uses of Tobacco by Native Americans." *Tobacco Use by Native North Americans: Sacred Smoke and Silent Killer.* Ed. Joseph C. Winter. Norman: University of Oklahoma Press, 2000. 9–58. Print.

Confrontational Content, Gendered Gazes and the Ethics of Adaptation in *Outlander* and *Game of Thrones*

Jennifer Phillips

The television adaptations *Outlander* (2014–) and *Game of Thrones* (2011–) are often compared because of their journey from sprawling novels to their current incarnations as popular additions to their premium cable networks (Starz and HBO, respectively). Additionally, while there are key differences in their settings, plot and characters, both series share similar features such as fantasy elements, depictions of war and brutality, and numerous scenes of graphic sexual content. In addition to these similarities, in May 2015, both series screened episodes in which a central character was brutally raped, provoking much controversy.

In the *Game of Thrones* episode, "Unbent, Unbowed, Unbroken" (E506), Sansa Stark weds Ramsay Bolton. Where Sansa is unaware of Bolton's brutality, viewers have already seen his gruesome treatment of Theon Greyjoy—torturing, tormenting, emasculating and ultimately erasing Greyjoy's identity. Thus, when it came to the wedding night, audiences were not expecting the gentlemanly treatment Sansa received during her ill-fated (and unconsummated) marriage to Tyrion Lannister.

In the same week as this *Game of Thrones* episode aired, the first season of *Outlander* aired the middle episode of a three-episode arc in which Highland hero Jamie Fraser is abducted, imprisoned, tortured and brutally raped by the villainous Black Jack Randall. Where the rape of Sansa Stark was mostly depicted off-screen and lasted only a few minutes, the violence inflicted on Jamie Fraser was graphically portrayed as the central focus of two entire episodes.

162

Despite the graphic visual detail of *Outlander*'s depiction of rape and its aftereffects, it was *Game of Thrones*' depiction which was criticized in the numerous online culture blogs that report on both series. A chief criticism of the *Game of Thrones* storyline was that it was not a part of the original novel—but was added by showrunners D.B. Weiss and David Banoff. This is in sharp contrast to the *Outlander* storyline, which is not only the climactic action of Gabaldon's first novel, but is a central event which leads to several other key moments in the novels to come.

In what follows, I consider not only the depiction of violence and rape in both *Game of Thrones* and *Outlander*, but the nature and effect of these events not only in the lives of the characters, but in the overall narrative of the shows. I also investigate the gendered nature of this violence, investigating the perpetrators and victims in each instance. I also analyze the nature of adaptation, and consider whether the origin of a scene within the original text justifies its inclusion in the televised adaptation—despite how horrific the filmed scenes themselves may be.

The Depiction of Rape in Game of Thrones

Over the first five seasons of *Game of Thrones*, the adaptation of the first five novels of George R.R. Martin's *Song of Ice and Fire* series, three of the central female characters become victims of rape: Daenerys Targaryen, Cersei Lannister and Sansa Stark.

Daenerys

In the opening episode of the series, Daenerys is raped on the evening after her wedding to Khal Drogo. Dany grimaces and cries throughout the entire encounter. While this scene has been adapted from the book, there is one pivotal alteration: in the novel, Drogo receives consent from his new bride. However, this consent is complicated by the fact that in the novel Daenerys is only 12 years old, which, as Frankel points out, is unquestionably still rape by modern standards, if not by medieval ones (149). Despite this, there is significantly more consent in the novel than in its adapted counterpart:

> He cupped her face in his huge hands and looked into his eyes. "No?" he said, and she knew it was a question.
> She took his hand and moved it down to the wetness between her thighs.
> "Yes," she whispered as she put his finger inside her [*A Game of Thrones*, ch. 11].

As Sonia Saraiya observes, the whole narrative trajectory of the relationship between Daenerys and Khal Drogo is altered by beginning their marriage with a rape instead of consensual intercourse ("Rape"). By taking control of her body and willingly choosing to have sex with her new husband, as she does in the novel, Daenerys is reclaiming some of the power that her brother robbed from her by arranging the marriage in the first place. In the television series, her wedding night is merely a continuation of her lack of power and control—but instead of her brother it is Khal Drogo who now controls her (Frankel 150). Daenerys is filmed naked in the second episode, exploited by Drogo as titillation for the audience.

Similarly, in the novels, Dany's development of feelings for the Khal demonstrates the beginnings of her power and agency. By receiving Drogo's love and respect, Daenerys grows into a confident woman, able to become the leader she eventually is. Despite empowering Daenerys, the love she develops for the Khal on the show also forms part of a contentious Television Trope—that of a woman who falls in love with her rapist. This problematic pattern has been seen in TV soaps such as *General Hospital* and *Days of Our Lives*, but was also part of a controversial storyline in *Buffy the Vampire Slayer*.

The adaptation of Daenerys' relationship with Khal Drogo also represents the first of what would become a series of "amnesiac" rape scenarios, where Daenerys and later Cersei show no memory or ill-effects from their abuse, nor do they express any ill-will towards their abusers. By giving their characters (apparent) amnesia, viewers are also able to forget how Daenerys and Drogo's relationship is based on a foundation of violence and abuse. Unlike Sansa's season two attack in King's Landing, followed by traumatic dreams, and Brienne's screams of anger and horror during her near-rape in "Walk of Punishment" (E303), these women's degradations leave no evidence of lasting trauma or the journey to healing that follow.

Cersei

Another controversial scene in the history of *Game of Thrones* is that in which Cersei is raped by her brother/lover Jamie Lannister while mourning the death of their son Joffrey (in "Breaker of Chains," E403). This scene, like the scene of Daenerys' wedding night, is also taken from George R.R. Martin's novel (in this case, *A Storm of Swords*). However, where in the book Cersei was a willing participant, in the episode, Cersei is without a doubt raped by Jamie. Cersei's enthusiastic encouragement of her brother/lover ("my brother, sweet brother, yes, like that, yes, I have you, you're home now, you're home now, you're *home*" [ch. 62]) is replaced with her screams and cries and pleas for Jamie to stop.

When the episode aired, Margaret Lyons called it "a new low for the deeply violent series" while Sonya Saraiya described the scene as "hyperbolically awful" ("Rape") due to the triune violations of Cersei's agency, the Westerosi religion and the death of Joffrey. Despite the outcry, both the director of the episode (Alex Graves) as well the actors who portray Jamie and Cersei (Nikolaj Coster-Waldau and Lena Headey) have argued that the scene is not one in which rape takes place. When asked if he thought the scene depicted a rape, Coster-Waldau took a decidedly fence-sitting position: "Yes, and no" (qtd. in Stern). Similarly, when asked, Lena Headey refused to make a stand either way (Pantozzi).

Director Alex Graves' perception of the scene is even more troubling; Graves believes that the sex "becomes consensual by the end" (qtd. in Sepinwall). Responding to Graves, critic Amanda Marcotte argues that "It's as straightforward a rape scene as you'll get on TV." Jessica Valenti has also taken exception to Graves' comments, as well as those of Headey and Coster-Waldau, arguing that "we need to call rape what it is, and not water it down with descriptors or replace it with inaccurate terms that make sexual violence and the people who perpetrate it seem more palatable." One reviewer summed up the issue perfectly: "If Graves and Coster-Waldau were attempting to portray something that viewers would perceive as consensual, they obviously didn't succeed" (Culp-Ressler).

So controversial was this episode when it aired that even George R.R. Martin, who had until that point sought to separate his writing from the promotion of the HBO series, felt the need to explain his take on the scene:

> If the show had retained some of Cersei's dialogue from the books, it might have left a somewhat different impression[…]. That's really all I can say on this issue. The scene was always intended to be disturbing … but I do regret if it has disturbed people for the wrong reasons [Martin, "Re: Jaime's Changes in Breaker of Chains"].

Without going so far as to say that the director, writers and actors made the wrong decisions when adapting his source materials, Martin is quick to point out that certain omissions, namely Cersei's words of consent, have had the effect of changing the central intention of the scene.

So problematic was the alteration in Meslow's opinion that he feared that it "single-handedly threatens to derail the arcs of both Jaime and Cersei Lannister." Of course, this wasn't the case. Like the rape of Daenerys, this event had little to no emotional impact on the lives of the characters involved.

Sansa

It is in the context of the already ill-received attacks on two central female characters, as well as numerous scenes of sexual abuse of other female characters (such as the violent death of Ros and Craster's abuse of his daughters), that the rape of Sansa Stark occurred in season five. Sansa, like Daenerys, is raped on her wedding night. However, where the figure of Khal Drogo is relatively unknown to the viewer when that scene occurs, the true character of Ramsay Snow/Bolton has been revealed in his brutal torture, emasculation and eventual brainwashing of Theon Greyjoy. In fact, it is Theon who becomes the focus of this scene. Theon is about to leave the room when Ramsay makes him stay. Ramsay then rips the back off Sansa's dress, exposing her skin. Sansa's face turns from passive to disgusted as Ramsay bends her over the bed. The remaining scene is played entirely off Theon's reaction accompanied by the sounds of Sansa's clear discomfort. Theon whimpers and cries as he watches what Ramsay does to Sansa and the audience hears her escalating screams, punctuated by a vibrato violin score as the episode ends.

Again, like the two previous examples, this scene is a deviation from the source material. Originally, a character named Jeyne Poole is disguised as Arya Stark and married off to Ramsay. It is she, not Sansa, who is raped and brutalized by him. As Jeyne is not a major or viewpoint character, this story arc follows Theon's struggle to reclaim his old self and rescue the distressed damsel—basically the rape plot is all about him. Sansa is a more significant character, but as she pleads for Theon to call Brienne to rescue her, and Theon must battle through Ramsay's conditioning, Sansa herself has little agency. It must also be noted that the brutality Ramsay shows Jeyne in the novels is far worse than the scene shown with Sansa. Regardless of the difference in Bolton's treatment of Sansa compared to what happens to Jeyne in the books, the question remains, if the scene was not in the source material, why add it at all? Showrunners D.B. Weiss and David Benioff claimed the decision to cut the character of Jeyne and give her storyline to Sansa was to give Sansa's character more of a narrative in season five (where, in the same point in the novels, she remains stuck at the Eyrie) (Hibberd). Because of these changes, an argument about narrative fidelity or accuracy of adaptation cannot be made to justify this scene. As Tom Ley observes "the show runners weren't in any way bound to put Sansa's rape on TV because it never happened in the books."

The addition of the marriage to Ramsay and Sansa's rape seemed especially gratuitous considering all of the horrendous events in which she has been a helpless victim throughout *Game of Thrones'* five-year run. She has had her direwolf executed, seen her father beheaded, and was then made to stare at his rotting head as it was strung up among other "traitors." Moreover, Sansa was the victim of Joffrey's sadism, including being stripped and beaten in front of the whole royal court. Later, Sansa is married off to Tyrion Lannister, and, along with him, accused of Joffrey's murder. After escaping, Sansa is manipulated and controlled and ultimately married off to Bolton because of Littlefinger's wishes. When these events are considered cumulatively, it's no wonder one critic entitled his review of the episode "Game of Thrones Will Not Stop Doing Horrible Things to Sansa Stark" (Rougeau).

As a result of Sansa's rape, feminist website *The Mary Sue* announced they would no longer promote *Game of Thrones* (Pantozzi "No Longer"). It is the outcry against this episode that is particularly interesting to read against *Outlander* because both episodes aired within a week of each other. As we will see, the rape and torture of *Outlander's* Jamie Fraser was far more disturbing, taking up more airtime and being depicted with far more graphic imagery; however, there was very little outcry about the scene. One reason for this could be due to how Ramsay's assault on Sansa sits not only as the third, perhaps unnecessary, scene in which a central female character is raped (in addition to many scenes in which secondary female characters are sexually abused). Likewise, it also sits within an ongoing systematic problematic depiction of women in *Game of Thrones*. *Outlander*, by contrast, provides a single villain who exists at the height of sadism, whose obsession with breaking Jamie and those he loves drives the plot in a way more poignant than gratuitous, as Jamie, Claire, and Jenny all learn to defeat him.

The Depiction of Rape in Outlander

The frequency of rape (or attempted rape) in *Outlander* has not escaped the notice of reviewers (see Soligan, Thomas). However, when compared to the depiction of rape in *Game of Thrones* there are several key differences in how these scenes' execution and narrative purpose. One key difference is the choice of victim: Whereas victims of rape in *Game of Thrones* are (almost exclusively) female, in *Outlander*, both men and women are attacked.

Also different from *Game of Thrones*, *Outlander* depicts women escaping from rape attempts—and not always relying on the tired heroic male "rescuer" figure, although that does occur at times. In the series opener "Sassenach" (E101), when Claire first arrives in 1743, disoriented from traveling over 200 years into the past, her first encounter is with Black Jack Randall. After Randall mistakes her 1940s dress for a shift and assumes she is a prostitute, he attacks her. Claire attempts to free herself, running away, only to find herself trapped between a rock and Randall's sword. Both in the book and the series, Claire is saved by Murtagh, a highland warrior.

This isn't the last time Claire is threatened by Randall. When Claire is taken to Fort William in the mid-season finale "Both Sides Now" (E108), she is almost raped by Randall for the second time. The scene plays out quite the same in the book as well as in the adaptation—with one clear difference. In the book, Claire observes that in the midst of his attack on her, Randall remains flaccid. Claire describes a "heavy, flopping movement" (*Outlander*, ch. 21) against her leg. This causes her to realize that Randall cannot take sexual pleasure unless his victim shows her fear, revulsion, and rejection of consent. This detail is missing from the adapted version. In both the novel and the series, Jamie rides to the rescue, interrupting the tableaux with the (almost clichéd) heroic phrase "I'll thank ye to take your hands off my wife" (*Outlander*, ch. 21).

While the characters in *Game of Thrones* (particularly Daenerys and Cersei) do not seem to be overtly impacted by the horrific acts they have experienced, nor are their relationships irrevocably altered; the attacks on Claire by Black Jack Randall are part of an accumulation of abusive and violent actions which paint this character as the primary villain of the season. In fact, although Randall is not the only perpetrator of sexual attacks in *Outlander*, the frequency of his attacks paints a picture of his character rather than a general depiction of the world, whereas, in *Game of Thrones*, rape appears more prevalent. More than these scenes revealing something about Randall, they are also part of the development of Claire's character. She is no passive victim; even in the scenes where she is rescued by Murtagh or Jamie, Claire has not waited uselessly for their arrival. When Randall first attacks her, she runs. In the later scene, Claire tries to convince him that she is his ally rather than his adversary.

Even though Claire is saved from Randall by the intervention of men, there are several other occasions where Claire herself is the agent responsible for evading unwanted sexual advances. In "The Gathering" (E104), Claire decides to escape for Inverness. On her way out of the castle, she runs into Dougal who drunkenly kisses her and reaches beneath her skirt. Before Dougal can go any further, Claire hits him over the head with a stool, incapacitating him. This scene, new to the show, allows Claire increased agency and foreshadows Dougal's unhealthy interest in her.

In "Both Sides Now," Claire also fights back against two redcoat deserters who attack her after discovering the newly-married Frasers having sex in a glade. The trauma of the event is clearly depicted. While Jamie and Claire are having sex, the only sounds are those of their mutual enjoyment. This is interrupted by the clicking of a gun being held to Jamie's head. One soldier holds Jamie still with a pistol while another climbs on top of Claire. From this point, time slows and events are presented impressionistically. As her attacker's face fills Claire's vision, Claire's decision to attack him is shown by her wide open eyes. Claire retrieves her newly received *sgian dubh* (a small knife hidden in her stocking) and stabs the soldier in the kidney, killing him. Jamie takes advantage of the other soldier's confusion to kill him, too.

The effects of the attack on Claire aren't erased the moment the threat has been eliminated. The threatening score as well as the fractured images continue as Jamie frantically lifts Claire up from where she is lying on the grass and carries her away to collect herself on a nearby rock. In the next scene, Jamie attempts to comfort Claire, who unconvincingly mutters "we're okay" before diagnosing herself as experiencing shock. Claire's voiceover informs the viewer that her thoughts are fractured, her mind "jumped and danced from thought to thought" while the filming itself is blurred. This scene is similar to the one in the book, but significant effort has been made onscreen to keep the trauma—something much simpler in a first person novel. Later, Claire refers to the events as a "pivotal" moment in her life. As Kaitlyn Soligan observes:

> Jamie's helplessness, her realization that he cannot save or protect her, and the knowledge that she must save herself. These realizations, and not the assault itself, will ultimately lead to a hugely important moment for Claire that drives the plot forward—her attempt to return to her own time, the twentieth century [Soligan, "Can We Talk About Those Rape Scenes in 'Outlander?'"].

The frequency of the attacks on Claire has not gone unnoticed (see also Rowles, Thomas, Mcalister among others). Sarah Hughes goes so far as to argue that *Outlander*'s use of rape as a shorthand for danger or peril is its biggest weakness. Despite issues with the prevalence of rape scenes in the series, on the whole, the depiction of sexual assault in *Outlander* has been judged more favorably by critics than the scenes from *Game of Thrones*. Jodi Mcalister cites one telling exchange between Claire and Colum MacKenzie as representing the series' subversive take on its depiction of a world where rape is considered an unfortunate norm. Colum asks Claire why a Redcoat captain such as Randall would attempt to rape her "for no good reason," to which Claire replies, "Is there ever a good reason for rape?" an exchange which does not occur in the novel (*Outlander*, ch. 5).

Jenny

Claire isn't the only female character who is shown fighting back against a would-be rapist. In the series' second episode, "Castle Leoch," Jamie tells Claire that he believes his sister was not only raped by Black Jack, but that Randall impregnated her with his bastard child. Jamie carries this fact with him for four whole years until he is reunited with his sister in the episode "Lallybroch" (E112), his sorrow culminating in his asking why she named Randall's bastard Jamie—after himself. Jenny sets the record straight for her brother. Not only is her son the legitimate offspring of her marriage to Ian Murray, but Randall did not rape her at all.

The scene of Randall's attack is shown in flashback, overlaid with Jenny's present- day narration of the events. As she tells the story, her eyes are averted from all present in the scene—she cannot look at Jamie, Claire or even her own husband Ian. The color palette in the flashback scenes has been muted—almost black and white, except for the color red, which has been emphasized.

Randall's red coat is vibrant. So, too is Jamie's blood on Randall's finger as he suggestively inserts it into Jenny's mouth, causing her to gag.

Jenny doesn't remain a passive victim of Randall's attack. After Randall has forcibly placed one of Jenny's hands on his crotch, Jenny uses the other to grab a large candlestick, whacking Randall over the head with it. This enrages Randall, who drags her towards the bed. Jenny's second act of self-defense is far more effective. Noting that Randall is struggling to achieve an erection, Jenny laughs at him. Randall's failure is clear to both Jenny and the viewer—the scene includes several shots of Tobias Menzies' flaccid penis, one of the first times full-frontal male nudity has been shown in a sexual context on television (Ryan "Radical").

The way Jenny fights back against Randall's attack adds to *Outlander*'s subversive depiction of attempted rape. In fact, one critic claimed never before to have seen a woman's laughter used as weapon against sexual assault in any television or film (Saraiya "Laughs"). Even in the midst of her attempted rape, Jenny reclaims her power. Thus, Jenny is no passive victim but rather an empowered survivor, one who has gone on to marry and have children, but, nevertheless, still carries some trauma from the assault, evident in the way that Ian reaches out to clasp his wife's hand in a sign of solidarity and support. This scene is roughly identical to the one in the book, though aspects like Tobias Menzies' nudity have far more impact onscreen than in the reader's imagination.

Jamie

By far, the most graphic and affecting depiction of rape in the first season of *Outlander* is the rape of Jamie Fraser by Jack Randall. Having the hero of a show, and one who is ostensibly the embodiment of the idealized hegemonic male, become a victim of such a brutal sexual attack is unlike anything previously depicted on television or in film. In film, Marcellus Wallace (Ving Rhames) is raped by The Gimp in *Pulp Fiction* (1994), yet in that context, he is the antagonist in opposition to Butch Coolidge (Bruce Willis). Brandon Teena is brutally raped and murdered in the conclusion of *Boys Don't Cry* (1999), but this depiction is complicated by Brandon's transsexuality. The attack is clearly a hate-crime; the very fact that Brandon does not have male genitalia causes Tom and John to assault and ultimately murder him. The rape of Andy Dufresne in *The Shawshank Redemption* (1994) is one of very few examples of the rape of a male protagonist, yet Andy's bookish, introverted nature does not encapsulate the idealized hegemonic male hero like Jamie Fraser does.

Aside from crimes depicted on *Law and Order: SVU*, the depiction of men raped on television is just as scarce. In a 2013 episode of *The Mindy*

Show, Dr. Paul Leotard (James Franco) gets "blackout drunk," only to wake up in the morning and find that a female character, Christina, has had sex with him without his consent. This event is played for laughs despite the fact, as one reviewer noted, "if the genders were reversed in this scenario—this episode would have looked completely different and likely Dr. L would be written as a predator" (Strom). Similarly, in an episode of *True Blood*, Jason Stackhouse is fed Viagra so that werewolf women can breed with him. Although Jason does later admit that he was raped and felt violated, there is no emotional fallout. Of course, what sets these scenes aside from *Outlander* is that these men are raped by women, rather than men. The television show *Oz* did depict numerous scenes of men being raped by other men—at least nine major characters were victims throughout the series' run. However, the setting of the series in a prison with inmates serving time for serious crimes is in contrast to the heroic tropes that surround Jamie Fraser.

As Esther Bloom observes, the rape of a "good guy" is "almost without parallel in pop culture." Sonya Saraiya believes that is the very goodness of Jamie, a character she describes as "more hunk than human," which makes the violence perpetrated against him so affecting (Saraiya "Torture"). More than just representing groundbreaking content, the representation of the physical, psychological and spiritual trauma Jamie undergoes puts the forementioned cases (particularly those in which the male victim shrugs it off) in sharp relief.

The attack is shown over the course of two episodes, "Wentworth" and "To Ransom a Man's Soul" (E115–116). "Wentworth" begins with Jamie about to face the noose for his (supposed) crimes, only to be saved by the heroic visage of Black Jack Randall—although viewers (who are aware of Randall's fixation on Jamie) know that Randall presents no real salvation. Over the course of the episode, the two face off in a darkened cell. The scenes are claustrophobic—the only light is the flicker of a fire—reflecting the inevitability of what is to come.

Over the course of the episode, Jamie is tortured by Randall. His hand is repeatedly struck with a mallet as well as pierced with a large nail (the latter as a trade to stop Randall attacking Claire). In terms of sexual assault, not only is Jamie forced to perform sexual acts on Randall, who forces Jamie's hand onto his penis, but Randall also takes control of Jamie's body, caressing and licking the scars Randall once inflicted and kissing Jamie while Claire watches on, helpless. However, as "Wentworth" concludes, readers of the novels know there is much worse to come.

The series finale "To Ransom a Man's Soul" begins with a jump forward in time to a shocking opener. Jamie is shown the next morning, naked, lying in a prison cot with his mangled hand dangling. Staring vacantly into space, he is a defeated man. Suddenly, Randall sits up from where he lies beside his victim. He, too, is naked (and Tobias Menzies' penis makes its second appearance in *Outlander*). Although Randall has raped and tortured Jamie, we soon learn that his goal wasn't only physical. Randall wanted to write himself on Jamie's very soul. Throughout "To Ransom a Man's Soul," Jamie is indeed haunted by Randall, oftentimes confusing Claire's face for his captor's in an example of severe PTSD. Ultimately, in book and show, it is only by taking on the role of Randall and allowing Jamie to fight back that Claire can bring her husband back from the brink. Unlike the characters in *Game of Thrones*, both Jamie and Claire have deep scars which need to be healed. In the case of Jamie, the mark Randall places on his very being is symbolized by Randall's branded initials in Jamie's flesh, which Jamie gouges out with a sharp knife.

Sonia Saraiya is quick to note that while the episode is one of the most upsetting hours of television she has ever watched, it is closely related to the source material ("Torture"). The only clear difference is how the scene is conveyed to the reader/ audience.

> But in the book "Outlander," this story is narrated to the reader as it is told to Claire, who discovers the details of Jamie's imprisonment in the weeks following, as he's struggling to recover. In the show, the torture is conveyed to the viewer directly ["Torture"].

This shift meant that these episodes had a profound impact even on those who had read the novels and knew what was in store. As Ester Bloom noted, "This isn't just the transition from text to TV; this is the transformation of second-hand story into firsthand experience, of hastily sketched characters into fully realized human beings." Not only does the mode of telling make a difference in the reception of the scene, but the very act of reading and viewing graphic depictions of rape vary the emotional impact. Readers of Gabaldon's novel can blur details, skip over events, and even vary the speed at which they read. For those watching these episodes of *Outlander*, the pace is achingly slow, the scenes are extremely claustrophobic, and the detail is presented with vivid (and revolting) realism.

Perhaps there is a willingness to forgive some of the problems within the rape-threat trope because of the depiction not only of Claire and her agency (as well as Jenny Murray's), but because the most brutal and affecting rape portrayed in the series is reserved for its hero. The brutal abuse of Jamie Fraser by Jack Randall doesn't minimize the trauma experienced by Claire and Jenny, but it does release the series from the impression of implied misogyny that dogs *Game of Thrones* (the show especially) and its sexual ill-treatment of characters who are, almost exclusively, women. One reviewer went so far as to say that Jamie's trauma in exchange for Claire's freedom is apropos of Christ's substitution—although instead of suffering for the sins of mankind, Jamie Fraser is taking the punishment for patriarchy's sins

(Seltzer "Dark")—an atonement for all of the times women have been raped and abused in film and on television. In fact, in his choice to surrender to Jack Randall, Jamie Fraser is enacting something Susan Bordo in 1999 believed our culture wasn't ready for, namely, a male cultural icon "passively" giving himself to another man (191).

Part of the further acceptance of the scenes of sexual assault in *Outlander* comes from the fact they originated in Gabaldon's novel. Unlike *Game of Thrones*, any additions or omissions do not add to the salaciousness of the encounter, nor do they have the effect of minimizing Claire's agency, or turning a scene of consent into a non-consensual encounter. Also, in contrast to the comments made by the director and actors in *Game of Thrones* denying the depiction of rape or the horrific nature of the events depicted, showrunner Ronald D. Moore and actors Caitriona Balfe, Tobias Menzies and Sam Heughan have all commented on the traumatic brutality and painful consequences of the scenes depicted (see Fretts, Debnath, Vineyard, Ge).

Two more key issues set *Outlander* apart from *Game of Thrones* in its depiction of rape and sexual assault. One is the narrative impact (or lack thereof) of these confrontational scenes. Another is the way these scenes are filmed—representing either the "male" or "female" gaze.

The "Male" and "Female" Gaze in Game of Thrones *and* Outlander

Much has been written about the "male gaze" in *Game of Thrones*. To summarize Laura Mulvey's seminal writing on the male gaze from 1975, such images are used to uphold gender dynamics (such as the active male and the passive female). The male gaze is also an act of projection, styling the female body in line with male sexual fantasy, although this act of styling and projection ultimately transforms the fantasy into a reality of expected sexual behaviors. In line with these fantasies, women are displayed, objectified, dehumanized and fetishized. They are looked at, rather than the ones doing the looking. In terms of depicting the sex act, then, women are dominated by their male lover, and used as a means to a singular end: his sexual pleasure.

Lili Loofbourow has written an extensive essay on the topic of the use of the male gaze in *Game of Thrones*. She observes that the show in its early seasons especially pins its "cinematic choices to a heterosexual male subjectivity," framing and filming scenes in such a way as to attend to male heterosexual pleasure rather than feminine or queer sexual pleasure. Reflecting on her own experience watching *Game of Thrones* as a heterosexual woman, she sees "breast after breast after buttock after breast while understanding that they're not there for me." Her experience is not new. In fact, it is eerily similar to what John Berger observed about the representation of women in *Ways of Seeing* in 1972: "Men look at women. Women watch themselves being looked at" (42).

Loofbourow contrasts this pattern in *Game of Thrones* with a single outlier—a scene as late as season four in which Daenerys watches lover Daario undress, and in fact orders him, "take off your clothes," claiming utter control over him and the moment (E407). Loofbourow describes the "The thrill of being invited by the camera to regard a naked man in an explicitly erotic context as a woman." Maureen Ryan hypothesizes that the lack of female writers, directors and directors of photography in Hollywood may have contributed to the phenomenon of the overwhelming norm of the male gaze. If those behind the camera are mostly male, then, as Ryan postulates, "What they don't want to see usually doesn't get shot." When the list of writers and directors of *Game of Thrones* season five was published, feminist website *The Mary Sue* was among the first to note that the list didn't include a single woman (Cox). In contrast, six of the sixteen episodes in *Outlander* season one were written by women—with four episodes directed by a woman.

It is in the context of criticism like this that not only are the problematic depictions of rape in *Game of Thrones* situated, but into which the first season of *Outlander* was welcomed—not only because of its more nuanced engagement with sexual assault, but its willingness to represent something that had been missing in the first four seasons of *Game of Thrones*: female sexual pleasure and agency.

In her first review of *Outlander*, Jenny Trout analyzed a scene in the series-opener "Sassenach" in which Claire invites her husband Frank to perform cunnilingus. The scene, Trout claims, feels like voyeurism not only because it focuses on Claire's pleasure, but it is missing all of the signs viewers have become accustomed to seeing in a "traditional" sex-scene—"there are no flickering candles, no slow strip-teases to reveal her gravity defying breasts or his rippling six-pack [...] the usual cues to the viewer that scream, 'you're watching something sexy.'" Claire's relationship with Jamie, while also notable for its focus on her sexual pleasure, also pushes the boundaries beyond typical Hollywood relationship dynamics. In fact, reviewer Maureen Ryan described the wedding episode (E107) as "nothing short of revolutionary" ("Wedding").

In the first place, Jamie, a virgin on their wedding night (which is a rarity in and of itself), is definitely given marks for enthusiasm and effort from his new bride, but their first coupling is less than satisfying. Viewers need not be told this; it is evident not only in the cinematography, which, as Maureen Ryan observes, contains "no 'sexy' camera angles, no golden light, no instant nirvana" but also in the sounds accompanying the couple's lovemaking, which are not those of enraptured pleasure, but of the awkward groans of two people who have not yet gotten used to each other's bodies.

Awkward first-time sex such as this is almost never depicted in film or on television—unless, perhaps, played for laughs. However, in *Outlander* the goal is the honest, real journey of these characters and the foundation of their marriage.

Moreover, where viewers of shows like *Game of Thrones* and *True Blood* are used to the male gaze of the camera fetishizing female bodies, much screen time in "The Wedding" (and in many *Outlander* episodes) is taken up with slow, meandering shots of Jamie's shirtless torso. As reviewer Roxanne Gay admits, "I objectified Jamie along with Claire and millions of viewers." The female gaze is not beyond the objectification of the male form. However, the focus need not be on the object's physical beauty. When Jamie stands naked before Claire for the first time, while there is an unmistakable element of fetishizing in the depiction of Jamie's body, the scene is also about Claire's agency. She orders him to take off his clothes while she remains clothed. She lingers, slowly circling his body, and while the objective and the external elements of sexual attraction are clearly on display, there is an unmistakable representation of Claire's internal subjectivity, her enjoyment and arousal and the anticipation of their mutual sexual pleasure.

Gaze

The female gaze in *Outlander* is often directly compared to the male gaze in *Game of Thrones*. Jenny Trout compares Jamie's mid-coitus pause to check on the reason for Claire's screams (which, as it turns out, is the first time he's heard a woman climax) as "a far cry from the violent thrusting and distressed shouts of a *Game of Thrones* sex scene," nor, as another reviewer put it is the sex in *Outlander* like "the usual joyless, furniture bumping HBO sex." Neither, as Trout observes, does *Outlander* use sex as shorthand for morality or window-dressing for scenes laden-down with exposition (as *Game of Thrones* has been accused of doing).

The difference between sexual scenes directed by women and men is clearest in *Outlander's* mid-season finale, "Both Sides Now" (E108). Although the director credit is given wholly to Anna Foerster, there was one key scene which she did not direct: the final attack on Claire by Black Jack Randall. Foerster, unable to film the scene due to scheduling issues, was replaced by Richard Clark (Ng). While the scene in which Claire is attacked by the Redcoat deserters captures Claire's trauma through tight subjectivity, the final attack has been criticized by one reviewer as an "offensive failure," citing the scene's "conflation of pornographical camerawork (deliberately cheating out to maximize the camera's access to the nipple) and love-scene direction (tear open bodice, expose breast, bend over desk, expose buttocks)" as sign of a heavy-handed director heightening the trauma and exploitation of the scene for titillation rather than echoing the emotional and psychological impact of the earlier scene (Soligan).

As this example shows, *Outlander* isn't entirely fixed within female subjectivity. However, *Outlander* has become known for its predominant focus on female pleasure rather than the objectification, dehumanization, and male domination for which *Game of Thrones* has been largely criticized.

Rape as a Narrative Device

Another difference in the depiction of sexual assault in *Outlander* when contrasted with *Game of Thrones* is the narrative impact of the scenes. As Jill Pantozzi of *The Mary Sue* argues in her article about the website's decision to stop promoting *Game of Thrones*: "using rape as the impetus for character motivations is one of the most problematic tropes in fiction." More problematic, however, is the sheer prevalence of rape not only in these two series, but in television more generally. This trend caused critic Sarah Seltzer to ask, "Has the Golden Age of TV Been Replaced by the Age of Rape and Torture?"

When contrasting the depiction of rape in *Outlander* and *Game of Thrones,* one clear element divides the two: in *Outlander,* these scenes are included in service of the narrative arc of the characters, and the unfolding plot of the series, whereas in *Game of Thrones,* these scenes could easily be excised without impacting either character or plot. As Sonya Saraiya observes, in *Outlander,* "if women were raped or near-raped, it was a part of their story" ("Torture")—and it has ongoing resonance.

Moreover, the lack of narrative impact of the scenes of sexual assault in *Game of Thrones* feeds into another issue in the discourses surrounding rape in our society. As Margaret Lyons argued when analyzing the Cersei/Jaime rape scene, without showing the emotional impact of such an attack, these shows support the lie that "women's feelings don't matter, that sexual agency isn't a big deal, that rape is something that just kind of happens and that healthy people simply move on."

If the depiction of rape in *Game of Thrones* has little or no narrative impact, the question must be asked: Why have these scenes been included at all? Certainly is it not because of fidelity to the source material—as we have seen, all three of the scenes from *Game of Thrones* have been altered in adaptation to remove the agency and consent of the female characters. In her analysis of rape in *Game of Thrones,* Sonya Saraiya believes that *"Game of Thrones* is falling into the same trap that so much television does—exploitation for shock value. And, in particular, the exploitation of women's bodies" ("Rape"). It is this exploitation which has problematic consequences not only for our televisual culture, but our culture in general. As Sonia Ossorio, president of a chapter of NOW, argues, "Gratuitous rape scenes feed the rape culture" (qtd. in Alcorn). In terms of additions in adaptation and failure to provide narrative justification for such scenes, it seems that *Game of Thrones* has been guilty of such gratuity.

Conversely, while *Outlander* has not escaped criticism for its far more frequent depiction of rape (and attempted rape) throughout its first season, these scenes do succeed where the scenes in *Game of Thrones* fail: in providing narrative resonance and in staying true to the source material. Every scene in which a character is raped or threatened with rape in *Outlander* season one has been taken from the source material and adapted with a high degree of accuracy. Moreover, the characters' lives are shown as impacted from the attacks: Jenny is depicted as a survivor, Claire suffers from PTSD after the attack from the British Redcoats, and Jamie's very soul is almost consumed by Black Jack Randall. In terms of narrative, these attacks are vital: Jamie stays away from his home at Lallybroch for four years in part because of his guilt about his sister's rape. Claire decides to run for the standing stones (and the twentieth century) as a result of Jamie's failure to protect her from her attack, and the narrative impact of Jamie's rape echoes throughout the rest of the novels and will play into key events in *Outlander* season two.

Conclusion

What can be learned from contrasting the depiction and reception of such confrontational content in *Game of Thrones* and *Outlander*? There are four particular elements in which *Outlander* succeeds where *Game of Thrones* fails in its depiction of such content.

In an adapted television series, scenes of rape and sexual assault are more likely to be accepted by viewers and critics if they were part of the original text. If, as in the case of all three *Game of Thrones* rapes, these scenes have been added in adaptation, it is hard to justify such an inclusion if the plot of the original survives without putting the characters though such trauma. Secondly, if there are scenes of sexual assault within the series, as problematic as it is to use rape as the impetus for character development, if the characters aren't changed as a result of the scene, then its inclusion seems merely gratuitous or sensational for mere sensationalism's sake. Thirdly, and relatedly, in order for the character to grow as a result of the scene, he or she must be depicted not as a mere victim, but as a survivor, not only after the scene, but within the scene itself—as *Outlander* shows, both Claire and Jenny fight back and even Jamie's passive acceptance of Randall's assault is a choice made for the sake of Claire. Finally, as the contrast between the two rape scenes in *Outlander*'s "Both Sides Now" shows, if these scenes include elements of the female gaze—focusing on subjective experience rather than objective dehumanization and bare body parts, these scenes are more likely to serve narrative impact rather than providing mere shock value.

While neither series is entirely successful in its depiction of such confrontational content, the process of adapting *Outlander* in season one and many of the choices made by Ronald D. Moore and his team have the potential to impact both original and adapted television for decades to come. Certainly, there is more that needs to be done to increase the number of women writers, directors and directors of photography in Hollywood to ensure that controversial content such as is depicted in these shows contributes more helpfully to the discussions and representations of rape in our culture—providing affective engagement rather than mere titillation.

Acknowledgment

With thanks to my partner in crime, Katharina Freund, for her feedback, comments and wise suggestions.

Works Cited

Alcorn, Chauncey. "More Women's Groups Condemn 'Game of Thrones' Rape Plotlines." *Daily News* 26 May 2015. http://www.nydailynews.com/entertainment/tv/women-groups-condemn-game-thrones-rape-plotlines-article-1.2236459.

Berger, John. *Ways of Seeing*. New York: Viking, 1972.

Beth. "My Top Ten Moments from *Outlander* Midseason Finale: Both Sides Now." *That's Normal* 27 Sep 2014. http://thats-normal.com/2014/09/top-ten-moments-outlander-midseason-finale.

Bloom, Esther. "Outlander Recap: Scottish History X." *Vulture* 30 May 2015. http://www.vulture.com/2015/05/outlander-recap-season-1-episode-16.html.

Bordo, Susan. "Beauty (Re)Discovers the Male Body." *The Male Body*. New York: Farrar, Straus, and Giroux, 1999. 168–225.

Cox, Carolyn. "*Game of Thrones* to Return for Season 5 with All Male Writers, Directors." *The Mary Sue* 16 July 2014. http://www.themarysue.com/game-of-thrones-no-women-writers-directors-season-5.

Culp-Ressler, Tara. "What That *Game of Thrones* Scene Says About Rape Culture." *Think Progress* 21 Apr 2014. http://thinkprogress.org/culture/2014/04/21/3429107/game-of-thrones-rape.

Debnath, Neela. "*Outlander* Star Caitriona Balfe on Filming Rape Scenes and Sexual Violence in the Show." *Sunday Express* 29 May 2015. http://www.express.co.uk/showbiz/tv-radio/580949/Outlander-Caitriona-Balfe-rape-scenes-sexual-violence.

Frankel, Valerie Estelle. *Women in Game of Thrones: Power, Conformity and Resistance*. Jefferson, NC: McFarland, 2014.

Fretts, Bruce. "The 'Outlander' Show Runner, Ron Moore, on That Harrowing Season

Finale." *The New York Times* 30 May 2015. http://artsbeat.blogs.nytimes.com/2015/05/30/outlander-finale-jamie-rape-ron-moore-interview/?_r=0.

Gabaldon, Diana. *Outlander.* New York: Bantam Dell, 1992.

Gay, Roxanne. "*Outlander* Recap: Our Bodies and Hearts Were Ready and So Were Theirs." *Vulture* 21 Sept 2014. http://www.vulture.com/2014/09/outlander-recap-season-1-wedding-claire-jamie-do-it.html.

Ge, Linda. "'Outlander' Star Sam Heughan on Jamie's Brutal Sexual Assault Scene, Major Changes for Season 2." *The Wrap* 19 June 2015. http://www.thewrap.com/outlander-star-sam-heughan-on-jamies-brutal-sexual-assault-scene-major-changes-for-season-2.

Hibberd, James. "*Game of Thrones* Producers Explain Changing Sansa's Storyline." *EW.Com* 26 Apr 2015. http://www.ew.com/article/2015/04/26/game-thrones-sansa-ramsay-interview.

Hughes, Sarah. "Highland Flings and Time Travel: Have You Been Watching *Outlander*?" *The Guardian* 20 May 2015. http://www.theguardian.com/tv-and-radio/tvandradioblog/2015/may/20/outlander-highland-flings-time-travel-have-you-been-watching.

Ley, Tom. "*Game of Thrones* Is Gross, Exploitative, and Totally Out of Ideas." *The Concourse* 18 May 2015. http://theconcourse.deadspin.com/game-of-thrones-is-gross-exploitative-and-totally-out-1705235364.

Looftbourow, Lili. "'Game of Thrones' Fails the Female Gaze: Why Does Prestige TV Refuse to Cater Erotically to Women?" *Salon* 17 Jun 2014. http://www.salon.com/2014/06/16/game_of_thrones_fails_the_female_gaze_why_does_prestige_tv_refuse_to_cater_erotically_to_women.

Lyons, Margaret. "Yes, of Course That Was Rape on Last Night's *Game of Thrones*." *Vulture* 21 Apr 2014. http://www.vulture.com/2014/04/rape-game-of-thrones-cersei-jaime.html.

Marcotte, Amanda. "The Director of Sunday's *Game of Thrones* Doesn't Think That Was Rape." *Salon* 21 Apr 2014. http://www.slate.com/blogs/xx_factor/2014/04/21/game_of_thrones_rape_director_alex_graves_says_the_sex_becomes_consensual.html.

Martin, George RR. *A Game of Thrones.* New York: Bantam, 1996. Kindle file.

_____. "Re: Jaime's Changes in Breaker of Chains." *Not a Blog* 21 Apr 2014. http://grrm.livejournal.com/367116.html?thread=19030284#t19030284.

_____. *A Storm of Swords.* London: Harper Voyager, 2000. Kindle file.

Mcalister, Jodi. "The Radical, Romantic Female Gaze of *Outlander*." *Overland* 23 Oct 2014. https://overland.org.au/2014/10/the-radical-romantic-female-gaze-of-outlander.

Meslow, Scott. "The Sexual Politics of *Game of Thrones* Just Got Enormously Worse." *The Week* 20 Apr 2014. http://theweek.com/articles/447693/sexual-politics-game-thrones-just-got-enormously-worse.

Mulvey, Laura. "Visual Pleasure and Narrative Cinema." *Screen* 16.3 (Autumn 1975): 6–18.

Ng, Philiana. "'Outlander' Director on Midseason Finale: 'we all went beyond our comfort zones.'" *The Hollywood Reporter* 27 Sept 2014. http://www.hollywoodreporter.com/live-feed/outlander-director-midseason-finale-we-735795.

Pantozzi, Jill. "Someone Finally Asked Lena Headey About That Controversial *Game of Thrones* Scene." *The Mary Sue* 29 Apr 2014. http://www.themarysue.com/lena-headey-controversial-game-of-thrones-scene.

_____. "We Will No Longer Be Promoting HBO's *Game of Thrones*." *The Mary Sue*

18 May 2015. http://www.themarysue.com/we-will-no-longer-be-promoting-hbos-game-of-thrones.

Rougeau, Michael. "'Game of Thrones' Will Not Stop Doing Horrible Things to Sansa Stark." *Mashable* 18 May 2015. http://mashable.com/2015/05/18/game-of-thrones-season-5-episode–6-recap.

Rowles, Dustin. "Dear 'Outlander': Please Stop with All the Raping (NSFW)." *Pajiba* 29 Sep 2014. http://www.pajiba.com/tv_reviews/dear-outlander-please-stop-with-all-the-raping-nsfw.php.

Ryan, Maureen. "'Outlander' Did Something Radical Again." *Huffington Post* 27 Apr 2015. http://www.huffingtonpost.com/2015/04/27/outlander-lallybroch_n_7155 096.html

_____. "'Outlander,' the Wedding Episode and TV's Sexual Revolution." *Huffington Post* 29 Sept 2014. http://www.huffingtonpost.com/2014/09/29/outlander-wedding_n_5896284.html

Saraiya, Sonya. "'Outlander' Shows Full Male Nudity—and Laughs in the Face of Rape." *Salon* 26 Apr 2015. http://www.salon.com/2015/04/26/outlander_shows_full_male_nudity_and_laughs_in_the_face_of_rape.

_____. "The 'Outlander' Torture Chamber: A Shockingly Brutal Rape Transforms a Hero into a Victim, but at What Cost?" *Salon* 1 Jun 2015. http://www.salon.com/2015/05/31/the_outlander_torture_chamber_a_shockingly_brutal_rape_transforms_a_hero_into_a_victim_but_at_what_cost.

_____. "Rape of Thrones." *AV Club* 20 Apr 2014. http://www.avclub.com/article/rape-thrones-203499.

Seltzer, Sarah. "Has the Golden Age of TV Been Replaced by the Age of Rape and Torture?" *Flavorwire* 19 May 2015. http://flavorwire.com/519467/has-the-golden-age-of-tv-been-replaced-by-the-age-of-rape-and-torture.

_____. "Outlander's Dark Exploration of Sexual Assault." *Flavorwire* 1 June 2015. http://flavorwire.com/521107/outlanders-dark-exploration-of-sexual-assault.

Sepinwall, Alan. "Review: 'Game of Thrones'—'Breaker of Chains': Uncle Deadly?" *Hitflix* 20 Apr 2014. http://www.hitfix.com/whats-alan-watching/review-game-of-thrones-breaker-of-chains-uncle-deadly.

Soligan, Kaitlyn. "Can We Talk About Those Rape Scenes in 'Outlander'?" *Bitch Media* 23 Oct 2014. https://bitchmedia.org/post/can-we-talk-about-those-rape-scenes-in-outlander.

Stern, Marlow. "Game of Thrones' Most WTF Sex Scene: Nikolaj Coster-Waldau on Jaime Lannister's Darkest Hour." *The Daily Beast* 21 Apr 2014. http://www.thedailybeast.com/articles/2014/04/20/game-of-thrones-most-wtf-sex-scene-nikolaj-coster-waldau-on-jaime-lannister-s-darkest-hour.html.

Strom, Hannah. "What Happened on 'The Mindy Project' This Week Was Not Okay." *Bitch Media* 26 Sept 2013. https://bitchmedia.org/post/what-happened-on-%E2%80%9Cthe-mindy-project%E2%80%9D-this-week-was-not-okay.

Thomas, Rhiannon. "Outlander, Rape and the Female Gaze." *Feminist Fiction* 3 October 2014. http://feministfiction.com/2014/10/03/outlander-rape-and-the-female-gaze.

_____. "Outlander: Would You Like Some Rape with That Rape?" *Feminist Fiction* 10 October 2014. http://feministfiction.com/2014/10/10/outlander-would-you-like-some-rape-with-that-rape.

Trout, Jenny. "Outlander and the Female Gaze: Why Women Are Watching." *Huffington Post* 22 Nov 2014. http://www.huffingtonpost.com/jenny-trout/outlander-and-the-female-_b_5859154.html.

Valenti, Jessica. "When You Call a Rape Anything but Rape, You Are Just Making Excuses for Rapists." *The Guardian* 24 Apr 2014. http://www.theguardian.com/commentisfree/2014/apr/24/rape-game-of-thrones.

Vineyard, Jennifer. "*Outlander*'s Tobias Menzies on Playing Torture Scenes, Going Full-Frontal, and Getting Back on *Game of Thrones*." *Vulture* 16 May 2015. http://www.vulture.com/2015/05/outlander-tobias-menzies-on-going-full-frontal.html.

The Heroine's Journey
Claire Beauchamp Reclaims the Feminine

PATTI MCCARTHY

> Strange, the things you remember. Single images and feel-
> ings that stay with you down through the years. Like the
> moment I realized I'd never owned a vase. That I'd never
> lived any place long enough to justify having such a simple
> thing. And how at that moment, I wanted nothing so much
> in all the world as to have a vase of my very own.
> —*Outlander*, E101

One of the controlling metaphors in *Outlander* is a vase. Locked away behind a window, Claire considers the implications of what it might be like to own one of her own, and a home in which to put it. It doesn't take a big stretch of imagination to realize what the vase represents to Claire. Full or empty, this vase is a symbol of those things in her life that Claire fears, has denied expression, or needs in order to become a fully balanced individual. This vase represents a journey then, that Claire needs to make in order to recapture something she has lost, something that has disappeared—something she once had, but is now gone.[1]

Many are familiar with what is called the Journey of the Hero defined by Joseph Campbell in his seminal work *The Hero with a Thousand Faces*. In the book, Campbell uncovers a deep structure that can be found in the great epics of every world culture that he believes to be the basis of all human narratives—from jokes to myths and everything else in between. Campbell explains that as these mythic stories are shared we integrate them into our own lives and into the very core and foundation of our being. These mythic narratives explore the basic questions of "who we are," and help us to create our own identities and our understanding of our place in the world. While these stories are as varied as the human race, according to Campbell, the basic pattern and form remains the same, is universal, and occurs in every culture, in every time (17–18). The Hero's Journey can be broken down into three separate parts, each part containing specific narrative and plot elements:

Departure	Initiation	Return
The Call to Adventure	Road of Trials	Refusal of Return
Refusal of the Call	Meeting with Goddess	Magic Flight
Supernatural Aid	Woman as Temptress	Rescue from Without
Crossing the First Threshold	Atonement with Father	Crossing Threshold
Belly of the Whale	Apotheosis	Master of Two Worlds
	Ultimate Boon	Freedom to Live

In the basic Journey of the Hero, or Quest Myth, Campbell determined the hero leaves his ordinary world and ventures to a place of supernatural wonders (Separation). He faces a series of trials, survives a supreme ordeal, is granted a boon or treasure (Initiation), and returns home, having learned from the ordeal, to share his treasure and knowledge with those he left behind (Return) (Campbell 17–18).

Journey of the Heroine

Unfortunately, many woman have judged themselves against the male definition of success and in spite of the woman's movement, the prevailing myth in our society is decidedly patriarchal. Certain people and certain positions have more value than others. Murdock, author of *The Heroine's Journey*, explains:

> Male norms have become the social standard for leadership, personal autonomy, and success in this culture, and in comparison women find themselves perceived as lacking in competence, intelligence and power. The girl observes this as she grows up and wants to identify with the glamour, prestige, authority, independence, and money controlled by men. Many high-achieving women are considered *daughters of the father* because they seek the approval and power of the first male model. Somehow mother's approval doesn't matter as much; father defines the feminine, and this affects her sexuality, her ability to relate to men, and her ability to pursue success in the world [29].

Many women seek power and authority either by becoming like men or becoming liked by men. Seeking the approval of men, women look in the mirror only to find they have no reflection of their own—only the internalized projection of what the patriarchy wants her to be.

To reclaim the part of the "self" that has been buried, splintered, split or replaced with the face of the father, she needs to dig into the depths of her unconscious to heal her wounded animus, or masculine side, and reclaim the feminine which has been sleeping—combined, these elements create the *Hieros Gamos*, the Sacred Union or Great Marriage, which, according to Carl Jung, represents the ultimate alchemical transformation within the individual. This union of opposites, yin and yang, logos and eros, represents the fully integrated individual who has achieved balance on a spiritual, mental and emotional level. Such a union allows women to touch the divine within themselves. This is the journey that Claire must take. She must come to terms with the negative masculine that has wounded her animus and integrate them before she can reclaim the feminine she has lost and enter into the Sacred Marriage of the self.

Comparison of the Hero/Heroine Journey Models[2]

HERO'S JOURNEY (Joseph Campbell)	HEROINE'S JOURNEY (Patti McCarthy)
DEPARTURE	**AWAKENING—The Maiden**
The Ordinary World	World of Illusions
The Call to Adventure	The Call to Adventure
Refusal of the Call	Refusal of the Call
Supernatural Aid	Harsh Mentor/Supernatural Aid/Talisman
Threshold Guardians	Threshold Guardians
Crossing of the First Threshold	Crossing of the First Threshold
The Belly of the Whale	Fortunate Fall
INITIATION	**TRANSFORMATION—** **The Lover and Great Mother**
The Road of Trials (Tests and Gains)	Road of Trials (Revelation and Losses)
The Meeting with the Goddess	Meeting with the Animus —Face Bluebeard *(Negative Animus)* —Meet Green Man *(Positive Animus)*
Woman as Temptress	Tempted to Abort Quest/True Path
Atonement with the Father	Atonement with the Mother Confront False and Powerless Father
Apotheosis	Apotheosis
The Ultimate Boon	Reward: Integrated Self/Family
RETURN	**REBIRTH—The Crone**
Refusal of the Return	Refusal of the Return
Rescue from Without	Supreme Ordeal: Rescue from Within
Crossing of the Return Threshold	Crossing of the Return Threshold
Master of Two Worlds	Rebirth: Power of Life and Death
Freedom to Live	Mother of the World

World of Illusions

Typically, the heroine's story begins with her living in a World of Illusions designed to protect her. Victoria Lynn Schmidt, author of *45 Master Characters: Mythic Models for Creating Original Characters*, observes, "This is a familiar world of things known to her and repetition brings her the illusion of security, but is a form of imprisonment" (186). Deep down, the heroine knows her perfect world isn't so perfect and creates any manner of coping strategies to live in it. This might include living in naïve denial (Dorothy, *Wizard of Oz*), becoming a people-pleaser (Thelma, *Thelma & Louise*), relying on men (Scarlet O'Hara, *Gone with the Wind*), trying to be one of the boys (Claire, *Outlander*; Clarisse, *Silence of the Lambs*), or, for the more self-aware heroines, being depressed, but feeling trapped (Claire, *Outlander*; Rose, *Titanic*; Katniss, *Hunger Games*) (Schmidt 193–195).

Our heroine typically stays put because she feels she has an obligation to do so or has bought into the role of martyr. Throughout World War II, Claire has done her duty and faithfully served King and Country. She's no martyr, but she has put her marriage on hold for the past five years, only seeing her husband, Frank Randall, ten days within that time period. She's tired, worn out. But now that the long war is finally over, she can look forward to being reunited with her "long lost" husband once again. Most heroines usually take the journey to protect the people and those things she loves most, and Claire is no exception, but she needs to learn, before she can take care of anyone else, she must first take care of herself and grow as a person.

Call to Adventure

As our heroine becomes more self-aware, the coping strategies that allowed her to live in her familiar or present day world begin to unravel (Schmidt 207). This early stage of the journey might aptly be called "Trouble in Paradise." For Claire, the ending of the war bodes a return to her past—her home, her husband, her life before the war. But after all she's experienced, can Claire's life really be the same? She has been changed by the experience—as certainly as has her husband. It is at this point in the narrative and in her life that Claire, like many heroines before her, begins to ask the questions, "Am I happy?" and "Have I *ever* been happy?"

She starts to see her situation as it really is. Even before she comes "home" to Frank after the war, we can see that Claire doesn't quite share the excitement of the soldiers celebrating around her—in the very beginning she's positioned as an outsider, an outlier—and appears to be a stranger in a strange land—a woman living in a man's world. The war that has been raging around her for the past five years, in many ways, parallels the conflict she feels within her own psyche.

Narratives work on a variety of levels, and *Outlander* is no exception. Just as the war has devastated Europe (The world is in chaos, old regimes have been upset or overthrown, people have been murdered, displaced, the world is a wasteland that needs healing, etc.), so too does it reflect not only the personal life of our character (Claire's relationship with Frank is in disarray and needs work, she needs to reconnect with her husband), but also her internal state of mind (She's in a state of dis-ease, she may have concerns about whether her marriage will work or not, or if she's ready to settle down and give up her independence experienced as a field nurse to be a "devoted" wife and self-sacrificing mother, both based on an unconscious fear of wedlock and perhaps childbirth.)

It is interesting to note that Claire mentions that while memories of V.E. day quickly fade for her, her memory of a vase, locked away in a store window, can be recalled in striking detail. It is apparent then, at this point in her life, she needs to consider and confront what other things she "has put on the shelf." Like those wounded men in the "outside world" she has tended, and the destruction in the world around her, she must now acknowledge the wounds within her own psyche and learn to liberate and heal the conflict she finds within herself—and her encounter with the vase starts this process.

The quest for the Grail, or vase, acts as a herald and triggers Claire's need to recognize that she has been wounded in some way (both Frank and she are both walking wounded), learn how to heal her wounded self, then integrate the healed self in such a way as to create balance in her life. For Claire, this vase represents nothing less than the Hieros Gamos, or the Sacred Marriage that integrates the self into wholeness.

Claire and Frank go on a road trip to Scotland on a "second honeymoon" to reconnect and reestablish their relationship. Claire sees it as "A way to celebrate the end of war and start life anew and discover the people we've become after five years apart" (E101, "Sassenach"). A road trip always signifies that our heroine has begun a journey of self-discovery, and this case is no exception. After serving as a nurse on the battlefield, being an independent woman and making her own decisions, Claire now has the opportunity to settle down. But does Claire want to "settle"? Frank is stable, secure, and somewhat boring. Is there more to life? To love? Again the question, "Am I happy?" hangs in the air between them. Claire seems to be respected as an equal by her husband, but when he finds a "ghostly" Highlander standing outside her window he quickly becomes jealous and questions her fidelity. Is this the reaction of a loving spouse?

It is interesting to note that Frank is on a search as well. Frank is a historian, trying to reclaim his-story. He is trying to piece together the puzzle and fabric of his past and track down his ancestors. This is a journey, for both Frank and Claire, of origins—a need to discover the missing "I." But whose "I" is it? Frank's search is the driving force of this road trip. So far in the narrative, it is his-story, not her-story that is the focus. In particular, Frank is tracking down Black Jack Randall, a notorious British officer who brutalized any rebellious Scotsman during the 1700s who posed a threat to his power and control. It's no small wonder Claire has unconscious concerns. The past, any historian can tell you, has a tendency to repeat itself. What does she really know about Frank after five years anyway? Is he the kind and gentle man she loved "in the past," or has he become someone else, someone who is jealous, possessive and may want to dominate and control on parallel to Black Jack Randall?

At this point in the narrative, during Frank's discussions with the Reverend about his ancestors, the historical tension between a rebellious Scotland and tyrannical England is established and foreshadows both the conflict Claire experiences in her current relationship, and then in the world to which she travels. The occupied faction fights to be free, the other seeks to dominate and control, reflecting the power dynamics and tension of an uneasy military occupation, but also a negative relationship as well. Again, the heroine's journey leads inward and this conflict clearly reflects Claire's sense of "dis-ease." She loves Frank, but can she ever really "go home" again to a place she may never have "felt at home" in the first place? The vase is representative of a journey then, that Claire needs to make in order to recapture something she has lost, something that has disappeared—not only her relationship with Frank, but even more importantly, the place she should most feel at home, but doesn't. She needs to seek the feminine in herself. Claire needs to find "her-story," the part of herself she has lost in the past, in order to find her place in the present.

Accepting the Call

Claire's "call" comes to her through a series of mystical events. First, her road trip leads to a bed and breakfast that has been marked by blood over the mantel. Clearly, while she can weather this storm, there will be pain and sacrifice. Her arrival here signals a threshold experience. The act of marking the mantels in the Highlands, called "Bleeding for St. Martin," was one of the most important feast days of the Church. It is interesting to note that this ritual, which occurred on Samhain, or All Hallows Eve, protected the home against disease. Perhaps it is time for Claire to consider what dis-ease she might be feeling and as a "healer, heal thyself" and ask, "what ails thee?" This is the question the drives both the Grail Myth and quest of the heroine. Claire may want to be "passed over," as indicated by the ritual, but the journey to self-discovery is often painful, especially if something has been repressed and what has been buried suddenly comes to light. Both the vase and the bloody mantel (both feminine spaces and places of the Great Mother) foreshadow Claire's mystical journey to "another world," a place in her unconscious where she must "go back in time" to a place where time does not exist, where ritual has the capacity to unbind time, and where dwells the old magic of the Goddess. The veil of Maya (illusions) is pulled back. This then is Claire's journey—In order to "go home," she needs to go into her psyche/unconscious and confront her fears and get in touch with her feminine side.

While the second honeymoon road trip, and the visit to the bed and breakfast set the stage for our heroine's Call to Adventure, the actual Call comes in the form of Mrs. Graham who Claire meets at Reverend Wakefield's house and invites our heroine into the kitchen for some tea. Mrs. Graham is a Druid mystic who offers to read Claire's tea leaves, then her lifeline. It's interesting that Frank (masculine) and the Reverend (formalized religion) discuss his family history (his-story) in the library (logos nourishes the mind), while Claire (feminine) and Mrs. Graham (pagan religion) discuss her-story (mystic arts) in the kitchen (eros nourishes the body and soul). There's something wrong with her lifeline (life). Mrs. Graham tells Claire that "she's here but not here" (a part of her has been lost, she's not completely present in this relationship), that she will be married twice, but it's an odd marriage. Her lifeline ends in a fork, not a break. She will not end one, then start the other—rather she will live both lives (loves) simultaneously, or be married to two men.

After her "reading," Claire sees the vase in the window, then goes home and gazes into a mirror while she waits for Frank to return from his visit with the Reverend. In film, a mirror typically signifies a need to "look at one-self," to confront the "I." It's not surprising that it is at this moment that a ghost (in 1700s Highland garb) appears outside her window. Her musings conjure the "other" man (perhaps symbolically a ghost of the past, or of the man Frank used to be, or of the "Frank" she longs to "find" again). Frank sees the ghost watching Claire through the window to her room from the street. He goes to confront the man, but he suddenly disappears. The ghost of the past, then, haunts them both. There *is* trouble in our honeymoon paradise. Claire worries about whether she and Frank can "go home again" and about an uncertain future. Frank worries about Claire's fidelity. We can see that Frank's suspicions make Claire uneasy. Is this the man she loved, wants to be with—a man who is jealous, suspicious, and potentially controlling?

Supernatural Aid/Crossing the First Threshold

Frank learns that there will be a sacred druid ritual performed at Craigh na Dun to celebrate the feast of Samhain/Beltane. It is a place where the sacred (spiritual) and profane (physical) world meet. Only here can the dualities that need to be integrated within Claire's psyche occur (spirit/body,

Mother Earth/Father Sky, yin/yang, masculine/feminine, head/heart, conscious/unconscious, circle/blade). Here, in this sacred space of the circle, the veil (Maya and all illusion) between the two worlds disappears. Frank asks Claire to go with him. She accepts.

Claire and Frank watch the druid ritual. It is hauntingly beautiful. Women dressed in white, whirl in circles among the circle of stones—circles within circles—an eternal return, an unlocking of time into infinity, creating a spiral, a labyrinth, the sacred Ouroboros, a place of wholeness and infinite possibilities—the mystic womb of the Great Goddess, a place of alchemical transformation which gives birth to individuation. Carl Jung saw the Ouroboros as an archetype and the basic mandala of alchemy, stating:

> The alchemists, who in their own way knew more about the nature of the individuation process than we moderns do, expressed this paradox through the symbol of the Ouroboros, the snake that eats its own tail. The Ouroboros has been said to have a meaning of infinity or wholeness. In the age-old image of the Ouroboros lies the thought of devouring oneself and turning oneself into a circulatory process, for it was clear to the more astute alchemists that the *prima materia* of the art was man himself. The Ouroboros is a dramatic symbol for the integration and assimilation of the opposite, i.e. of the shadow. This "feed-back" process is at the same time a symbol of immortality, since it is said of the Ouroboros that he slays himself and brings himself to life, fertilizes himself and gives birth to himself. He symbolizes the One, who proceeds from the clash of opposites, and he therefore constitutes the secret of the *prima materia* which [...] unquestionably stems from man's unconscious [para. 513].

While the circle of stones at Craigh na Dun represents the receptive feminine principle (chalice/vase/urn), the erect stone in the middle symbolizes the fertile masculine (blade), which together brings forth life out of nothingness—the great Ouroboros.

This then is Claire's call. Nothing less than the descent into her unconscious toward self-discovery and transformation where she must rectify and confront the fears and pain of her past in order to love in the present. Loving others first always, however, begins by loving oneself, and only Claire can take the first step in this direction.

The women in white (who prefigure Claire as the White Witch) also dance holding vessels filled with the flame of creation; this is the dance of life, but as part of the Ouroboros, also the dance macabre (of death). These women in white also hold what looks like cocoons. This is truly a place of transformation and change, from pupa (child) to chrysalis, then to butterfly and thus, transformation and individuation. Claire must transform in order to be reborn. She must realize her true potential that has been sleeping (chrysalis). Finally, these women in white represent the Grail Maidens who guard the Holy Grail and appear when the world has been spiritually wounded and needs healing (Goodwin 27).[3]

Claire and Frank watch the druid ritual until the sun rises (a transitory time) that ends as a whiteout on screen (symbolizing death and rebirth). Both have been touched by the ritual and they go to explore the ruins. Claire notices a blue flower, a forget-me-not, growing near one of the stones. Forget-me-nots have both magical and healing properties. It is said that on Beltane the flower can be used to walk between worlds, reveal karmic connections, and create a bridge between those that have departed us and for those we have yet to meet in this life. One of the flower's many healing properties is stopping bleeding and healing the wounded. It's not surprising both the vase and the flower are blue, connecting both to Claire. A bit later, Claire decides to go back to the stones to retrieve the forget-me-not. While Claire invites Frank to join her, he lets her know he has an appointment with the Rev. Wakefield. It is interesting to note that Claire decides to leave when Frank is busy finding and connecting with Black Jack Randall—a foreshadowing of what happens later.

When Claire touches the forget-me-not, it acts as a key to her unconscious and unlocks those things she has denied or buried, transporting her through the stones to another time and place. Claire's is not an easy "fall." Her world is literally turned upside down, broken and torn apart. The experience approximates the chaos of a car wreck. Glass shatters, the car flips over, she's thrown off the familiar road and falls into another world, another place, a different time (her unconscious). It hurts sometimes to wake up to the truth. Sometimes you have to break down to break through.

Fortunate Fall/Meeting the Animus

Claire "falls" into the middle of a battle, paralleling her "old" world. The fall signifies nothing less than a descent into the battle she's been fighting in her unconscious. Love, for Claire, is a battlefield. It's not surprising the first person she meets is a physical representation of her husband. She soon learns this man is not Frank, he's Black Jack Randall—Frank's monstrous double. At first Claire is stunned by his appearance, and looks to him for help, but then quickly becomes horrified when he calls her a whore and tries to rape her. She learns that looks can be deceiving. It's not uncommon in the unconscious to split good and bad qualities of an individual into separate parts, especially if an individual is experiencing anxiety about a particular person or situation (Freud 37–41). These good and bad parts of her husband (and her marriage) manifest in the characters of first, Black Jack Randall (bad), and then Jamie Fraser (good).

Black Jack Randall feeds on control. He rapes, destroys, murders, he demands complete obedience and submission and takes what he wants. He represents everything Claire fears in her marriage—the controlling and destructive male. Jamie on the other hand, is everything Black Jack is not—compassionate, supportive, trusting, sensual, just, intuitive. On a mythic level, these two aspects represent Claire's animus, or what Carl Jung, called the male aspect of her psyche. These "people" represent aspects of the individuation process in her psyche that must be healed and integrated before she can "go back" to join with her husband in a loving marriage as an equal and fully balanced and "whole" individual. To grow on her journey, and reconnect to the "lost" feminine in herself, the heroine must experience these aspects of the negative and positive masculine (or her animus) personified as both Bluebeard and the Green Man. Claire's journey in *Outlander* is no exception.

Road of Trials/Allies and Villains

The heroine is tested on the Road of Trials. From Episode #101 ("Sassenach") through Episode #105 ("Rent"), Claire meets a variety of allies who will support, but not rescue, antagonists who will provoke thought, and villains that will force decisions and/or double as mentors. Schmidt writes that our heroine must face Issues of Attachment, Fear, Guilt, Lies, Shame, Grief, and Illusion (220–221). During these trials the heroine needs to: (1) learn to depend on herself and confront her fears; (2) find her voice, say "no" and overcome feelings of guilt; (3) forgive herself and others and accept her strengths and weaknesses; (4) accept love from others and love herself for who she is; (5) refuse to conform; (6) overcome denial; and (7) trust herself and learn not to blindly obey. She must also learn, through it all, to remember to ask "why?" but also "why not?"

After first escaping rape by Black Jack Randall, Claire barely escapes the same fate at the hands of her rescuers. Taken to a safe house to hide from the British after her close escape from Jack Randall, Claire soon meets Jamie Fraser, her future husband and lover, who has been wounded in the recent skirmish. His shoulder has been badly dislocated. She refuses to "hold her tongue" and stand by and watch Jamie suffer disfiguration under the misguided ministrations of his countrymen. Although she is suspected of being a spy, in an uneasy alliance, Claire joins with the rebels (Highlanders) who stand against the tyrannical British. Over time, she also refuses the unwanted sexual overtures of Dougal MacKenzie (Jamie's uncle), overcomes the ranting of a misguided and misogynistic Parish priest, and holds her own against Laird Colum MacKenzie who "allows" her, since she is a healer and he is afflicted with a crippling malady, to stay under his protection.

Saying "no" *is a dangerous narrative because it is subversive. It threatens the status quo and those in authority.* To reclaim her true self and power our heroine must learn during her journey to say "no," question authority, grow up and make her own path, rather than follow the one prescribed for her.[4] However, there is always a price to pay for saying "no." Those in authority will fight to regain their power and will stop at nothing to get it back. Once the genie is out of the proverbial bottle, however, it's hard to stuff it back in again. When one woman says "no" this knowledge is shared with other women will have the strength to do the same. For instance, Mrs. FitzGibbons allows Claire to treat her nephew with herbs to cure his poisoning, thus undercutting the power and authority of the parish priest who believes the boy is possessed by demons and needs to undergo exorcism. Claire's refusal to obey and submit to the priest's authority saves the boy, but has dire repercussions later.

It is also during this time of trials, that our heroine will encounter her shadow. The shadow tests our heroine and represents the energy of the dark side, the unexpressed, unrealized or rejected aspects of herself, all the dark secrets she can't or won't admit—all our dark wishes and even darker thoughts. We think them, but as soon as they reach consciousness, we push them back down into the darkness. We tell ourselves, "I can't believe I even considered that option, thought that thought, desired that outcome." So we tell ourselves otherwise and pretend it didn't happen. We pretend so well that we forget we even thought such a thing, or remember it as something someone else said or did. Then we pretend we are shocked when confronted with the thought or deed personified in another individual.

However, the shadow can also shelter positive qualities that are in hiding or that we have rejected in ourselves for some reason. Characters that trigger the ire of our heroine usually represent that aspect of the personality she is trying to deny. Based on psychoanalytic findings of Sigmund Freud, Otto Rank, and Carl Jung, et al., author Robert Bly, suggests that each of us has some part of our personality that is hidden from us.

"When we were one or two years old we had a 360-degree personality," author Robert Bly observed, "but one day we noticed that our parents didn't like certain parts.... They said things like: 'Can't you be still?' Or 'It isn't nice to try and kill your brother.'" (17) So, to keep our parents' love and approval, we stuff these "ugly," unwanted, or forbidden parts of ourselves into an invisible bag that we drag behind us. When we enter school our bag is already rather large and grows bigger and darker each time we stuff another part of ourselves into it. Teachers tell us, "Nice girls don't get angry,"—so we stuff our anger in the bag. Religions may say sexuality is bad ("Nice girls don't do that!"), so that goes into the bag as well. We even do more bag stuffing in high school when peers pressure us into being something we are not. (Bly 17) "We spend our life until we're twenty deciding what parts of ourselves to put in the bag," noted Bly, "and we spend the rest of our lives trying to get them out again" (18).

The negative face of what we've stuffed in the bag, better known as the Shadow, is projected in stories onto characters called "villains, antagonists, or enemies" (Vogler, *Writer's Journey* 65).

Often, the shadow shows up in the heroine's quest, when she needs to confront something that she has stuffed in her "bag," allowing her to experience alternate possibilities, decisions and outcomes. Geillis is Claire's "shadowy sister" who allows Claire to confront and "live out" her darker desires or fears. Claire first meets Geillis gathering mushrooms not long after she arrives at Castle Leoch (E102, "Castle Leoch"), having gained a new "pleasure in touching growing things again." It's a nice change, considering Claire has been tending to the dead and dying for the past five years. Geillis tells Claire that she has experience with medicinals and potions—those that heal and those that kill. She lets Claire know that the mushrooms she gathers will get rid of an unwanted child, suggesting that Claire not only still carries the taint of death with her and needs to find balance with "growing things," but may be harboring unconscious fears about childbirth as well.

This is our first hint that Claire may fear childbirth and motherhood as well as her marriage. Every woman, at one time, or another has doubts and fears when facing these stages in her life, but none so much as those without modern medical care. Childbirth was the leading cause of death for women during pre-modern times (and even today childbirth is the sixth leading cause of death in women) and Claire, a nurse, would be fully aware of these medical risks. Further, being raised by an uncle, living most of her life among men, Claire has not had much of an opportunity to be around women who have given birth and raised children. She's a stranger in a strange land (not only in the Highlands in 1743, but also in the role of mother). She knows how to get pregnant and deliver a baby, but may not feel as secure in her knowledge about raising a child. Geillis, as shadow, lets Claire know that there are options besides being saddled with bearing "an heir," as Claire and Frank had discussed only weeks before at the bed & breakfast during their second honeymoon. While Claire may consciously think she wants a child, Geillis gives voice to Claire's unconscious fears. Later in the series (E109, "By the Pricking of My Thumbs"), Geillis again reminds Claire of her "options," when Claire goes in search of a child crying in the woods who has been exposed and abandoned in the crotch of a tree. Geillis explains that the parents have exposed the sick child because they believe it is a changeling—a fairy child that was exchanged with their own. It's a custom, Claire realizes, that allows parents to deny their guilt and diffuse the responsibility for killing their own unwanted, sick child. Claire reaches the child, but it is too late. She cradles the baby in her lap and mourns the baby's death.

While the previous episode with Geillis and the mushrooms suggests a fear of pregnancy and childbirth, this reflects a fear of perhaps not wanting the child once it is born. The fear that you will not want your child for whatever reason is a horrifying thought. At one time or another in a mother's life she may feel overwhelmed by a child that is too demanding, too difficult, takes too much time, or acts in ways that the parent did not bargain for. Being a parent requires sacrifice. Will she be able to nourish and support the child? Be willing to sacrifice her own desires for the child? Will she abandon her child the same way she was abandoned by her own, dead mother? Can Claire raise a child that will replace her in every way—grow in strength and beauty, while she grows old and dies? A good mother celebrates the life of her child, wishes her the best, and nourishes her throughout her life without resentment, or jealousy. The sacrifices she makes along the way are worthwhile—and she knows she will live forever through the many generations to come. The bad mother, on the other hand, resents the child and will not make sacrifices on her behalf. During her journey, Claire needs to decide whether she is ready for a child and what kind of mother she will be, or at the very least, recognize that her feelings toward pregnancy, childbirth, and motherhood are "normal."

Soon after her arrival at the Castle Leoch, Claire also meets her rival, Laoghaire, who has been brought forward for her father for "judging." Her father wants her beaten for suspected sexual indiscretion. Here then we first see the negative father, or patriarchy, in action that seeks to punish or control the sexual aspect of the feminine. Women, throughout the ages, have been stoned, burned or beaten to death and told they are "bad" or "unclean" or "wicked" by men (via some form of authority such as religion) seeking to control their bodies. Claire, we realize in Episode 101 ("Sassenach"), is a woman who enjoys sex and doesn't have a problem about letting her husband, Frank, know how he can please her. But like Laoghaire, Frank suspects Claire of sexual infidelities. Both women have been accused unfairly. No proof is brought forward in either case—it's enough that a man has suspected them of sexual wantonness—it condemns them. It is noteworthy that Jamie Fraser steps in to take Laoghaire's place and accepts the punishment on her behalf. Jamie throughout most of the series is bandaged, beaten, flogged, broken, shot, raped, or otherwise wounded, as to protect various women (Jenny, Laoghaire, Claire) at the hands of the negative and perverted masculine (Black Jack Randall). While the archetypes of Bluebeard (in this case Jack Randall) and the Green Man (Jamie) battle over the heroine (since they are competing aspects of Claire's animus), the Green Man will bear the brunt of our heroine's fear and pain. He will be wounded—badly. He bears the agony of her wounded animus—and throughout the series personifies all her emotional and psychological hurts, her "wounds" that need healing. The Green Man teaches the heroine that compassion is not weakness or vulnerability—but strength. *And it is this strength and courage of the feminine (willing to sacrifice for another) that will, in the end, prove to be her core and will ensure our hero-ine's survival.* Jamie, as Green Man, teaches Claire to face her fears instead of running from them (Episode 104 "The Gathering"; i.e., oath taking cere-mony), or use them as a source of rebellion (Episode 105 "Rent," i.e., the Jaco-bite cause). He does what she as of yet cannot. In the act of healing his wounds, she begins to heal herself. It is not up to the Green Man to rescue our heroine, but up to the heroine to learn how to rescue the Green Man from the brutality of Bluebeard and in doing so, rescue herself.

We are now at the midpoint of our narrative. The story will spin on a decision our heroine must now make. Claire is now offered a choice. Marry Jamie Fraser (for protection) or face the horrors of Black Jack and imprison-ment. Either way, she is trapped. As counterpart to Black Jack (Bluebeard), Jamie appears as "positive" rescuer. The problem is Claire is still being res-cued. While the wedding promises protection, Claire is torn. The fear of wed-lock is one of the things that sent her on her journey in the first place. Although she is attracted to Jamie, she still loves Frank (or the Green Man aspect of Frank Jamie represents). If she marries Jamie, will she forget her past? Is this wedding just another form of escape?

As the episode (E107, "The Wedding") opens, Claire muses that she has begun to forget her old life. "The life I had before and cherished and held dear, like pearls on a string," Claire states in voiceover, has been broken until the individual pearls "roll around in the dark corners of my memory, until I forget what the pearls ever looked like." (Her gold wedding ring from Frank actually does fall off her finger and roll into the crack on the floor—so this is what she is afraid of forgetting). Here appears again the fork in the road referred to in her palm reading. Will she forget why she started this journey in the first place? It is not enough to just embrace the positive aspect of her animus; she must also reconcile her fear of the negative aspects of the mas-culine (Bluebeard) and rescue her own wounded feminine. How can she do this?

Early in the episode we see Claire in her wedding gown. The dress is so tight it looks painful. It's hard for her to "breathe" (the wedding dress, on parallel to her feelings, is bound so tightly it looks as if she's bursting at the seams). Claire gets drunk (another form of escape), descends into the womb/tomb of Mother Earth (underground church) and marries Jamie. Jamie's ring fits. It's not surprising that during the ceremony both Claire and Jamie are cut and bleed. They repeat the vows of marriage together, stating, "You are blood of my blood and bone of my bone. I give you my body that we two may be one. I give you my spirit … 'till our life shall be done."

Both, we already know, are wounded … but now those wounds join them—they recognize a part of their pain and selves in the other—Claire is approaching the grail (in herself). While not fully asking the question "what ails thee?" she had taken a step closer to facing her fears. While she does say yes to Jamie and marriage, and no to the British and Black Jack Randall, she is still not at ease with her decision—she still has doubts. She cares for Jamie, but she still loves Frank. Rather than joining in this union for love, it is a marriage of convenience and protection—this is not the Hieros Gamos that will heal her life and on a higher plane of existence, the world and universe.

It is only after the wedding and they begin talking, sharing memories, and family history, and getting to know each other, is Claire allowed to finally "breathe." Jamie makes her feel more comfortable and shares with her his three "requirements" for the wedding: a priest, a ring and a wedding dress. Rather than see this marriage as a sham, Jamie, Claire finally realizes, has entered into the union with sincerity. The marriage ring has been forged from a key to the estate he has left behind and abandoned after being brutalized by Black Jack Randall. Like Claire, Jamie has been trying to get back home. The ring he gives her is literally the key. Jamie unties her dress, waits until Claire does the same for him, then asks him to bed. Sexually, Claire is more experienced than Jamie and he proves to be a poor performer on their wedding night, Claire doesn't make fun of him, but instead she initiates him into the sexual mysteries (as the sacred prostitute) and teaches him how to not only please himself, but please her as well. No longer a blushing maiden, our heroine fully experiences and enjoys the lover aspect of the Goddess. Jamie asks, "Are men and women usually so ... connected?"

"No," Claire replies ... sex with Frank (the most powerful thing she shared with him) is a fading memory and the true ghost of the past—temporarily replaced with the pleasure she enjoys in the present with Jamie.

While Jamie's understanding empowers her, he also reminds her what she is seeking—a place of completion. It's not just about sex (which she shared with Frank on her second honeymoon), but love. The Green Man seeks to nurture and support her unconditionally. It's not surprising that this episode opens with her marriage to Frank in the 1940s. It is through her union with Jamie that she can once again connect to the love she shared with Frank before the war—the Frank she knew and fell in love with. Her marriage to Jamie heals her for the time being and helps her to believe in herself again. He teaches her to overcome her fears of the negative patriarchy. With Jamie she finally can relax and feel safe. At this point, the heroine as Maiden experiences the Lover aspect of the feminine in the form of animus. Our heroine learns to more fully trust her own judgments and, consequently, moves toward healing the masculine aspect within herself (the animus). As a wedding gift, Jamie presents Claire with his mother's pearls, his love acting as a balm that helps her reconnect and string back together the parts of her past life and "lost" self that have rolled into the "cracks of her unconscious" that she's been trying to remember. The Green Man reminds the heroine of the true path she must follow. He forces her to ask herself what she truly wants … why she is taking his journey. Does she really know?

After the wedding, at the eighth episode and midpoint in the narrative ("Both Sides Now"), Claire does begin to reevaluate her journey. She's presented with a gift from a man with no tongue—a dragonfly in amber. In a cross-dissolve, Claire's dragonfly in amber links to a similar image of a dragonfly on a child's cup from Frank's point of view in the 1940s. Both Frank and Claire are dragonflies stuck in amber. She in the past, and he in the future, both unable to move from their present realities to find the other: They are not much different from two people in a marriage who, while in the same relationship, are stuck in their ways and either long for a life they once lived or wish for a life they should have lived. During this episode, we cross-cut between Frank's search for Claire in the 1940s with scenes of Claire falling more in love with Jamie. Frank's fear is that Claire has stopped loving him (and found a lover), while Claire fears that she has fallen out of love with Frank, but also that she is trapped in a marriage where she is unable to take control of her life and path.

During the next episode (E109, "The Reckoning"), Claire experiences another, more insidious and socially acceptable, form of the negative masculine. Once they escape from Fort William and Black Jack, Jamie spanks Claire and begins to personify Claire's fear of the "angry husband" archetype—how Frank might react if she were to return through the stones.

It's not surprising that Geillis, Claire's shadow, shows up at this point to remind Claire of her darker options. Jamie's actions as the "angry husband" have provoked Claire's shadow. There's not only a way to get rid of an unwanted child, but also an unwanted husband. In Episode 110 ("By the Pricking of My Thumbs") Claire seeks out Geillis in the woods where Geillis is performing a Druid ritual (a perverted parallel to the Druid women in Episode 101), asking for the freedom to wed another—meaning she wants her husband dead. Claire learns that Geillis is having an affair with Dougal MacKenzie and pregnant. Again, this is a personification of Claire's own fears (pregnancy, a loveless and controlling marriage, the accusation of having an affair, lack of choices) and current marital situation (in love with one man and married to another). Soon after, Claire tries to manipulate the Duke of Sandringham, only to have it blow up in her face. This is the second time manipulation hasn't worked. It failed on Bluebeard when Black Jack trapped her in "The Garrison Commander" (106) and "Both Sides Now" (108), and now fails with the "Father," in this case, Duke Sandringham who arranges a duel between Jamie and his second—and again Jamie is wounded (taking on Claire's punishment as scapegoat/Green Man). Colum is angry with both Jamie, for the duel, and Dougal, for getting Geillis pregnant, and they are banished for the time being. Geillis and Claire are left alone under the protection of Laird Colum.

Although separated from Jamie, Claire has, for the moment it seems, overcome Bluebeard, the Big Bad of the Patriarchy and has learned to stand alone without the help of the Green Man. She finally arrives at the point of her journey where she believes she will get the answers she wants and rest for a time. Things could be worse. Then things get worse.

Confront False and Powerless/Impotent Father

During her journey the heroine must also confront the powerless and impotent Father (either personified as a father figure or as a representation of the patriarchy). On her road of trials she will discover that the Father is not all-powerful, or infallible. In fact, in many instances he is the perpetrator of the lie that our heroine needs to obey him to survive. Before she can truly participate in the Hieros Gamos, the sacred marriage of the masculine and feminine in herself (which is foreshadowed in her marriage to Jamie), she must abandon the father and learn to look within for approval, to obey her own desires and intuition, and trust her own judgment. Therefore, the heroine will go through a series of trials and tests that reveal the "Father's" impotence and destructive nature.

It's not surprising that once Jamie attempts to force Claire into the role of the "good," submissive wife and demeans and spanks her like a naughty child that the need to confront the Impotent Father stage is triggered. After Colum banishes Jamie and Dougal, it isn't long before Claire and Geillis are accused of witchcraft, arrested, imprisoned and put on trial.[5] Colum is noticeably absent. The "father" of the Clan who has promised to protect the women, especially Claire, in this case is impotent[6] (in more ways than one) to act—and in fact, may have provoked the arrest, or at the very least, remained silent in order to get rid of the women whom (he believes) are at the root of both Jamie and Dougal's misguided actions. Cages, chains and other constrictive images proliferate during the trial, signaling a need for our heroine to break out of the enslavement of a patriarchal ideology. Offers of protection will not provide safety, but imprisonment instead. This is the third time our heroine needs to say "no," specifically to the lies of the Father that make our heroine feel she is helpless.[7] She has been duped into believing so.

This is the danger of groupthink, and the tyranny of the majority, which our heroine must defend against. Most notably, Claire is accused of killing the baby she found exposed earlier in the woods. Ironically, Claire, the healer, is accused of being a murderer. Rather than face the truth of their own complicity, or wrong thinking, the people want to believe that their child is a changeling and lives in a wonderful land free from pain and sorrow. Claire reminds them that the world is filled with lies and unless the people realize the truth, and stop believing in fairytales perpetrated and supported by the authorities, they will never be free. This is what the heroine teaches and must learn herself, to trust her own judgment and break free from the shackles of an ideology that doesn't protect, but instead enslaves.

Ironically, the circular court room parallels the circle of stones of Craigh na Dun—here the circle is not the great Oubourous, the womb of life and possibility, but a manufactured ring of lies, a circle of Hell—a trial by fire, where the transformation is no less significant. Our heroine, faced with the poor judgment of those in authority, needs to face her accusers and reveal the truth while refuting the lies and in doing so, see her situation like it really is.

As shadow, Geillis represents Claire's unspoken desires, fears, anger, and dark aspect. She also represents the fear the patriarchy has of the Great and Terrible Mother (she killed her husband, took a lover, and is pregnant with a child outside of wedlock sanctioned by the church, thus becoming both creator and destroyer). Eventually Claire will learn that these unwanted aspects of her hidden self are her strengths, but not yet. She still fears the destructive power of the Goddess within. Geillis asks Claire, "Why are you here?" Although Claire has found the strength to stand up to the patriarchy, she still hasn't accepted who she is and why she is on this journey—there is still more she needs to discover about herself. Geillis exposes her "devil's mark," to the crowd and by showing the small pox vaccination scar reveals that she and Claire are both travelers on the same journey. Claire is certainly not the first to be accused of being a witch, or a threat to the patriarchy, and certainly won't be the last. Both are condemned to burn for their "crimes" if they don't confess their "sin" and accept the judgment of the Father.

It is interesting that for the first time, rather than Jamie being around to take on her pain, Claire is beaten at this point of the narrative and forced to actually feel the pain of her wounded feminine/animus. To learn that the Father has lied is an extremely painful experience. It hurts to learn that someone or something you trusted and believed in has betrayed, abandoned, or failed you in some way—especially if you have identified with that person, or ideology. Our heroine is a survivor and doesn't bow down to the authority figure, but there has been a cost. Jamie arrives to rescue Claire, but Geillis takes on this role of "savior" and sacrifice at this point of the story. She willing confesses that she is a witch—seemingly to protect Claire, but instead of groveling for forgiveness, she fully embraces the power of the Goddess and is carried to the pyre, pregnant belly exposed for all to see.

Once away from the courthouse, Claire confesses not her "sin" to Jamie, but her secret. Secrets can be deadly and are often built on our shame and fear. It is that part of ourselves we are ashamed to admit or share—lest we face abandonment and loss. She's been afraid to admit "Why she is here,"—not only to Geillis and Jamie, but also to herself. Unlike the "bad" fathers who wanted to destroy her, Jamie believes her and takes her back to Craigh na Dun to go home. This has always been a story about Claire "going home," learning to be at home in her own skin, being at home with her self and decisions, being at home in the world. Claire is reluctant to go, but Jamie tells her to trust her own decisions. This is the true power of the Green Man and the Circle—a place of unconditional love that heals the "sin" of dualism and fear of the feminine. It is a place of acceptance, understanding and compassion where we drink from the sacred cup of our shared humanity. Magic always occurs in the circle. Jamie does not pretend everything will be "okay," or that he can protect her. He has listened to her truth and he shares his as well. He warns her, "There is only danger and pain on this side." True enough.

The journey could end here for our heroine. Claire could go back to Frank. She's exposed and denied the power of the impotent Father (if our heroine has Daddy issues) and defeated Bluebeard for the time being (if our heroine has sex/relationship issues). However, she has further to go. Women help bury the Goddess when they act like men and belittle the feminine in themselves. Until she is at home in herself as a woman, Claire will never find the Grail that she is. To do this, our heroine must descend deeper into the labyrinth of her unconscious and face the next stage of her journey, the Atonement with the Mother.[8] Claire makes her decision to continue on her journey and stay with Jamie.

Atonement with the Mother

"The hero journeys off to the Chapel Perilous or innermost cave on his journey as preparation to face his supreme ordeal," states Vogler (Writersjourney.com). But our heroine must learn on the road and during her descent into the cave that *she is the cave*. All she has ever had to do was look inside herself—and recognize her own power. She is giver of life and vessel of death. As womb/tomb, the center of the labyrinth, she needs to realize and accept she is the mother of her own life, makes her own path, and creates or destroys her own reality.

The Atonement with the Mother always forces the heroine to undergo a symbolic death experience. For Claire this occurs in Episode #115 ("Wentworth Prison") and is symbolized by Jamie's capture, torture, and imminent death at the hands of Jack Randall who has grown in strength and power. On parallel to a fear that has been locked away in the dark of our unconscious and repressed, yet grows in strength, Black Jack returns with a vengeance, cutting and beating his way to conscious thought. Also buried in the unconscious is the Dark Mother. When we go down into the darkness—or confront those things that have been repressed—we are forced to cast away all that is not true about our lives and ourselves. The old self, outworn and constricting, usually based on the false goals, dreams, or desires of others, must die, before the whole self can be reborn. This requires a painful stripping off of the layers of our false selves. The Atonement with the Mother forces us to look at ourselves with utter, naked honesty. This is one part of her Terrible aspect—she strips us bare of all illusions and false pretensions. She is our shadow sister—that bag of insecurities, fears, worries, and self-loathing that we drag behind us and try to forget and repress. These are the things women have been taught that make them, "unclean, sinful, and terrifying," when in truth they are the very attributes that make them strong (Frankel, *Buffy* 132).

From the very first, both Black Jack Randall and Jamie Fraser have represented Claire's hope and fears in her marriage with Frank. This was why she made the journey in the first place. Black Jack represents the brutalization by the masculine by war, the negative masculine that kills, tortures the feminine and demands complete obedience and submission. His appearance from the very beginning is a physical embodiment of Claire's fears about the man that Frank may have become during the war. This is a perversion of the male/female, masculine/feminine relationship.

Jamie on the other hand, only represents the compassionate and supportive side of Frank (that Claire remembers from the past and longs to find in her marriage), but he also represents her own wounded animus. But can compassion and love survive the brutalization of war? Claire must first heal her own wounds before she can love another. Throughout the narrative, Jamie as Green Man and Claire's positive animus has embodied the wounds of the feminine. As stand-in for Laoghaire, Jamie bore the pain of repressed sexuality (beaten for Laoghaire's "bad" reputation). As his sister Jenny's stand-in and protector from rape and brutalization, Jamie was beaten because he represented strength and courage and the ability to resist rape by Bluebeard (penetration by negative masculine ideology) and to defend his home against oppressive "colonization" by destructive forces (within the self). For Claire, Jamie took a shot from the negative patriarchy via the dual (her manipulations of the Father fails), then is captured and imprisoned by Black Jack at Wentworth Prison. Throughout it all, Jamie has personified the pain, subjugation, peril and wounds of the feminine around him, specifically Claire's unconscious fears. It is in Wentworth Prison, however, when Claire, and subsequently Jamie as her "other half," or double, experiences their deepest wounds, and not only come close to death, but even begin to long for it. Claire, using her strength of will, enters the prison and rescues him, uniting their friends (representing parts of her personality) in a desperate quest.

To find the Mother, our heroine must first heal the split between her negative masculine (Black Jack) and positive masculine (Jamie), then find, accept and restore the woman and Goddess buried beneath.

Supreme Ordeal

In Episode #116, "To Ransom a Man's Soul," Claire does just that.

Jamie is taken to a place of sanctuary with the monks. Having rescued her wounded animus from the destructive aspect of Bluebeard, Claire is ready for her Supreme Ordeal. Just acknowledging her fears, isn't enough. Claire must actually face them—and does so during this episode. While Claire was mustering the troops, using her wits to manipulate the Warden so she could rescue Jamie (it finally works because she is on the "correct path" and trusts herself, whereas before she used it to escape from the journey before it was "time"), she didn't actually see what Jamie experienced at the hands of Jack Randall. Once again, our heroine could deny her fears, but the Supreme Ordeal forces our heroine to face her demons. For the fourth and final time, our heroine needs to embrace these fears as her greatest strength. Gaining this wisdom and clarity is what the entire journey has been all about.

In this episode, Claire has rescued Jamie, but the man Claire knew is gone, "missing." Claire faces the dark night of her soul—the Green Man is gone. The Jamie we knew before, strong and noble, has been stolen away—held prisoner by the destructive masculine. Power is what attracted Black Jack to Jamie in the first place—his courage, his strength, his noble soul, his willingness to sacrifice and protect the weak, and his love of life and freedom—everything Black Jack was not. Black Jack craves it, but rather than joining in union, he seeks to control and destroy, so he makes Jamie believe this courage is weakness. This is Black Jack's masterpiece, his work of art—to take the beautiful and pervert it into a reflection of his own shortcomings.

Claire's secret, the one she's tried to pretend isn't there, which may have wounded her most deeply, is her struggle with the "negative" masculine she wants to be "like." This need and desire chafes at her, but she seeks it out anyway and, in fact, "loves it." Again, Jamie parallels in flesh the unconscious workings of Claire's mind.[9] Throughout his ordeal, Jamie hates Randall for beating him into submission, leaving him nothing to hold on to but Randall's perverted "love." Jamie hates himself even more than his torturer, however, when he becomes aroused by the approval Randall offers. Jamie begins to loathe himself for *his* weakness. But we know it is not Jamie's weakness, but Jack Randall's. Likewise, Claire, throughout the series, has identified with the masculine and, it appears, has lost a vital part of herself because of it. She realizes she's been duped all along. How can she find balance if she continues to deny her "feminine" side? And in this case, Jamie personifies her psychological gender bending and subsequent wounding. *This then is the true battle, Claire's supreme ordeal—it's not about whether she can love Frank, but whether she can forgive and love herself.* This is the true test. This is the strength she must find and use to rescue not only Jamie's soul, but her own ("You only respond to strength!" Episode #116). Claire must learn to internalize the Green Man now—become the Green Man, and heal.

She confesses everything to a monk, Fr. Bain, while Jamie is recovering at the monastery. As another kindly Green Man, the priest shows her a way to love herself again. He comforts Claire and asks her the all-important question, "What ails thee?" and in doing so experiences a "miracle." In this moment of compassion and grace, Claire is freed from her feelings of guilt ("It's all my fault."), and the priest assures her that whatever her "sins," they have been replaced with love. Indeed, they have.

Apotheosis

To find balance, to fully reach wholeness within the self, an individual must harmonize the masculine and feminine within. Somewhere in her past, Claire allowed part of herself to die (or else she wouldn't be so threatened by the negative masculine). And the aspect of Dark Mother who has died with her grieves for lost opportunities, broken dreams, childhood hopes and potentials neglected. However, the Great Mother in all of us remembers that having given birth, she can do so again. To be the Great Mother, Claire needs to embrace her ability to nourish as well as understand her capacity to destroy. Once absorbed and acknowledged, these fears become strength: "independence, assertiveness, sexuality, power, and worldly accomplishment" (Frankel, *From Girl to Goddess* 133).

Because Claire has gone into the cave and learned from the Dark Mother not to loathe who she is, but embrace the beauty and strength of the feminine, she is able to overthrow Jamie's longing for death (a surrender to the patriarchy and Refusal to Return from the underworld), cut out the lies that won't support a balanced life, and heal Jamie's soul and in doing so, save her own. She finally banishes the face of Jack forever, replaces it with her own, and joins with Jamie in both body and soul, having made love and finally found completion in the Hieros Gamos. Healing the world within and between, above and below, linking the sacred and profane, mortal and immortal, joining the masculine and feminine, in an eternal dance of integration, completion and balance—this is our heroine's reward.

Our heroine needs no other talisman now, having been forged in the fire of her own destructive and creative knowledge, and rises as the Great

Mother, harbinger of both life and death—a synthesis of Maiden, Lover, Mother and Crone.

The Return

Most heroines make the decision, after saving themselves and those around them, to go home. It's not usually an easy choice. Where once this land (of our heroine's unconscious) was filled with fears, villains and impossible tasks, now it is populated with newly found friends and allies. The demons have been tamed and the tasks completed—for now. Claire makes this decision as well, but rather than go back to Frank at this time, she has learned that home is not a place, but a state of mind. She decides to stay with Jamie and continue on her journey. There are still things she needs to learn, wounds that need to heal, and the dragon (Black Jack) has not been slain, only incapacitated for now. As she continues on her journey, Claire must not forget she has the power to do it again.

Mother of the World

The heroine's reason for going on the journey has always been to pass along her knowledge to the next generation—a regenerative act—leaving the world a better place than before. Anyone can kill, but not all can give life. By acknowledging her "super" power, our heroine reclaims the life force in her self. We have come full circle. And in this case, Claire continues on her journey to help liberate the Scots from the British, or at the very least, help to prevent the Battle of Culloden that will claim the lives of the people she loves and holds most dear, including her husband, Jamie Fraser.

This is a matrilineal story. One story begets another. And, we learn, at the end of Episode #116 ("To Ransom a Man's Soul"), Claire is pregnant with Jamie's child. Where her life was once a wasteland, filled with the dead and dying on the battlefield, now, after taking the journey, her life is filled with the promise and hope of new life. Her vase, or cup, is no longer empty, but filled to overflowing. Claire has taken the journey, sought the Grail, asked the question "what ails thee?" and healed herself. The heroine's tale is a story about walking the labyrinth, battling and taming inner demons, and finding one's center. It's a story of birth, life, death, resurrection, and regeneration. All this, Claire has accomplished on her own inner journey.

NOTES

1. The heroine's journey in many ways parallels the mythic quest for the Holy Grail. Typically, its appearance heralds that some "thing" or someone has been deeply

wounded and needs healing. For each heroine the quest for her "Grail" is different depending upon what has lost in her life. For Claire, in *Outlander*, the vase symbolizes the Grail, and the quest is focused on her marriage or lack thereof. She's not sure if she can, or still does, love her husband the way she did before the war.

2. I am greatly indebted to the women who have forged the path and created their own *Heroine Journey* models before me—specifically Valerie Estelle Frankel, Maureen Murdock, and Victoria Schmidt. After consideration and study, I have put forward my own interpretation of the *Heroine Journey* model (based not only on mythic structures, but screenwriting principals as well). While many of the stages I have listed above are similar to other models, there are slight, but significant, variations.

3. The essence of the early matrilocal cultures of Old Europe can be best expressed as the sacred Chalice of the Womb. The image representing the nomadic invaders would have been that of the lethal blade. Together, they are a combined object, both masculine and feminine, yin/yang, the symbol of the fully integrated individual. Interestingly enough, the fiercest upholders of the lethal blade, the Celts, somehow understood the necessity of the balance between a Sky God and an Earth Goddess—it is out of that intuitive understanding that the Grail legend grew.

4. In fact, throughout the course of the journey, our heroine will need to say NO four times, reflecting the four part aspect of the Great Goddess (maiden, lover, mother, crone). First, our heroine will need to say "no" when she Crosses the First Threshold and decides to follow her own path. Next, she will need to say "no" when she is tempted to allow a man to rescue her, rather than trust her own insights and better judgment (Tempted to Abort the Quest). Thirdly, our heroine will need to say "no" to the False and Powerless Father who teaches her that she is weak and needs protecting. Her challenge is to see past that lie and slay the patriarchal myth of female inferiority. Finally, she will need to say "no" to her deepest fears when she faces her Supreme Ordeal and finds that what she thought were weaknesses are, in truth, her greatest strengths. Each NO pushes our heroine from external expectations (the life she "should" live), toward inner strength and wisdom (the life she "wants" and has been born to live).

5. The witchcraft trials were an effective method of patriarchal control. Independent women who possessed property and didn't have a husband or son to "run their affairs" were often targeted (as they challenged patrilineal inheritance laws). Women healers and midwives were also under attack—usually from the Church—since they threatened male authority. The trials were also used to control women's sexuality, often condemning women for lasciviousness and "vile" and "sinful" practices—demonizing women's bodies, sexual enjoyment, and procreative power.

6. In *Outlander*, Colum MacKenzie serves as the Fisher-King in the Grail myth. His country has been laid waste by the British and his people suffer. He is diseased ("dis-eased") and bears the pain of "a wound that will not heal." He is impotent (since he cannot sire a child and is unable to act against the British) and everyone in the Clan knows it (in a parallel to the Emperor's New Clothes), but is afraid to say anything because it would threaten Colum's ability to rule. When Claire unknowingly calls attention to Colum's "impotence" at their first meeting and mistakes his heir for his brother's son, she calls into question both Colum's ability to rule (according to Celtic law an impotent man was proscribed) and the laws protecting patrilineal ascension. Rather than admit his "secret," and face his demons, Colum, it appears, decides to "burn" away any potential threat Claire or Geillis might represent.

7. Typically, this stage of development for our heroine can go several ways: (1)

betrayal: Either the promised protector is ineffectual (he asks her to do something for him, because he can't, so sends her on another quest as in *Wizard of Oz*); (2) won't help her, or will sell her out in some way (this is where Colum appears to fall on the spectrum); (3) doesn't exist, dies, or disappears (again like the Wizard, like in *Wizard of Oz*); (4) might demand the heroine do something she knows is wrong, and so forces disobedience (Claire also faces this aspect); (5) or turns out to be the villain himself. This father aspect teaches our heroine that she can't rely on a "Daddy" figure to make decisions for her. She doesn't need protection because she isn't weak and powerless. She's also not a "bad" girl for standing up to the Father. *At this stage of the journey, our heroine needs to realize that she doesn't need to ask her father's, or anyone else's, permission to live her own life.*

8. Since Jamie arrives to "save" Claire, it is clear our heroine has not yet fully "let go" of the need for a man's protection, so she needs to experience all the ugly consequences. In Episode # 111 "Lallybroch," Claire sees the ugly side of Jamie in the role of Laird. On arrival, Jamie calls his sister a whore, tells her to mind her tongue, and takes over the running of the estate to the detriment of the people and community. Jamie as Laird is patriarchy run amok. In Episode #112 "The Black Watch," we see the generalization of the "bad father" extend from the family and estate to the larger community and country. Negative "fathers" who promise protection, instead destroy. There is always a price to pay—one's soul, or at least the procreative aspect of the feminine. Jamie is forced into "service."

9. On another, more archetypal level, Jamie represents the feminine part of Claire that has been beaten down, oppressed, and wounded by the negative patriarchy in the form of Black Jack. But it's even more than that—the negative patriarchy has succeeded in burying the feminine so deep in the collective unconscious that the face of the Goddess has been replaced by that of the Father. And this is what we experience in *Outlander*. Black Jack replaces Claire's face with his own, so that Jamie, while bearing the wounds of the feminine is also a reflection of the damage done by the negative patriarchy. Women, over time, believing the negative masculine narratives that taught them that the feminine was weak, passive, unstable, bad, ugly, stupid, crazy or of no value, have tried to distance themselves from the Mother. Often, the Mother is often buried so deep, under layers of scar tissue (scars left by layers of self-loathing and denials paralleling the scars on Jamie's back) and replaced by the masculine, that when a woman looks into the mirror of her psyche she sees not the face of the Mother, *but the Father reflected there instead.* This process—the pain and scars left by burying the feminine-and the self-loathing that occurs once a woman realizes she's been unknowingly complicit in the "crime" (on par with Jamie)—is what Claire needs to face in Wentworth prison, accept, and forgive to find peace and gain her freedom.

WORKS CITED

Bly, Robert. *A Little Book on the Human Shadow.* San Francisco: Harper & Row, 1988.

Campbell, Joseph. *The Hero with a Thousand Faces.* New York: MJF Books, 1949.

Frankel, Valerie Estelle. *Buffy and the Heroine's Journey: Vampire Slayer and Feminine Chosen One.* Jefferson, NC: McFarland, 2012.

_____. *From Girl to Goddess: The Heroine's Journey Through Myth and Legend.* Jefferson, NC: McFarland, 2010.

Freud, Sigmund. "Family Romances." *The Uncanny.* New York: Penguin Books, 2003.

Goodwin, Matthew. *The Holy Grail, Its Origins, Meaning and Secrets Revealed.* New York: Viking Studio Books, 1994.

Jung, Carl. *Mysterium Coniunctionis, The Collected Works of C.G. Jung,* Vol. 14. Trans. RFC Hull. New York: Princeton University Press, 1977.

Murdock, Maureen. *The Heroine's Journey.* Boston: Shambhala Publications, Inc., 1990.

Schmidt, Victoria Lynn. *45 Master Characters: Mythic Models for Creating Original Characters.* Ohio: Writer's Digest Books, 2001.

Vogler, Christopher. "The Practical Guide to Joseph Campbell's The Hero with a Thousand Faces." 1985. www.thewritersjourney.com.

_____. *The Writer's Journey: Mythic Structure for Writers.* Studio City: Michael Wiese Productions, 2007.

Appendix A:
Series Reading Order

Outlander (1743, 1945)
Dragonfly in Amber (1743–1745, 1968)
Voyager (1746–1767, 1968)
The Drums of Autumn (1767–1770, 1968–1971)
The Fiery Cross (1770–1772)
A Breath of Snow and Ashes (1773–1776, 1978)
An Echo in the Bone (1776–1778, 1978–1980)
"The Space Between" (March 1778) [short story]
"A Leaf on the Wind of All Hallows" (October 1941, 1739) [short story]
Written in My Own Heart's Blood (1739, 1778–1779, 1980)

These can be read at any point and provide additional backstory for book one:

"Virgins" (October 1740) [short story]
The Exile (1743) [graphic novel]

These take place within Jamie's Helwater years in *Voyager* and should be read before *An Echo in the Bone,* where characters begin to cross over:

"Lord John and the Hellfire Club" (1756) [short story]
Lord John and the Private Matter (June 1757–August 1757)
"Lord John and the Succubus" (September 1757) [short story]
"Lord John and the Haunted Soldier" (November 1758) [short story]
Lord John and the Brotherhood of the Blade (January 1758–October 1758)
"The Custom of the Army" (1759) [short story]
The Scottish Prisoner (1760)
"Lord John and the Plague of Zombies" (1761?) [short story]

Appendix B:
Television Episode Guide

Season One

101	09 Aug 2014	Sassenach
102	16 Aug 2014	Castle Leoch
103	23 Aug 2014	The Way Out
104	30 Aug 2014	The Gathering
105	06 Sep 2014	Rent
106	13 Sep 2014	The Garrison Commander
107	20 Sep 2014	The Wedding
108	27 Sep 2014	Both Sides Now
109	04 Apr 2015	The Reckoning
110	11 Apr 2015	By the Pricking of My Thumbs
111	18 Apr 2015	The Devil's Mark
112	25 Apr 2015	Lallybroch
113	02 May 2015	The Watch
114	09 May 2015	The Search
115	16 May 2015	Wentworth Prison
116	30 May 2015	To Ransom a Man's Soul

Appendix C:
Television Cast and Crew

Producer/Showrunner
Ron Moore

Costume Designer
Terry Dresbach

Cast
Annette Badland as Mrs. FitzGibbons
Caitriona Balfe as Claire Beauchamp Fraser
Simon Callow as the Duke of Sandringham
Liam Carney as Auld Alec
Steven Cree as Ian Murray
Finn Den Hertog as Willie
Laura Donnelly as Jenny Fraser Murray
James Fleet as The Rev. Reginald Wakefield
Roderick Gilkison as Young Hamish MacKenzie
Prentis Hancock as Uncle Lamb
John Heffernan as Brigadier General Lord Oliver Thomas
Douglas Henshall as Taran MacQuarrie
Sam Heughan as James (Jamie) Alexander Malcolm MacKenzie Fraser
Kathryn Howden as Mrs. Baird
Nell Hudson as Laoghaire MacKenzie
Duncan Lacroix as Murtagh Fraser
Gary Lewis as Colum MacKenzie
Aislín McGuckin as Letitia MacKenzie
Tim McInnerny as Father Bain
Graham McTavish as Dougal MacKenzie
Simon Meacock as Hugh Munro

Tobias Menzies as Frank Randall and Jonathan (Black Jack) Randall.
Lochlann O'Mearain as Horrocks
Grant O'Rourke as Rupert MacKenzie
Bill Paterson as Ned Gowan
Lotte Verbeek as Geillis Duncan
Stephen Walters as Angus Mhor
Tracey Wilkinson as Mrs. Graham

About the Contributors

Valerie Estelle **Frankel** is the author of many books on pop culture. Many of her books focus on women's roles in fiction, as in *From Girl to Goddess, Buffy and the Heroine's Journey, Women in Game of Thrones* and *The Many Faces of Katniss Everdeen.* Once a lecturer at San Jose State University, she now teaches English at Mission College. Her research can be found at www.vefrankel.com.

Katharina **Freund** works as an eLearning designer at the Australian National University in Canberra, designing and supporting education technology initiatives. She completed a Ph.D. on fan video editing communities at the University of Wollongong and researches fandom, television culture, and digital communication as an independent scholar.

Michelle L. **Jones** is a graduate student at the University of Regina, pursuing a Master of Arts degree in English. She is writing her thesis on Diana Gabaldon's *Outlander.* She has had a number of publications on varying topics in newspapers and magazines across Canada and has been working as copyeditor at the University of Regina newspaper.

Jessica R. **Matthews** is an associate term professor of English and the associate director of the composition program at George Mason University. She has presented papers about the romance novel at the International Association for the Study of Romance Conference, the Popular Culture Association Conference, and the Popular Romance Author Symposium at Princeton University.

Jodi **McAlister** is an Honorary Associate in the Department of Modern History, Politics and International Relations at Macquarie University in Sydney. Her Ph.D. research looked at the history of representations of female virginity loss and love in popular literatures. She is the Area Chair of Popular Romance Studies for the Popular Culture Association of Australia and New Zealand.

Patti **McCarthy** is a visiting assistant professor teaching film studies at the University of the Pacific, Stockton, California. She holds a Ph.D. (critical studies) and an MFA (film production) from the University of Southern California. She worked for RASTAR Productions at Sony Pictures Entertainment and was involved in projects such as *Harriet the Spy, Random Hearts,* and *American History X.* She has been a keynote speaker for many events, including *Star Wars 30th Anniversary Conference* and *Wizard World Comic Con.* Her book, *Outlander and the Heroine's Journey,* is forthcomig from McFarland and Co.

Stephenie **McGucken** graduated from Dickinson College (Carlisle, PA) with a degree in medieval and early modern studies before earning an MA in the history of art at the University of East Anglia in Norwich, England. She has worked in museums and at heritage sites in the United States and the United Kingdom. She is a Ph.D. candidate at the University of Edinburgh in the history of art.

Stella **Murillo** is a blogger on several topics, including fashion, wellness and *Outlander.* She is fluent in both English and Spanish, and earned a B.A. at the University of Toronto in Spanish and anthropology. Some of her academic achievements include the Governor General's Academic Medal, earned when graduating from high school, and two scholarships, one of them received at the university level.

Anthony Guy **Patricia** is a lecturer in English at Concord University in Athens, West Virginia. His book, *Queering the Shakespeare Film: Gender Trouble, Gay Spectatorship and Male Homoeroticism,* is forthcoming from Bloomsbury/*The Arden Shakespeare.* He has presented papers at numerous annual meetings of the Far West and the Southwest Popular/American Culture Associations.

Jennifer **Phillips** is a research associate at the University of Wollongong and a visiting lecturer in the School of Foreign Languages and Literatures at Wuhan University, China. Her research areas are literature and culture with a particular focus on masculinity and narration.

Sandi **Solis,** as a Chicana/American Indian, womanist, essayist and activist, is interested in cultural survival and ethnic identity. She has taught courses in women's studies, sexuality studies, critical race theory, Chicano and American Indian Studies.

Eleanor **Ty** is a professor of English and film studies at Wilfrid Laurier University in Ontario. She has published on cultural memory, Asian North America and on 18th century literature. She has authored several books and has co-edited two volumes on cultural memory. Her edited paperbacks, still in use in classrooms, include *Memoirs of Emma Courtney* (Oxford 1996; rev. ed. 2000) and *The Victim of Prejudice* (Broadview 1994, 2d ed. 1998), both with Mary Hays.

Index